To my Daddy Christmas 1989 – and many miles
may we walk together.
                    With love from
                            Alexander.
                                    αα.

Walking Britain's Coast

· AN AERIAL GUIDE ·

WALKING BRITAIN'S COAST

• AN AERIAL GUIDE •

Richard Sale · Bob Evans ·
Martin McClean

UNWIN

HYMAN

LONDON SYDNEY WELLINGTON

First published in Great Britain by the Trade Division of
Unwin Hyman Limited, 1989

UNWIN HYMAN LIMITED
15–17 Broadwick Street
London W1V 1FP

Allen & Unwin Australia Pty Ltd
8 Napier Street, North Sydney, NSW 2060, Australia

Allen & Unwin New Zealand Pty Ltd with the Port Nicholson Press
Compusales Building, 75 Ghuznee Street, Wellington, New Zealand

British Library Cataloguing in Publication Data
Sale, Richard, 1946–
    Walking Britain's coast : an aerial guide.
    1. Great Britain. Recreations : Walking – Visitors'
    guides
    I. Title   II. Evans, Bob   III. McClean, Martin
    796.5′1′0941

    ISBN 0–04–440481–6

Designed by Julian Holland
Typeset from disc by Columns of Reading
Printed in Italy

Acknowledgements

The production of this book covering the whole of Britain's 6,000 mile coastline could not have been achieved without the assistance of many people both on the ground and in the air.

Neil Ray and John Jefferies deserve special thanks, the former for assistance with all aspects of the project, the latter for the drawing of the maps.

Mention is also due to the following for their invaluable help – Tony Baines, Alan Dean, Paddy Dillon, John Hilton, Keith Kellett, Timothy Kendall, Andrew Mayhew, Colin Miller, Keith Noble, Roy Rainford, Jim Shean, Jack Simpson and Danny Walsh.

Thank you.

Contents

Acknowledgements 4
Introduction 6
The Dorset Coastal Path 8
The South Devon Coast Path 18
The Cornish Coastal Path 28
The North Devon and Somerset Coastal Path 41
The Bristol Channel. South Wales and the Gower 48
The Pembrokeshire Coastal Path 55
Cardigan Bay and the Lleyn Peninsula 63
Anglesey 72
North Wales and the Wirral 74
The Isle of Man 79
Lancashire and Cumbria 81
From the Solway to the Clyde 88
Arran 98
Towards the Islands 99
The Outer Hebrides 108
The Inner Hebrides 110
Skye 112
North Scotland 114
Orkney 122
Shetland 124
Pentland Firth to Moray Firth 126
Moray Firth to Firth of Tay 134
Firth of Tay to the Borders 146
Northumbria 156
Cleveland Way 164
Filey to Hunstanton 168
The Norfolk Coastal Path and North-east Norfolk 176
The Suffolk Heritage Coast 183
Essex 188
The Saxon Shore Way 196
Sussex 204
Isle of Wight 212
The Solent Way 214

Introduction

The walker of the coastline of Great Britain is treated to some of the finest and most spectacular scenery to be found anywhere on the island. The scenery is also remarkably varied: from the immense shingle bank of Dorset's Chesil Beach to the huge cliffs of Cape Wrath, from the dunes of Anglesey's Newborough Warren to East Anglia where the land merges with the sea so gradually that it is sometimes difficult to know where the boundary lies. Between these extremes there are 6,000 miles (9,600 km) of coast to be explored and enjoyed.

The Countryside Commission, a body empowered by government to set up National Parks in England and Wales and to designate 'official' long-distance footpaths in the two countries, recognised early the merits of the coast. Not only was the scenery magnificent, but the walking was comparatively straightforward, with few difficulties over access. Consequently they designated four coastal paths in England: the Dorset, South Devon, Cornwall and North Devon and Somerset Paths, the combination of which gives the South-West Peninsula Path, Britain's longest official way, a 520 mile (830 km) route from the outskirts of Bournemouth to Minehead. This Path, though only a fraction of the total British coastal mileage, is a fine introduction to coastal walking. It passes cliffs of chalk and granite, and of rock covering most of the range of hardness between: it passes Chesil Beach and goes through Torquay; it passes the ruins of tin mines, the sites of early Christian settlements and some much older; and it continues past Tintagel, the reputed site of King Arthur's castle.

Another official long distance path traces an equally spectacular route around the coastal perimeter of the Pembrokeshire National Park, passing the oil refineries of Milford Haven, the bird sancturies of Skokholm and Skomer and St David's cathedral, spiritual home of Christian Wales. And on the north-east coast of England part of yet a third official route, the Cleveland Way, traces a route along the seaward edge of the North York Moors National Park, passing the ruins of Whitby Abbey before going along Scarborough's holiday sea front. Between these 'short' sections of official paths, a route can be followed, sometimes with ease, sometimes – as, with the coastal sections of the remote north-west of Scotland – with difficulty.

For many people the covering of a section of coast each year assists in the exploration of a new area of Britain. This guide helps those people by offering advice on how to walk right around the mainland. Since some parts do have access problems, while others are less than appealing, it offers occasional alternatives to walking: a good train ride, or a bus around the odd eyesore. What is achieved, therefore, is an exploration not a route march. To reinforce this point, together with the route description for an area there is a brief description of each area's history, industrial archaeology, legends and wildlife. For completeness the larger offshore islands and island groups are included. Some of these – most notably the Isle of Man – have waymarked coastal circuits. The suggested routes for others do not always represent complete circuits but, rather, offer a view of the best of the available scenery.

When on the coast the walker frequently has a magnificent panorama, particularly if standing on a local high cliff, but there are also many times when the view, though excellent, is more local, the sweep of the coastline being obscured by cliffs, estuaries or towns. To overcome this occasional drawback, and to underline the more spectacular panoramas, there are a series of aerial photographs. These were taken specifically for the book and illustrate not only the diversity of British Coastal Scenery, but the changes brought by the seasons, the time of day and the weather. In addition many show the coastal path itself, so that the walker can retrace his walk section back at base, to relive the experience.

For the convenience of the walker the book is divided into geographical sections, each illustrated with its own maps. These maps are at a scale of approximately 10 miles (16 km) to the inch. While adequate to show the relevant places within an area and to give an overview of the suggested path, these maps cannot give an exact route. Therefore, at the start of each section there is a list of the Ordnance Survey Landranger (1:50,000) series sheets that cover the route, and these must be used in conjunction with the section route description. Those starting out on a coastal walk might consider that carrying a map is a luxury rather than a necessity – all you really need to do is follow the cliff-edge or the high-water mark. In one sense that is true, but in certain remote areas, especially in Scotland, the best route leaves the water's edge on occasions and in some areas Ministry of Defence property or urban and industrial development force the walker away from the shore. On those occasions a large scale map is indeed a necessity.

Finally, to ensure that the walker does not feel completely excluded by the bird's-eye views offered by the aerial photographs, there are a series of superb line drawings to accompany the text. These not only illustrate places of interest along the way, but some of the wildlife – animals, birds and butterflies – that the lucky walker might encounter.

The Dorset Coastal Path

(OS sheets 195, 194, 193)

Bournemouth to Durlston Head (9 mls, 14.5 km)

BEYOND THE CHINES – the narrow, deep clefts in Bournemouth's western cliff that are such a feature of the town – is Sandbanks, a thin finger of land crooked across Poole Harbour. By repute Sandbanks is the best of England's southern bathing beaches – though it is best to avoid the tidal drag at its tip, where the sea rushes into the harbour. From the north-western tip – Northern Point – the harbour view is dominated by Brownsea Island, where Baden-Powell held his first trial camp for boys in 1907.

South Haven Point, on the other side of Poole Harbour's entrance which is reached by ferry from Sandbanks, is the official start of the Dorset Coastal Path. The route begins on soft, wet sand, between dunes and sea, curving gently around Studland Bay. To the right here, behind the dunes, is Studland Heath, one of the last remaining tracts of Dorset heathland. The plant life supported by the poor soil of the heath seems equally poor and stunted: from its edge Studland Heath is a sombre mixture of dark brown and dark purple scrub. But amongst that scrub are some fine rarities, the marsh orchid and the Dorset Heath (*Erica cilioris*), the carnivorous sundew and other exotic bog plants. The nature reserve that covers the best of the heath is famous as one of the last refuges of the smooth snake, and the sand lizard on which it feeds. Otters still swim in Little Sea, as the freshwater lake at the heart of the nature reserve is known. The grayling butterfly and pine hawkmoth are found here, though the rare Dartford Warbler, most famous of the heath birds, is more likely to be found at Arne, about 5 miles (8 km) to the west.

Beyond Studland village there is a sudden and dramatic change of scenery as the coastal path crosses a band of chalk. One of the delights of Dorset is its diversity of scenery; such is the range of its underlying geology. In the space of 6 miles (9.5 km) from Studland we shall go across sand, pass chalk cliffs and arrive at cliffs as angular as any in Cornwall or Scotland. At Foreland, or Handfast, Point the chalk pinnacles of Old Harry and Old Harry's Wife are as spectacular as the more famous Needles which, on a reasonable day, can be seen across Poole Bay, as the chalk belt re-emerges from the sea on the Isle of Wight. Old Harry's Wife, the further and smaller stack, was virtually destroyed in a gale in 1896, and the little that remains will go in some future storm no doubt. Old Harry himself, for all his virginal whiteness, is named for the Devil and was undermined in the same gale. It is an interesting thought that the solid British coast, that changeless vista of a million clichés, is so fluid. By the next time you arrive here Old Harry might be gone, and that secure piece of cliff you are standing on might have gone with him.

South from the stacks the path is close to the cliff edge, with magnificent views to the sculpted chalk wall. There are other smaller stacks, sharp edged arêtes and graceful arcs like bite marks. At one point the sea has undermined the cliff to form a huge cave called the Parson's Barn. The name is local and shows well the feelings of healthy irreverence that the locals had for their clergy. When the tithes were due, they said, there was nothing bigger than the Parson's Barn!

The path turns west from Ballard Point to cross a section of Ballard Down, one of Britain's best sites for butterfly watching because of its position on a migratory route. Most of the species are familiar – red admiral, peacock – but the number of insects here is amazing, and there is the occasional rarity, the clouded yellow being the most noticeable. Beyond the down the coastal path slips quietly into Swanage.

In its earlier years the town was witness to the destruction of a Danish invasion fleet by Alfred the Great, in a battle fought in Swanage Bay. Its fame and prosperity were based on later stone quarrying. South of the town, near Durlston Head, the geology changes again and here the hard Purbeck Marble, a pearly, pale grey limestone, was much sought after as a sculpting stone. Many English churches have fonts, pillars and effigies of the stone. Salisbury Cathedral is perhaps the most famous.

The coastal path reaches the quarries by traversing the town, now a pleasant seaside resort, and taking the cliff path between Peveril Point and Durlston Head. Near the head is a globe, a 10 ft (3 m), 40 ton (40,642 kg) world constructed of 15 segments of

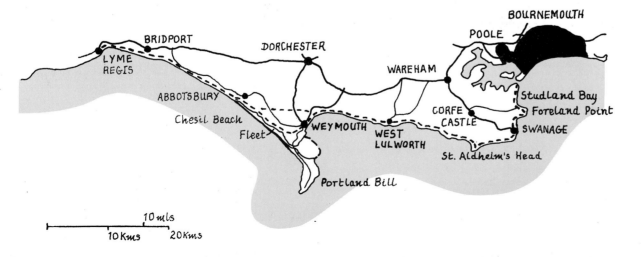

Peverill Point, at the southern end of Swanage Bay

Portland – not Purbeck! – stone. The Great Globe, as it is modestly called, was engineered for George Burt, a local stone merchant, and he also had the stone tablets set up nearby on which are inscribed snippets of information the good merchant thought worthy of a wider audience. Be careful here, some of the snippets owe more to enthusiasm than they do to fact.

It seems sad that Mr Burt did not construct his globe of local stone, but at least he was consistent in his placing of inappropriate rock. He also raised an obelisk on Ballard Down to commemorate the bringing of pure water to Swanage. The obelisk is granite, hardly in keeping with the local geology, and it is noted, was brought from a source near to London's Mansion House. The source was not a quarry – how could it be in London? – but an old lamp post!

Most famous of the sea quarries are those of Tilly Whim. The odd name derives from Tilly, the quarry owner, and whim, the wooden derrick used in the hazardous procedure of lowering the huge quarried blocks into ships waiting at the base of the cliff. Watching the water that thunders around the base of the cliffs even on relatively calm days it is difficult to believe that this loading operation was so *infrequently* disastrous.

Tilly Whim Cave to Worbarrow Bay (15 mls, 24 km)

There are old caves from the quarrying at several places along the cliff as we approach St Aldhelm's Head. One sits above the enchantingly named Dancing Ledges, so-called because the rock shelves at the base of the cliff makes the incoming tide appear to dance as it covers them. In these caves the fugitives in Meade Faulkner's *Moonfleet* waited to be transported to an unknown future. Since the coastal path also calls in on Fleet village and Chesil Beach, a walk along it really brings the book to life.

About a mile from St Aldhelm's Head a stream runs in from the village of Worth Matravers, a village of extravagant beauty and tranquillity. To the side of that stream and a little from the coast is a piece of flat land called East Man. Here are buried some of the 170 people who were drowned when the East Indianman *Halsewell* was wrecked in a January snowstorm in 1786. The wreck was at night, but over 70 people managed to reach the cliff and cling on until morning brought rescue. Most of the dead that

St Aldhelm's Chapel

the sea threw up were appallingly battered, but the ship's hourglass also came ashore not only unbroken but barely scratched.

St Aldhelm's Head, marked on the Ordnance Survey and other maps as having the alternative name St Alban's Head, a name that does not find local favour, is topped by the remains of a chapel dedicated to the saint, Sherborne's first bishop. It is a most uncharacteristic chapel, more a fortress with its stout square shape, 3½ ft (1 m) thick walls and formidable buttresses. Legend has it that its construction followed another shipwreck. In the twelfth century a Norman knight stood on the headland to wave goodbye to a newly married son or daughter bound for honeymoon in Normandy. The newly-wed's ship was caught in the treacherous waters at the base of the cliff and torn apart on the rocks. The knight watched, helpless, as his child drowned, and swore he would build a chapel in which to pray for lost souls, with a turret where a fire could burn to warn seafarers of the headland.

Beyond St Aldhelm's Head the coastal path switchbacks its way past the cliffs of Emmetts Hill and Houns-tout passing, between the two, Chapman's Pool, a marvellous cliff-hung cove with safe bathing on calm days. Beyond Houns-tout cliff are the Kimmeridge Ledges where the coastal path manages to stay closer to the sea for a while. Clavell's Hard is a fine, if short, waterfall onto the beach and soon we reach Clavell's Tower. The Clavell of the names refers to a family once resident in nearby Smedmore House. One family member, Sir William, is credited with having been the first to realise, in the first third of the seventeenth century, that the shale rock of the ledges could be burnt as a fuel. The idea of burning rock seems so unlikely – the Kimmeridge shale does

not, after all, look a lot like coal – that it begs the question of why Sir William did it. Perhaps there had been a fire, as there was in 1973 when the cliff near Clavell's Hard caught fire and burned for several months. Whatever the reason, Sir William then used the rock to fuel salt extraction from brine boilers, thereby foreshadowing the discovery of oil in the Kimmeridge shale. The tower that bears the Clavell name was not built by a family member though, but by the Rev. John Richards, resident, in 1820, in Smedmore House. The exact reason for the tower's construction is not known. It could have been an observatory, a watch-tower or just a folly. It is now ruinous and should be avoided.

Kimmeridge Bay is a magnificent spot, though children need to be dissuaded from climbing on the retaining shale cliffs which are very unstable. Beneath the bay's sheltered waters the marine reserve draws divers from all over Britain. One of the best features of the reserve are the great wrack and kelp forests.

The 'Nodding Donkey' oil pump, Kimmeridge

At the back of the bay is an oil well, its nodding-donkey pump looking like a giant mosquito relentlessly probing for oil – the blood of the Kimmeridge shales. It is a strange sight, almost surreal, but it is a quiet operation, with no great acreages of pipes and tanks, and no burning gas flares.

Distinctly less benign is the army gunnery range which starts on the western extremity of the Bay. Entry to the range is not controlled in the sense of there being fences and turnstiles, but the walker must read the range notice boards for exact information on access. **Once in the range, and others that we shall cross, please obey all warning notices,**

Mupe Rocks and Mupe bay, east of Lulworth Cove. In the distance are Arish Mell and Worbarrow Bay

keep to the paths, do not enter any building or go through any locked gate, do not touch anything and keep dogs and children under control. It is, by definition, inadvisable to enter the range if the visibility is poor, that is, in fog or at night.

It is almost an article of faith that the army's presence has preserved the clifftop landscape, an article best not discussed with the ex-inhabitants of Tyneham. The village was evacuated in 1943 and the exhibition in what once was the church is a sad reminder of the village's previous life. It is true, though, that the flowers in this area are quite superb, and certainly the coastal scenery is no worse for the range – Broad Bench with its flat square of cliff-base ledges; the curiously chopped-off face of Gad cliff; Brandy Bay, named from the smuggling that was rife on this coast; and the beached whale of Worbarrow Tout. The lack of access to the cliff-line from inland roads and villages, and the lack of inland activity also means that there is a peacefulness along this section of the coastal path that is worth the effort of finding.

Rings Hill to Osmington (11 mls, 17.6 km)

At the far end of Worbarrow Bay, Rings Hill brings the Purbeck Hills to the sea. The sea has worn away the hard rock here and half of Flower's Barrow hill-fort has disappeared. When it was in its original state it must been have one of the most impressive of Dorset's many fine forts, the more so for being the only one that used the sea as part of its defences. Rings Hill is famous as a site for the elusive Lulworth Skipper butterfly, first identified nearby as late as 1832 and still mostly confined to the area. The hill is also famous for an even more elusive sight, a ghostly army that marches across the defences of the hill-fort. Some reports speak of Roman legionnaires – though the fort pre-dates the Romans by several centuries. A seventeenth century sighting led to a panic when the locals, convinced that the army was real and that England had been invaded by Papists, barricaded Wareham and sent messengers to alert the government in London. The local militia waited behind their makeshift fortifications. And waited, and waited. . . .

Beyond Rings Hill the coastal path drops down to the cove of Arish Mill, beautifully named, beautifully set, but still off limits to the tourist. Beyond, the path rises steeply again up onto the high down of Bindon Hill, going south off of the Down to Mupe Bay, with a view of the Mupe Rocks with their fine seabird colony. Soon, the walker loses his military escort, but

Lulworth Skipper butterfly, only found near the Cove

before the barbed wire look for a sign to the fossil forest. This is reached by steps, but surprises the visitor by appearing out of the limestone cliffs rather than being confined to the cliff-base. The trees were, in fact, cycads, fern-like plants that flourished when dinosaurs roamed the area.

Beyond the forest and the barbed wire, is Lulworth Cove, one of the most famous seaside sites in Britain. The path here gets lost in the car-park and the tourist traps, and the beach is not Britain's least crowded spot, but the cove really is magnificent. The ceaseless war between land and sea – one which, on this coast at least, the land can never do more than lose slowly – has formed the archetypal cove, almost circular and almost fully enclosed by spits of land like crab's pincers. The cliffs that form the back wall have been twisted beyond description. Local legend tells of a woman walking the cliffs at twilight in the early 1800s and hearing voices in the cove. England was at war with France, and the woman's husband was French. Worse yet he was a smuggler, and the Dorset coves were a favourite landing spot for contraband. Fearing a trap set by excise men she crept close. A group of men were huddled over a map and, to her surprise, were talking in French. To her even greater surprise Napoleon himself walked clear of the group stared up at the cliffs, shook his head and said 'Impossible'. The men returned to a rowing boat and were gone. The lady lived to be over 100, and was never shaken from her belief that Napoleon had been on Lulworth beach that night.

West from Lulworth Cove, and nearby Stair Hole, a secret spot with a long smuggling history and an enclosing loop of even more tortured rock, the coastal path rounds the magnificent St Oswald's Bay to reach Durdle Door, one of the highlights of the entire British coastline. As can be clearly seen from the headlands of St Oswald's Bay we are back in chalk country, and once the sea has penetrated the harder Purbeck stone it eats away at the chalk to form the smuggling caves that abound in the cliff base near Lulworth. At Durdle Door this eating away has produced a natural hard-rock arch through which the sea pounds delightfully when a heavy tide is running. The angle of the arch and its barn door of a hole, and the excellent coves to each side, make this a memorable spot even if, in high summer, there are quite a few others to share the marvel with you.

West from Durdle Door the chalk headlands of Swyre and Bat's offer superb views, both locally – the switch-back cliffs here are more amenable to viewing than the steeper ones near Old Harry – and across Weymouth Bay to Portland which looks very much like an island from here. White Nothe, occasionally, but wrongly, written as White Nose, is equally good, topped by an ancient row of coastguard cottages. The undercliff area beyond the cottages is a reserve of the Dorset Naturalists' Trust, prized for its plant life, which includes the beautiful yellow-horned poppy and the rock rose, and the rare and exotic Nottingham Catchfly. To the right of the footpath above the reserve, the chalk downland is again famous for its butterflies. The reserve ends at Burning Cliff the name recalling the time, in the 1820s, when – as at Kimmeridge – the cliff's oil shales caught fire.

Burning Cliff lies midway along Ringstead Bay, named after a medieval village the outline of which can still be seen at the western end of the bay. No one knows the reason why the village was abandoned: some say that Black Death killed all the villagers and the houses were never settled again, while others maintain that a violent storm in the bay caught the village's fishing fleet, killing all the menfolk, and that in despair the women left. Happier times are ahead, near Osmington Mills, where the thirteenth century Smugglers' Inn is a favourite refreshment spot. John Constable honeymooned at nearby Osmington village, and the spot where he worked his painting of Weymouth Bay can be located – the Portland breakwaters being the only change to the scene.

Looking westward over Lulworth Cove

Osmington Mills to Abbotsbury
(29 mls, 46.5 km)

From the Mills an alternative path – not only official but also bearing the name Dorset Coastal Path – to the cliff path runs inland, visiting Osmington, passing the huge chalk cut figure of George III and the memorial to Dorset's other Thomas Hardy, Nelson's captain on the *Victory*, to reach Chesil Beach at West Bexington.

The cliff path, however, rises up another switchback, this time over Black Head, descending to a holiday camp-filled hollow before rising again to Redcliff Point. Beyond, Bowleaze Cove is a delightful mix of sand, shingle and rocks, enclosed on its western edge by Furzy Cliff, named for its covering of gorse and scrub. The path carves its way through the gorse to emerge onto a main road that is followed to Weymouth.

Weymouth is an excellent seaside resort with a long tradition. To here, in 1789, came George III to try sea bathing from one of the new-fangled bathing machines. As the King entered the water many held their breath, and a band played *God Save the King*. To register their thanks to the King, not least for the stream of rich Georgians who followed their monarch to Weymouth, the town-fathers erected a very elaborate statue to him on the occasion of his Golden Jubilee in 1810. On the whole it is a more pleasing reminder of the King than Osmington's huge chalk relief. The rich Georgians have left an array of excellent houses which, combined with the older narrow streets, make Weymouth an interesting town. Lately, the rise in ferry traffic to France has brought a new prosperity to the area.

The coastal path leaves Weymouth along the northern shore of the Fleet, the salty finger of water held from the sea by Chesil Beach, but the shore of the Isle of Portland can be comfortably followed by path and road. The massive breakwaters of Portland harbour were built by convict labour: the prison that held the men – some awaiting transportation to Australia – is still there, and the old quarry scars have yet to heal. Some of the quarries supplied the best building stone – Wren used it in St Paul's Cathedral, and Buckingham Palace is also made of Portland stone – and there are still working quarries where one man and a machine now do the work that once gave a whole village a living.

Portland has two castles, the Norman Rufus Castle near Church Ope Cove, and the more complete one

by Henry VIII at the northern end, each built to defend this vulnerable spit of land. It is ironic that later, after the harbour had been completed, Portland defended Britain as a naval base of renown, sharing, with Scapa Flow, the distinction of being able to hold the complete Grand Fleet. From the harbour, American troops left for the D-Day landings in Normandy.

The Chesil Beach – *chesil* is Saxon for shingle – ends at Portland. The beach is one of the most extraordinary sections of the British coast; 50 million tons of pebbles of varying size thrown up in a narrow – never more than 200 yards (182 m) – and high – sometimes over 40 ft (12 m) – band along the 13 miles (21 km) of coast from Portland to West Bexington. The pebbles vary in size and colour from one end to the other. The changes, though gradual, are so predictable that local smugglers were able to work out where they were by handling them. Or so it is said. No real understanding for this grading process, or even for the creation of the beach, exists and in the absence of theory a local legend maintains that it appeared during the course of a ferocious night-long storm.

It is possible to walk the whole length of the beach, but that is more a feat than a pleasure, and the coastal path takes the shore line of the Fleet, a brackish lagoon that reaches back to Abbotsbury's Swannery. Due to a change in salt content along its length, the Fleet has a most interesting ecology. At the village of Fleet is the old church where Meade Falkner set the early part of *Moonfleet*, while Abbotsbury itself is a picture book English village: a hilltop chapel, dedicated to the patron saint of spinsters; a tithe barn of monumental dimensions beside the ruins of an old abbey, a village pond, and, within short walking distance, the delightful Abbotsbury gardens and the Swannery.

Chesil Beach to Lyme Regis (17 mls, 27 km)

Near Abbotsbury the coastal path joins Chesil Beach, which is followed to its western end, somewhere near Burton Bradstock. I say somewhere near, because the true end point of the beach is a matter of opinion rather than fact. Certainly, the beach has finished when Burton Cliff is reached, where the path drifts inland to a foot–bridge over the river Bride for those unwilling to ford the river on the beach below. Either way, East Cliff and Bridport Golf Club are reached en route for the little seaside village of West Bay. The path crosses the River Brit at West Bay and

heads off along a section of less interesting, shattered coast to Seatown, a delightful village of thatched cottages grouped around a pub. From the village the pathway is badly eroded, evidence of further battles between the sea and the land, as it approaches Golden Cap, the highest cliff top in Southern England, at 625 ft (190 m) above sea level. Golden Cap is a huge jumble of ochre sandstone studded with yellow gorse, crowned with windcut grass. From it the views are arguably the finest on the Dorset coast extending not only out over Lyme Bay, but inland to the Marshwood Vale.

Stile on the Coastal Path between Seatown and Eype

From Golden Cap the path drops through meadow and bracken, the cliffs becoming increasingly unstable and tumbled. At Cain's Folly there is evidence of real and chaotic landslips just off the path to the left, and it is almost a relief to reach the stability of Charmouth. The Queen's Arms in the town is named after Catherine of Aragon who stayed there, albeit briefly, in 1501. Equally brief was the stop of Charles II following his defeat at the Battle of Worcester. The King hoped for a boat to France from the harbour, but was discovered and forced to flee.

West from Charmouth – a delightful town really, much spoiled by the car – are the famed Blue Lias cliffs of Lyme Regis, called, a little oddly, Black Ven.

Looking south over Weymouth and Weymouth Harbour. Beyond is the Isle of Portland, Portland Harbour and Chesil Beach

Here, in 1810, Mary Anning, an 11-year-old local girl, found the complete skeleton of an ichthyosaur. It took 10 years to finally persuade the fossil from its rocky tomb, and the British Museum, which still has it, bought it for the princely sum of £23. Later, she also discovered the plesiosaur and pterosaur in these Blue Lias beds. The cliffs can be viewed at close quarters if the path is deserted in favour of a walk along the beach to Lyme Regis. But do be careful: if the tide comes in the cliffs are too unstable to climb. And please do not indiscriminately hack away at the face, it may collapse on you and the activity is, in any case, vandalism. Those anxious for a fossil momento need only scour the beach where ammonites, of all sizes, abound.

Lyme Regis, at the end of the Dorset Path and the start of the South Devon Path, is a quaint place, seeming occasionally to be about to choke on a surfeit of cars and visitors. As a port it has a famous history – its vessels helped disperse the Spanish Armada, while a century later the Duke of Monmouth landed his army here at the start of his attempt to wrest the throne from his uncle James II. The people of Lyme and Dorset rallied to him, but there was no glorious outcome. For both Duke and people there was the Battle of Sedgemoor after which he went to London and the scaffold, while they went home to Judge Jefferies and the Bloody Assize.

The Cobb, the town's fourteenth-century breakwater, is a fitting last section to our Dorset walk. It offers a good view of Lyme Bay, and the chance to relive a sequence from *The French Lieutenant's Woman* by John Fowles, which was written, set and filmed here.

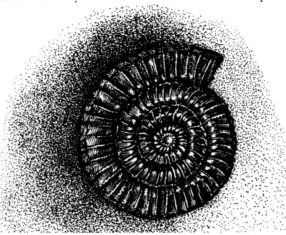

Ammonite, a fossil common in the rocks near Lyme Regis

Looking east along the length of Chesil Beach. To the left of the beach is the Fleet

The South Devon Coast Path

(OS sheets 193, 192, 202, 201)

Lyme Regis to Sidmouth (16 mls, 25.5 km)

THE SOUTH DEVON COAST PATH, another 'official' path, starts unpretentiously from a car park in Lyme Regis with a stiff climb to the top of Ware Cliff.

From the top the path goes through landslips which are among the most extensive and spectacular in England. The two easterly slips, Ware and Pinhay, are thought to be several hundred years old but the westerly ones, Bindon, Dowlands and Whitlands are only early nineteenth century. The biggest slip, and the best documented, occurred at Christmas 1839 between Dowlands and Bindon when around 20 acres of land subsided. The landslips have left the ground rough and broken, making the area inaccessible except via the path. Consequently, a number of nature reserves have been established and these are heavily wooded in parts with ash, hazel and maple. Elsewhere, there is scrub with the occasional sheltered pond and boggy area interspersed with scree. The area abounds in fossils, plants and birds.

The path through the landslips is strenuous, twisting and turning and offering little view of the nearby shoreline, but eventually grasslands are reached at the approach to Seaton, where the path crosses the fairways of Axe Cliff Golf Club before descending to a bridge across the River Axe. The bridge, built in 1877, is the oldest surviving concrete bridge in England. Bird watchers will want to leave it to walk up river a short way to the tidal mud flats which attract a fine collection of waders.

Roman remains have been found in the Seaton area and there may have been a Roman port. Today, the town is a popular, though comparatively quiet, resort with a pleasant promenade along the length of a shingle beach. At the western end, if the tide permits, it is best to walk along the beach to Beer.

Beer, once a busy fishing village renowned for its lace and infamous for its smugglers, is an unspoiled place, though busy in the holiday season. The beach is still used by local fishing boats as there they are sheltered from the westerly winds by Beer Head, the westernmost chalk outcrop in the British Isles. The coastal path goes over Beer Head, past a coastguard lookout, to Hooker Cliffs, though an alternative route is along the undercliff path. This is a more interesting route with the cliffs to the right, good views seaward, and a section of rough ground and thick vegetation ahead through a landslip dating from 1790. This path also passes the Pinnacles, enormous blocks of chalk which have broken away from the cliff.

Inland, about a mile from here, are Beer Quarry Caves. Beer stone was prized in Roman days and was used in the Middle Ages to build churches and cathedrals: Exeter and St Paul's Cathedrals and Westminster Abbey each have sections in Beer stone. Its creamy-white colour and smooth texture made it excellent for heraldic shields and monuments, and it was favoured by stonemasons because when newly quarried it was soft and easily carved but hardened after being exposed to air.

Beyond the landslip is Branscombe Mouth, and inland from that is the attractive village of Branscombe itself, well worth a visit for its church, dating from Saxon times, its old forge and bakery, thatched cottages and pub.

The fine unspoiled stretch of coastline from Branscombe Mouth to Sidmouth is tough going in places, but very rewarding. Along Coxes Cliff, where there are traces of an Iron Age or Roman encampment, the path climbs up to Weston Cliff and then

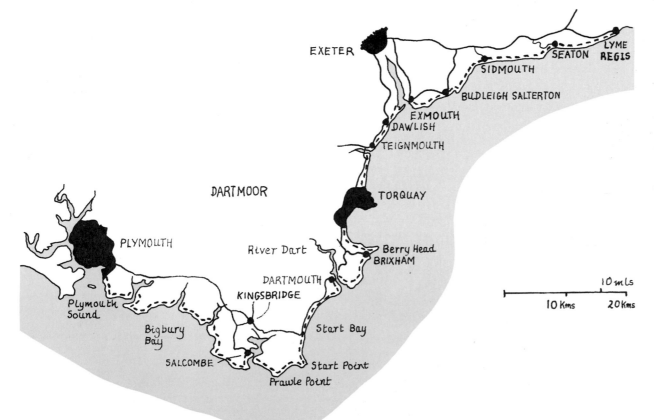

Beer, at the western end of Seaton Bay

down to the lonely beach of Weston Mouth. Climbing inland again through woods and around flinty mounds, which are the remains from lime burning over hundreds of years, you cross the 500 ft (153 m) Dunscombe Cliff before dropping steeply down to Salcombe Mouth. Here, a short inland detour will take you to Salcombe Regis where there is a fine church, part Norman and part Early English.

Beyond, a steep climb up Salcombe Hill above Chapman's Rocks reaches cliffs which support a rich variety of plant and bird life, with blackthorn, hawthorn, bramble and ivy making good habitats for the yellowhammers and finches. From here there is also a fine view of Sidmouth, well set between red sandstone cliffs with fishing boats drawn up on its attractive shingle beach. The path descends steeply to a foot-bridge across the River Sid over which there is a good example of a Victorian seafront. Outside the main holiday season the town has a quiet charm with many examples of Regency and Victorian houses. Queen Victoria stayed here as a child. At the western end of the seafront Chit Rocks has many rock pools with limpets, barnacles and sponges. Crabs, shrimps and small fish are trapped here until the next tide releases them – if they escape the nets of holidaying children.

The path from Sidmouth climbs a steep wooded bank onto Peak Hill, from which there are fine views back to the town. Westward the sea is hidden for a time by a bank of thick scrub though there are pleasant views inland of rolling Devonshire hills.

Sidmouth

Peck Hill to Bundle Head (21 mls, 33.5 km)

The approach of Ladram Bay brings more spectacular red cliffs, here with equally impressive sandstone sea stacks. The gulls and fulmars gliding overhead, and the statuesque cormorants on the rock stacks enhance the view, which cannot be said of the large caravan site even if it does offer holiday accommodation in a fine situation.

Beyond, pleasant undulating fields are crossed before the path drops down to the River Otter at the eastern end of Budleigh Salterton. There is no bridge across the mouth of the river and, although the river is only a few yards wide, wading across is not recommended. Instead a 1½ mile (2.4 km) detour inland is necessary, the compensation being a pleasant riverside walk, especially rewarding for the bird watcher. The estuary birds can be viewed from both sides of the river and a hide has been erected at one vantage point.

Budleigh Salterton is a quiet seaside resort with a shingle beach. The sea wall here was the setting for the well-known painting, 'The Boyhood of Raleigh' by Sir John Millais. Sir Walter himself was born 2 miles (3 km) away at Hayes Barton, in 1552, though his birthplace, a fine thatched farmhouse, is not open to the public.

At the western end of the seafront the coastal path follows the boundary of West Down Golf Course to West Down Beacon. Seaward here is a wild stretch of undercliff called The Floors, covered by thick bramble and gorse which provides a good habitat for birds. From the beacon, which is 400 feet (120 m) above the sea, there are splendid views in all directions.

Beyond Littleham Cove, the path has to bypass Straight Point headland, which is a firing range, and takes a detour through a caravan park at Sandy Bay before climbing again to the 250 ft (75 m) High Land of Orcombe which is owned by the National Trust. Orcombe Point is another good viewpoint. The estuary of the River Exe below is a good area for the bird watcher, especially during the winter months, but is a barrier for walkers who must go on past Orcombe Rocks to join the road for Exmouth.

Exmouth has an interesting and ancient history. In Saxon times it was known as Axenmouth and there was a harbour in Roman times. The town started to develop as a resort in the mid-eighteenth century and today many eighteenth- and nineteenth-century buildings survive. Lady Nelson and Lady Byron lived here

for a time on the fashionable Beacon, a terrace of Georgian houses overlooking the seafront. 'Point in View' is a delightfully named group of early nineteenth-century almshouses, while the curious 'A La Ronde', a circular house from the late eighteenth century, is decorated with thousands of shells.

The river can be crossed by ferry from Exmouth Dock to Starcross between May and September, though enquiries should be made locally to make sure it is operating. The alternative, a lengthy detour via Exeter, is usually made by public transport. However, since road walking is necessary between Starcross and Dawlish Warren, many will prefer to take the train as far as the Warren, where there is a nature reserve for the salt-water flora and bird life. Those determined to walk can reduce the road walking to a minimum, by taking the seaside route round Langstone Rock along the promenade, or the beach if the tide permits, to Dawlish. This was a fishing village, recorded in the Domesday Book as Doelis or Doules, which became a small seaside resort in Regency times. The railway station was designed by Brunel and through it runs the main Paddington to Penzance line. To the west of Dawlish, beyond a rock pillar known as The Parson and Clerk, is a raised beach that reaches as far as Teignmouth, the railway taking advantage of it to offer a fine ride along the shore line. This section of the line was engineered by Brunel in 1846. Providing the sea is not too rough, there is a pleasant promenade walk alongside the railway.

Teignmouth is an old port whose historical records date back to Ethelred the Unready in 1002. It was one of the first resorts to be developed in Devon: John Keats lived here for a time and Jane Austen and Fanny Burney also stayed here in the early nineteenth century. There is a good sandy beach and the port is still active. To cross the River Teign there is a busy road bridge a ½-mile (0.8 km) up river but walkers will find the ferry service near the river mouth a much more pleasant and convenient way to reach Shaldon.

Labrador Bay to Dartmouth (28 mls, 45 km)

After a short stretch of road walking through Shaldon, the path goes up to the Ness headland which offers a good view over Teignmouth, the Teign estuary and

Looking east over Brixham Harbour towards Berry Head

the coast beyond. The Ness has a 100 yd (91 m) tunnel bored through it which allows the visitor access to the delightful Ness Cove. Continuing across fields to the cliffs around Bundle Head brings the walker to Labrador Bay, named after a house built here by an eighteenth-century North American trader. Sadly only the name remains.

Beyond Labrador Bay are a number of hanging valleys, relics of the Ice Age, and the going is strenuous in places. Herring, Mackerel and Blackaller's Coves, are passed as the path dips and rises to reach Maidencombe, an attractive unspoiled village with thatched cottages where Rudyard Kipling lived for a short time. Here, too, there is a fine sandy beach.

The path continues along the cliffs, passing Shackley Bench and Bell Rock to reach the Valley of Rocks, a strange, enchanting bowl with boulders covered in ivy. A steep descent leads to Watcombe Beach in a wooded setting and then up again onto the cliffs past Petit Tor Point to Oddicombe and Babbacombe. There is a cliff railway at Oddicombe, built in 1926, while inland from Anstey's Cove, at Wellswood, is Kent's Cavern, an important palaeolithic site, explored between 1825 and 1829 by J. MacEnery who was convinced that man had existed for much longer than the teaching at that time indicated. Later, between 1865 and 1880, William Pengelly made a complete excavation and confirmed MacEnery's findings of man's bones alongside those of woolly mammoths and sabre-toothed tigers. The man-worked flints and bones of the extinct animals found in the cavern are now in Torquay's Natural History Museum.

Bishop's Walk, named after a nineteenth-century Bishop of Exeter, Henry Phillpotts, who lived nearby and took the walk frequently, takes the path around Black Head to Hopes Nose, passing nearby Thatcher Rock. From here many walkers will want to take the bus to cross built-up Torbay to reach Brixham. In 1968 Torquay, Paignton and Brixham were amalgamated to form Devon's largest holiday resort – Torbay – which stretches for about 22 miles (35 km) along the bay. Torquay had been growing since the nineteenth-century when it was regarded as one of the principal genteel watering places on the south coast, thanks to its mild climate and its setting. Paignton and Brixham, though, have a longer history, both having been fishing and commercial ports. The transition from ports to resorts began in 1880 and tourism has been developing ever since. Cockington,

Net-mending in the harbour at Brixham

near Torquay, is a justly famous village, to the east of which are the ruins of the twelfth-century Torre Abbey, while Brixham has a memorial stone to the landing at the port of William of Orange on Guy Fawkes Day 1688. The whole 22 miles (35 km) can be walked, a local guide *Torbay Coast Paths* helps keep road walking to a minimum.

A good place to start on the official path again is Shoalstone Point to the west of Brixham. The path from here leads to Berry Head with its lighthouse and air navigation beacon. The headland is a country park, and the cliffs are a breeding place for a variety of sea birds – kittiwake, guillemots, razorbills, fulmars and gulls. There are traces of an Iron Age cliff-fort and the remains of fortifications erected against the French, the latest set being built in 1803 at the time of the Napoleonic wars.

Continuing past a holiday camp, the path hugs the cliff-edge around Durl Head, an interesting crag of folded limestone. A descent to St Mary's Bay takes the path to a beach of pebbles and sand before climbing to Sharkham Point and over Southdown Cliff to Man Sands. Here there are remains of lime kilns from the times when Berry Head limestone was burnt to produce quick lime.

A comparatively new stretch of coastal path skirts Scabbacombe Head and has some strenuous gradients. Much of it is dedicated to the memory of the late Lt Col. Jones, the Falkland Islands' VC who owned the estate here. The path passes Mill Bay Cove to reach Kingswear, famous for its crabs and lobsters. Here

there is the terminus of the privately run Torbay Steam Railway which goes to Paignton. Kingswear Castle was built around 1491 as a defence against the French and sits opposite Dartmouth Castle. A ferry service across the River Dart operates all the year round.

Dartmouth is a deep water port in a beautiful setting and has a long history. It was a departure point for the Crusades and, in the Middle Ages, there was a good deal of trade with the Continent. In 1620 the Pilgrim Fathers' ships, *Mayflower* and *Speedwell*, were repaired in the port prior to their Atlantic crossing, although, as we shall see, further problems required a berthing at Plymouth. The castle here was completed in 1494 and was the first in England to be equipped with gun platforms and ports. A chain could be stretched between the castles of Dartmouth and Kingswear to seal off the River Dart. The imposing Brittania Royal Naval College, standing on a hillside above the town, was designed by Sir Aston Webb and completed in 1905 to replace the *Brittania* training ship that had been moored in the river. Less imposing, but arguably more elegant, is the seventeenth-century pillared Butterwalk, which houses one of the town's museums.

Dartmouth Castle to Salcombe (23 mls, 39 km)

The coastal path leaves Dartmouth towards the castle, continuing to Blackstone Point and Compass Cove. It then turns inland and along the road to Stoke Fleming, where St Peter's church, which was built in the fourteenth century, has two of the earliest brasses in Devon. From the village a bus to Torcross is an alternative to walking the busy stretch of road in high season.

En route to Torcross is Blackpool Sands, a very attractive bay out of season. In 1404 the French landed here but were driven off by local men. Equally good, especially for the naturalist, is Slapton Ley, the largest freshwater lake in Devon. It is a nature reserve leased to the Field Studies Council who have a centre at Slapton and run courses there. The Ley, which is divided from the sea by the road and a narrow spit of deeply shelved beach is particularly good in spring and autumn for migrating birds and for ducks in winter. There are many insects including no less than 17 species of dragon-fly.

Prawle Point, the southernmost tip of Devon

Slapton village has a fourteenth-century church and the ruins of a college. In 1943 the village was evacuated and used as a training ground by American forces preparing for the D-Day landings. A tank, recently hauled from the sea, and a statue, commemorate this period. A surprise U-boat attack during one training run resulted in the loss of many lives.

Beyond Torcross, if the tide permits, the beach can be used to walk to Sunnydale and on to Beesands where again there is a large caravan site. At Hallsands there are the remains of the fishing village which collapsed during a violent storm in 1917. The collapse was said to have been due to the dredging of shingle from the beach to build Devonport Docks at the turn of the century, which undermined the foundations of the buildings.

Climbing from the beach the path follows an undulating route towards Start Point which provides fine views both east and west. The lighthouse here was built in 1836 and warns of the dangers of Blackstone Rock which has seen many wrecks. The area around the Point is a nature reserve and the rugged headland is another good place to view migrating birds.

Turning westards the path passes many jagged rock formations, including the Pinnacles near Mattiscombe Beach. The scenery here is wild and rugged and offers first class walking. Lannacombe Beach may have a few cars but space is limited and so the number is small even in high season. Ahead is a section of raised beach, the original cliffs being a field width back from the present shoreline. The 'shelf' was once the sea bed, one theory being that the beach level rose after the last Ice Age. Here, look too for the many stone slabs set on edge that mark old field boundaries.

Prawle Point, the next major objective, is the most southerly point in Devon. The word 'Prawle' means 'lookout hill' and it has frequently been used to guard against possible sea-borne invaders. It is another excellent area for watching migrant birds and there is also a rich variety of flowers, heather and thrift.

Precipitous cliffs and jagged rock formations above the pounding white surf around Maceley Cove and Gammon Head make the next section of path very exciting. The views are excellent, and the whole section is well known for its abundance of butterflies: Small Coppers, Silver Studded Blues and Pearl Bordered Fritillaries to name but a few. Beyond the gorse on Rickham Common the path continues through woods to the estuary shore. In the mouth of the estuary lurks The Bar, a sandy hazard beneath the sea which is especially dangerous to deep-keeled craft at low tide. The Salcombe lifeboat was wrecked there in 1916 and 13 crew members were lost. The path follows the line of the estuary inland through Mill Bay to the ferry, which operates all year round, at East Portlemouth for the crossing to Salcombe.

Salcombe, the most southerly resort in Devon, was a port in early times but The Bar in the harbour mouth restricted its development. However, it is now a very busy yachting centre and has a reputation as a good spot for fishing. There are many interesting buildings along the main street and the ruined castle, Fort Charles, was built by Henry VIII. Walkers can take the summer ferry to South Sands to bypass some of the road and so make early progress towards Bolt Head. However, a visit to Overbecks museum and Sharpito Gardens is recommended. They lie on the path route and there is a National Trust shop and youth hostel on the same site.

Sharp Tor to Plymouth (41 mls, 66 km)

After a steady climb up to Sharp Tor, the triangulation point here is at 406 feet (122 m), there is an excellent view of Salcombe and the estuary that heads inland to Kingsbridge. Below is Starehole Bay and Courtenay Walk which was cut through the pinnacles of Sharp Tor by a member of the Tor family in the last century. From here it is worth walking out to Bolt Head, another fine view point, if only to see the strange parasitic plant, the Dodder, whose red tendrils appear to choke the host plant.

Back on the path, there is now a very fine stretch of clifftop pathway with spectacular scenery and an undulating and rugged coastline. The coast here had a deadly reputation in the days of sailing ships when many were wrecked on the rocky shoreline in the strong southerly gales. The section is also one of the longest stretches of coastline owned by the National Trust, a 6-mile (9.5 km) piece from Salcombe to Hope Cove.

On the way to Bolberry Down there are more upright slabs of the local stone, mica schist, forming old field boundaries. The original rocks were transformed through volcanic pressures and heat to leave a form of shining slate with white outcrops of quartz. Masses of stonecrop flower on the rocky ground, while the evocatively named Vernal Squill grows on the seaward side of the Cathole Cliff slope. Bolberry Down was named after a nearby hamlet which is mentioned in the Domesday Book. From it, on a clear day the Eddystone lighthouse, now automatically controlled, can be seen, across the South Hams.

Round Bolt Tail the path passes an Iron Age cliff fort, colourful in early summer with pink thrift and yellow gorse. In the winter in 1760 there was a terrible sea disaster here when *HMS Ramilles* was wrecked with the loss of 800 lives.

The path drops steeply to Inner Hope, by the old Methodist chapel, and leads to the quaint and attractive square. The twin villages of Inner and Outer Hope were once fishing communities trading in lobsters and pilchards. Today they are busy spots in the holiday season but still retain aspects of old Devon; Inner Hope in particular having a cluster of

Burgh Island, which is separated from Bigbury-on-Sea at high tides

Thatched cottage, Thurlestone

cottages which are good examples of mid-nineteenth century village buildings.

The walking becomes less strenuous from this point, across Great Ledge, with Thurlestone Rock on the shore below, and on past the golf course to the picturesque village of Thurlestone. From Bantham, where dunes and a sandy beach attract holiday makers, a ferry crosses the river Avon to Bigbury which has a fine ancient church well worth the visit. At low tide it is possible to walk along the sands to Bigbury-on-Sea, though the official path along the road gives better views. From the sands Burgh Island can also be reached by walking at low tide. At higher tides the very odd-looking tractor-drawn ferry bus can be used.

The next section of the path to Beacon Point has several very steep gradients. At Ayrmer Cove, a short detour to the attractive village of Ringmore is recommended. Here R.C. Sherriff wrote his famous play *Journey's End*, about the First World War, in the pub of the same name. The thirteenth-century church is also of interest. Back on the coast a particularly steep gradient leads down to Westcombe Beach and then equally steeply up the other side. From the 300 ft (90 m) Beacon Point the path turns Ferrycombe Point to Wonwell Beach on the River Erme, often described as England's most unspoiled river mouth. As there is no bridge or ferry over the river it is best

to wait for low tide and to wade across to Mothercombe. The alternative is a 10 mile (16 km) detour inland!

The path climbs out of Mothercombe to Stoke House, where it is worth taking a detour seaward to St Peter's Church, the church of Noss Mayo until the roof collapsed in the 1860s. Now partially restored, it is a fine weatherswept ruin.

A track round Stoke Point rejoins the official path and goes along an old carriage drive for several miles. From the 200 ft (60 m) cliff tops of Gara Point seals and porpoises may be seen in the summer, and on a clear day there are fine views from here to the Cornish coast and back eastwards to Prawle Point.

The path reaches the River Yealm which is only crossed by ferry – from Noss Mayo to Newton Ferrers or Warren Point – in high summer. At other times most will regard the Yealm as the end of their walk

on the South Devon Coast Path, taking a bus inland to Billacombe and Plymouth, although it is possible to take another bus back to pick up the path again.

The path section from Wembury to Turnchapel offers good views across the Sound to Cornwall, Plymouth and The Hoe. The Hoe famous for its lighthouse and Sir Francis Drake's bowls game, has been called the finest urban viewpoint in England. Plymouth Sound below, sited at the mouth of two rivers, the Tamar and the Plym, is a magnificent anchorage which developed as a military port in the Middle Ages. In the sixteenth century both Drake and Hawkins lived here and from here the fleet sailed against the Spanish Armada. In June 1620 the *Speedwell*, which was carrying the Pilgrim Fathers to America, had to pull into Plymouth with a leak. The 102 passengers transferred to the *Mayflower* to complete the historic voyage. Later, in 1772 James Cook left from Plymouth to circle the world, and to here, in 1967, Francis Chichester returned from his own, solo, circumnavigation. The city suffered badly from air raids in 1941 and extensive rebuilding was necessary after the war. Plymouth is now a busy city, the West Country's biggest thriving port and a major resort.

Plymouth. Smeaton's lighthouse on The Hoe can be seen at the left edge of the picture

Smeaton's Lighthouse on The Hoe, Plymouth

The Cornish Coastal Path

(OS sheets 201, 204, 203, 200, 190)

Mount Edgecombe Park to Fowey (33 mls, 53 km)

CORNWALL IS REACHED by taking the ferry from Stonehouse to Cremyll, a crossing noted with horror by Celia Fiennes who spent an hour in the boat despite having five men to row it. She claimed that at one point they were stationary in the current for 15 minutes and thanked God for safe delivery.

The Cornish Coastal Path is unusual in that although it is of no great antiquity it is a real path, dating from the 1700s, when it was patrolled by the Custom and Excise Service to deter smuggling. Later the coastguard used it to watch for shipping in distress, and to prevent wrecking. After falling into disuse, it was cleared in the 1970s to become one of the best of Britain's long-distance footpaths.

Our first steps on the path are into Mount Edgecumbe Park, once considered the best-sited house and garden in Britain. Both were to have been given to the Duke of Medina Sidonia if the Spanish Armada had been successful.

Beyond, easy walking leads past Kingsland and Cawsand to Penlee, extensively fortified during the First World War. Ahead now is Rame Head, a prominent landmark, with a chapel to St Michael that once served as a beacon.

The path reaches a group of chalets from which a road is followed to a path for Tregantle Fort. The Fort, beyond which firing ranges force the walker to use the road if the red flags are flying, is one of 'Palmerston's Follies', built to protect Plymouth in the 1860s, and soon rendered obsolete by improvements in naval gunnery. Because of this, a tunnel was constructed, leading inland to another fort at Anthony, to enable the garrison to escape in the event of a French attack!

At the eastern end of Whitesand Bay is Portwrinkle, a hamlet with a decayed harbour, beyond which the beach can be safely walked, at low tide, to Looe. There are high cliffs east of Downderry and one or two rocky outcrops, but chiefly the cliffs are shale, prone to landslips which occasionally divert the path.

Looe is a prosperous fishing port, not as spoiled as some Cornish villages, for instance nearby Polperro, and with fewer tourists. Like Fowey to the west, Looe developed as a trading port in the fourteenth century and was a military port for the campaigns of Edward III, until 'pestilence' caused its decline. The town continued as a fishing port, and was involved in the early Newfoundland fishery, but was destroyed by French and Spanish ships in 1405, and never recovered its former importance.

East Looe and West Looe are connected by a ferry for those not anxious to walk through the towns. The path leaves West Looe southward, rounding Hannafore Point for Portnadior Bay. On the cliff top of Talland Bat beyond, there are many mushrooms, but beware, they are yellow-staining mushrooms, and you will not walk far tomorrow if you eat them. Here too are posts measuring a nautical mile for boats in the bay.

Polperro was once a remote fishing settlement connected to the outside world by a muddy footpath, but times change, and although some boats still fish from here, the harbourside village is now given over to tourism, being crowded in summer and a ghost town in winter. Old buildings once connected with the fishing industry still stand and the village is unquestionably picturesque, but it is no place for the sensitive.

From Polperro to Polruan is an attractive and rather isolated stretch of coast, with only tiny hamlets inland. There are inviting coves for swimming, and rockpools full of marine life. The valleys are warm and sheltered, with early flowers in spring, and many

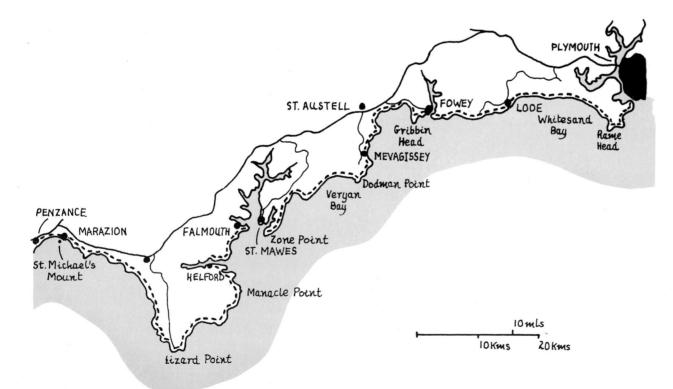

Looe, a typical Cornish fishing village, divided into two halves, East and West, by the River Looe

butterflies in summer. At Lansallos a track leading inland has been cut into the rock behind the beach. It was built to carry seaweed for use as a fertiliser. Such sunken tracks, there are others in Cornwall, also offered shelter for those taking illicit cargoes inland, and a watchtower for the Revenue Service was established nearby at Pencarrow Head. From it the view extends from Bolt Head to Dodman Point.

Polruan, a very pretty and well-set village, is connected by ferry with Fowey, its larger neighbour across the river. Fowey owes its origin to Edward I, who was advised to develop a maritime region in the south-west, to supplement the East Anglian and Cinque ports, all of which were vulnerable to foreign attack. The ancient harbours were at Golant, at the south end of the trans-peninsular route to Padstow, and Lostwithiel, at the tidal limit, which became silted as a result of tin-working activity in the Middle Ages.

Fowey traded with Bordeaux from about 1300, dealing in cloth, wine, iron, salt and tin, but it became a centre for piracy, and after a particularly destructive attack on the Cinque Ports, which ended their maritime supremacy, the king, Edward IV, was obliged to suppress the activities of the 'Fowey Gallants', and employed the men of Dartmouth to destroy the harbour and ships. They also carried off the great chain which had protected the river mouth, slung between the two forts, whose remains are still visible. The bulk of the town's trade then passed to Truro. Today Fowey is still an active commercial port. The walker should spend time among the old buildings, especially the church of St Nicholas, built in 1336, and the early sixteenth-century Place House, seat of the Treffry family.

Gribbin Head to Cadgwith (68 mls, 109 km)

From the southern end of Fowey the path leads easily to Gribbin Head where it turns north, reaching Polkerris with its tiny harbour and a section of trampled dunes to the road for Par. Par is the principal port for shipping china clay, and the sea is stained with the waste. Inland there is a huge expanse of white spoil heaps.

From Par the industrial scenery is maintained through Carlyon Bay, now a resort but once an area of intense mining activity. The scene is brightened by Charlestown's little harbour, built in 1791. It was considered unremarkable and backward, 40 or 50 years ago, but is now valued for its eighteenth-century appearance. The harbour, named after Charles

A Kissing Gate on the Coastal Path

Rashleigh, its builder, was designed by John Smeaton, builder of the Eddystone lighthouse, and was used for exporting copper before the china clay boom. Inland from here is St Austell, centre of the china clay industry.

Southward, the cliffs at Ropehaven are a good place to watch wintering birds, while Black Head is a quiet interlude before the tourist trap of Pentewan. Southward is Mevagissey, its name deriving from two Saints, Meva ag (and) Issey, of whom little is known. The first stone pier here was built in the fifteenth century, to protect the fishing boats. The inner harbour was added in about 1770. Mevagissey is a beautiful village, but not in summer when it can be jammed with visitors moving in a slow circle round the streets and back to the car-park.

Badrugan's Leap is named for the leap, on horseback in 1485, of Sir Henry Treworth of Badrugan en route for a boat to France, and his escape from the pursuing Sir Richard Edgecumbe. Sir Henry had backed the wrong side at Bosworth Field. From the Leap – cliff erosion means that the exact spot cannot be located – walk round Chapel Point for Gorran Haven and Dodman Point, the outstanding feature along this section of coast, a high, flat-topped promontory of pale grey slate. The southern half has a very large cliff castle, still with impressive ramparts, and commanding extensive views.

Hemmick Bay is a secluded spot, road access being steep and difficult, while Porthluney Cove beyond is an excellent sandy beach overlooked by Caerhays

Castle, an early nineteenth-century building by John Nash. Beyond, Portholland, Portloe and Portscotho are typical small fishing villages on a coastline known as Roseland, from the Celtic *ros*, meaning a peninsula. The birdlife is good here, and there is even a chance of seeing a chough, never common, but once a resident. Nare Head, an excellent viewpoint, can be used to watch the gulls and auks on Gull Rock a half-mile offshore.

Towan Beach, owned by the National Trust, has a good shingle beach, while nearby St Anthony Head is a magnificent viewpoint. There are usually seals at the base of the cliffs here. From Place Manor there may be a ferry to St Mawes. If not, there is a long walk inland to reach the village.

St Mawes had a castle built, like Pendennis opposite, in the time of Henry VIII. Unlike Pendennis, which held out for six months, it fell to the Parliamentary forces after only one day, at the end of the Civil War, because it had no landward defences.

A ferry takes the walker to Falmouth, a port on one of the world's finest natural harbours. For many years it was the first port of call in Britain for Atlantic shipping – news of the victory at Trafalgar was first heard here. The maritime museum is excellent for those wishing to learn more about the history of the town and harbour. Be sure also to see the Queen's Pipe – once called the King's Pipe – an incinerator used to burn captured contraband tobacco when smuggling was rife.

Another ferry is needed southward at Helford Passage, close to the beautiful National Trust gardens at Glendurgan. Helford, across the water, is an equally beautiful village, as is the smaller St Anthony-in-Meneage to the east. St Anthony is said to have been founded by shipwrecked Normans who vowed to build a church to the saint if their lives were spared. The addition to the name means 'monk's land' and probably derives from earlier, Celtic, monks. Dennis Head, close to the village, is topped by an Iron Age hill-fort.

Gillan Creek can be forded, at low tide, to avoid a long detour, the path then reaching the coast again at Porthoustock, a village spoiled by disused quarries. The Manacles, near the village, are best seen from Lowland Point to the south. These are an extensive group of rocks and reefs, once much-feared by

St Michael's Mount set in a sheltered bay off Marazion is reached by a tidal causeway

vessels making for Falmouth. The shipwrecks are too many to list here, though a visit to St Keverne churchyard will give you some idea of the losses over the years. Today, the area is popular with skin-divers. It is also frequented by sharks, which can sometimes be seen from the clifftop, not only basking shark, but smaller ones too, even mako.

Coverack, a pretty village, is passed en route to Black Head, from where the path turns westward for the Lizard. Carleon Cove has a serpentine quarry, much of the stone being finished locally, and some being available in the shops. Cadgwith is around the next corner, still a pretty village, with thatched roofs, most unusual in Cornwall, and testifying to the village's remoteness, not merely from the slate quarries of Delabole, but also from a small harbour where coasters might call.

Devil's Frying Pan to St Michael's Mount (26 mls, 42 km)

The romantically named Devil's Frying Pan further on is a hole caused by a collapsed cave. Another, the Lion's Den, caused by a collapse in 1847, lies closer to the Lizard itself. The tip of the Lizard is Britain's most southerly point, and not surprisingly was once the site of numerous shipwrecks. Ships had to rely on taking soundings if visibility was poor, searching for the 'forty-five fathoms and a fine sandy bottom', which told them they were east of the headland and safe. To reduce the danger, a lighthouse was built in 1619, a project opposed by the locals who made a good living from wreck salvage. The original lighthouse was replaced in 1752, and modified in 1903. The Point is a good place to watch birds and to see other less well-known migrants, such as Clouded Yellow butterflies.

A little north of Lizard Point is Kynance, a picturesque and popular cove. The name means 'a narrow valley', from the valley that brings the stream to the sea, not from the rock cleft – also known as the Devil's Bellows – where eroded soft rock allows the sea to roar in. Offshore is Asparagus Island, where the rare wild asparagus grows.

Soft rock re-appears at Soap Rock and Gew Graze where soapstone (steatite) was mined in the eighteenth century and used in the manufacture of porcelain. Mining ceased here when china clay was discovered. Northward, the path by-passes Vellan Head, skirting the evocatively named Pol Cornick and Ogo-dour Cove for Predannack Head. The cliffs here are lichen-covered, while the downs behind the Head are jointly administered by the National Trust and the Cornish Trust for Nature Conservation, and are home to a host of rare plants, including several species of orchid and heather.

Mullion Cove has a pretty harbour and a natural rock tunnel that leads, at low tide, to a sandy beach. Offshore, Mullion Island is a sea bird sanctuary, closed to the public.

North again the path is easily followed to Poldhu, with a memorial to Marconi, whose first transatlantic broadcast – the single morse letter S – was sent from here in December 1901. Inland, is Goonhilly Down where the transmitters are a little more sophisticated. Nearby Dollar Cove is named for the treasure washed ashore when a Spanish galleon sank.

Beyond the headland are Porthleven Sands, a long beach that is very unsafe for swimming, and dangerous even to walk along; the unwary are often caught by large waves, and too many have been drowned. In its earlier stages, by Loe Bar, the beach is safer and good for beachcombing, with many curiosities from warmer water – beans from the Caribbean, or innumerable floats of the jellyfish *Velella spirans*, commonly known as 'By the wind sailor'. Loe Bar, a sand bar, was formed during a storm, sealing off the former port of Helston by blocking the mouth of the River Cober. The freshwater lake formed by the blockage is a refuge for many water birds, especially in winter.

Beyond the sands is Porthleven, a picturesque fishing harbour, not at all spoiled by tourism, then a short stretch of rocky shore, with good rock pools, before two headlands are passed. Rinsey and Trewavas Heads are outcrops of granite in the surrounding metamorphic rocks, and bear the scars of copper mining. Rinsey Head is topped by the shell of the Wheal Prosper mine.

West of the headlands are Praa Sands, a popular family beach where it is best to walk along the beach, rather than to follow the path through the built-up area behind. Another, smaller beach is crossed to Prussia Cove. Formerly known as Porthleah, it was renamed after a notorious smuggler, nicknamed 'the King of Prussia', active from 1777 to 1807, and who, by all accounts, gave the Revenue men a hard time. The cove is also remembered as the place where the old battleship *Warspite* went aground on her way to the breakers, in 1947. It proved impossible to refloat her, and she was scrapped *in situ*.

Turning the long nose of Cudden Point the walkers get their first view of St Michael's Mount, losing sight of it again at Perranuthnoe at the end of Perran Sands. St Michael's Mount, offshore from Marazion, is said to be named after the saint who had a vision here in the eighth century. Edward the Confessor gave the island to monks who then established a priory. At the beginning of the Civil War the island was fortified by the then owner, Sir Arthur Basset, who, conscious of the likely damage and expense that would result from a siege, promptly surrendered it to the Roundheads, without resistance, when called upon to do so. Later, Basset sold the Mount to Col. John Aubyn, an ancestor of Lord St Levan, who lives there still, though St Michael's is now owned by the National Trust. The island is connected to the shore by a causeway, passable at low tide, a fact that has led to its identification with *Ictis*, the ancient tin exporting port described by the Roman Diodorus Siculus. Unfortunately there is little else to support this idea.

Marazion to St Ives (45 mls, 72 km)

From Marazion, or the Mount if it is visited, the coastal path follows the shoreline to Penzance. In spite of being trampled, the dunes here still support some interesting plants. This area was probably an ancient river-mouth which was blocked by sand and, when the resulting lake silted, was converted to marshland. In winter, grebes and divers can be seen.

Penzance is a pleasant town, no longer a major port, but not entirely given over to tourism. From here boats leave for the Scilly Isles, all that remains of the legendary Lyonesse, King Arthur's Kingdom. The 100 islets offer splendid walking on fine sandy beaches. Sir Humphrey Davy was born in Penzance in 1778 and his statue now stands in front of the Market House. The exotic Egyptian House is the office of the National Trust, appropriate in view of the Trust's preservation efforts in Cornwall. Near the town the Trust owns Trengwainton, a garden of Himalayan and Burmese shrubs.

Road walking is necessary to reach Newlyn and Mousehole (prounounced Mouzel), the latter a little fishing village with serious car-parking difficulties, which should make walkers feel superior. Both Newlyn and Mousehole were burned by the Spaniards in 1595. Close by Mousehole the Penlee Point lifeboat house is passed, recalling the day in 1981 when the *Looking south past Gurnard's Head on the north Cornish Coast. Inland can be seen the village of Porthmeor*

Levan there is a cleft rock, split by the staff of St Levan himself, who prophesised that the world would end if a ladened pack-horse ever walked through the cleft.

Westward, at Porthwarra is a bird observation and ringing site. Migrating birds arrive from March to May, and leave from August onwards, and there is an impressive list of sightings. The cove is sheltered and inviting, and the walker may wish to linger before tackling the exposed, but majestic, granite cliffs ahead that offer the best seascapes on the path.

The granite cliffs, though spectacular, support little vegetation, and few birds nest on them. There are sea birds, including skuas, to be seen offshore though. The view is of the Longships light and the more distant Wolf Rock, and, if the weather is clear, of the Scilly Isles. Land's End itself, England's most westerly

St Michael's Mount

The Longship's Lighthouse off of Land's End

boat overturned in a gale with the loss of all eight crew.

Next is Lamorna Cove, a romantic spot where, in the nineteenth century, granite from the Kemyel Wartha quarries, was loaded into ships for export. Tater-du lighthouse beyond became the first British automatic light in 1965. Westward, Penbarth Cove is the most perfect of all Cornish coves, according to the National Trust, and is the first in a series of interesting but varied spots.

On the next headland is a cliff castle, Treryn Dinas, and the famous Logan Rock. Logans – from the Cornish *log*, to move – are delicately-balanced boulders which will rock at the slightest touch, their rocking foretelling the future to those who can interpret the movement. In April 1824, in an act of mindless vandalism, one Lt Goldsmith RN – nephew of the poet – and a group of friends, dislodged the rock. Such was the public outcry that he was forced to replace it at his own expense – it ruined him – but it has never been the same since. At Porthcurno, is the celebrated Minack open air theatre, while at St

The Logan Rock, near Treen

point, almost as far west as Mallaig, has a new owner, and there is hope for improvement, with repairs to the damage done to cliff and vegetation by the feet of millions of tourists.

Nearby, Sennen Cove – beyond Maen, or Mayon, Castle, another cliff castle, with a single rampart of stone and a well preserved entrance – is preferred by

St Ives, one of Cornwall's most popular resorts

many to Land's End, as the seascapes are equally spectacular but less intruded upon by people. The village, too, is a quiet spot, while Whitesand Bay is a mecca for surfers.

Low granite cliffs lead to a diversion inland at Lower Bosavern, and on to Cape Cornwall, just south of which, and close to the path, is the Carn Goose Barrow, also known as Carn Gluze or Ballowall. It is a complex chambered tomb from the middle Bronze Age. Cape Cornwall, the only 'cape' in England and Wales, is topped by ancient mine chimneys, and mine ruins abound on the next cliff section. Inland, there is a museum to the local industries on the old Geevor site at Trewellard.

From Pendeen Watch, where a path leads to the lighthouse for a view of the sea stained red by ore deposits in the granite at the cliff base, there is a spectacular 5-mile (8 km) stretch of coast to Zennor.

Bosigran, now a favourite haunt of climbers, was a wartime training cliff for commandos, while Trereen Dinas, an Iron Age cliff-fort on Gurnard's Head, holds the remains of 13 huts within its banks and ditches,

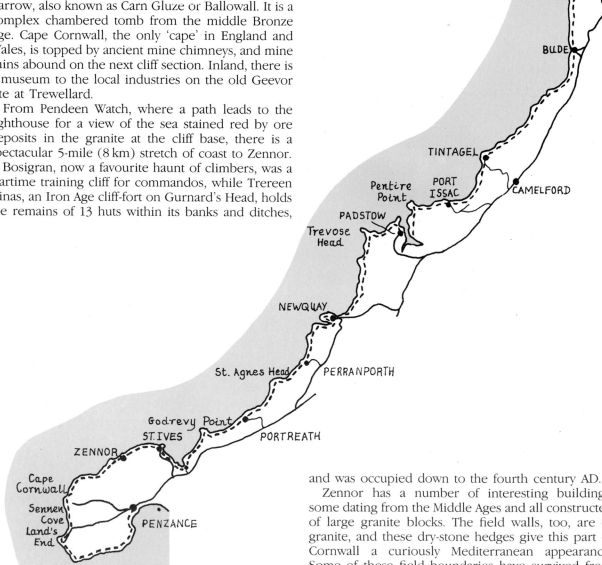

and was occupied down to the fourth century AD.

Zennor has a number of interesting buildings, some dating from the Middle Ages and all constructed of large granite blocks. The field walls, too, are of granite, and these dry-stone hedges give this part of Cornwall a curiously Mediterranean appearance. Some of these field boundaries have survived from the Iron Age, and a little way inland darker green lines in the grass indicate where the Bronze Age boundaries ran. Here, as further south, the land is thickly strewn with ancient remains, though most are

well away from the coast.

D.H.Lawrence wrote part of *Women in Love* in Zennor during the First World War, but he and his German-born wife were forced to leave, the locals accusing them of being German spies. The path from Zennor Head follows a plateau between the granite moors and the sea, taking the walker into St Ives.

St Ives was a small fishing port, but is now a busy resort, at times crowded beyond belief. It is famous as an artist's village, a fame resting in large part on its association with Dame Barbara Hepworth; one of her sculptures stands outside the Guild Hall.

River Hayle to Crantock (33 mls, 53 km)

From the village the Path follows the railway eastwards, a messy detour around the Hayle estuary being necessary as there is no ferry over the few yards from Port Kidney to Towans. Hayle itself has little to offer though the estuary is of great biological importance, having an unusual mix of mud and sand which supports a rich fauna, with plenty of wading birds. An osprey and a stork, too, were seen here in 1988!

Much of archaeological interest, dating from the Bronze Age to Medieval times and including an early Christian site of some importance, is buried beneath the sands that the route follows to Godrevy Point. The Point has a bad reputation for shipwrecks, one wreck reputedly being the vessel carrying all Charles I's personal possessions, lost on the day of his execution, though cynics will note the comparison with the story of the loss of King John's treasure, shortly before his death. Both Godrevy Point and The Knavocks to the east are part of a large promontory of sandstone, harder than the surrounding shales, and are excellent for sea birds and ravens. Grey seals are common here throughout the year.

At Reskajeage Downs the clifftop is nearly flat, with good coastal scenery for several miles, though occasional land slips force the walker onto the road. Beyond, there are steep cliffs, and the going is slippery in wet weather, so care is needed. There are a steep climb, and a very steep-sided valley before Portreath.

Portreath is a curious little port, with inner and outer harbours, constructed originally in the mid-eighteenth century to export copper, principally to

Looking north-west along Trevose head, to the west of Padstow. Off shore to the left are the rocky Quies

South Wales. A tramway was constructed in 1809 to connect the mines with the harbour, and its route can still be traced. Portreath also imported coal to serve the extensive industrial region inland, around Redruth and Camborne. Pebbles on the beach here sometimes contain interesting minerals.

From Portreath the path skirts Nancekuke, once infamous as a chemical warfare centre, to reach Porthtowan from where, at low tide, the beach can be followed to Chapel Porth. But please be careful, it is easy to be cut off by rising water.

Chapel Porth takes its name from a chapel that once stood here, and is the start for an interesting nature trail that mixes natural history and industrial archaeology, passing noted bird haunts and the remains of the Wheal Coates mine, as well as much more.

The area north of Chapel Porth, both before and after St Agnes Head, a fine viewpoint, is also dotted with the remains of mining activity. The shell at Trevellas Porth is of a tin mine, while Cligga Head is extensively scarred with tips, old quarry workings, and the ruins of a dynamite factory belonging to Nobel, a desolation favoured by peregrine falcons.

North of Cligga Head was a copper-mining area, though traces of other minerals can be found in the tips, including wolfram (tungsten) and even gold.

The ruin of the Wheal Coates mine, near St Agnes Head

Perranporth, the next village, is a small holiday town named after St Piran, the Patron Saint of Cornwall, an obscure figure said to have sailed to Cornwall from Ireland on a millstone. Perran Beach is an impressive stretch of sand, with lifeguard patrols at the south end. The walker should beware of quicksand, particularly if the temptation to ford the river is overwhelming.

In the dunes of Penhale Sands – at 270 ft (82 m) the highest in Britain – that back the beach are buried the remains of St Piran's Oratory, dating from the seventh or eighth century, and one of the oldest Christian buildings in Britain. Some crosses associated with the foundation are visible above the sand. The soil here is lime-rich, and supports a good flora and a fascinating range of snail species. Penhale Point, at the northern end of the sands, is an army training area and access is sometimes restricted, though there is usually no problem on Sundays. **Please read the entry notices carefully.** Holywell Beach, beyond the Point, is heavily used in summer, and the dunes behind are much worn.

Kelsey Head, at the northern end of Holywell Bay, is a Site of Special Scientific Interest, with a varied fauna, including hares, while Porth Joke, the next inlet, lies at the mouth of a little valley with a very interesting flora, the soil here having a high calcium content. In May, the valley is covered with cowslips, and there are rarities to be found, including orchids, and Shepherd's Needle.

Crantock is named for a Celtic Saint. The village was once a religious centre, with a famous collegiate church, but a report from 1352 states that it had declined and was serving as a tavern and brothel! The Gannel, the shallow, sandy estuary beyond Crantock, is crossed by an occasional ferry, by means of a causeway at low tide, or by a lengthy detour. Either way, Newquay, the largest Cornish resort, is reached.

Newquay has been given over to tourism, but the harbour is still pretty, and Huer's House, on the cliff above it, is a nice link with history. In the eighteenth century a look-out here watched for shoals of pilchards in the bay and then guided the town's boats with instructions bellowed through a huge horn.

Newquay to Marsland Mouth (68 mls, 109 km)

Newquay ends at Trevelgue Head which has another cliff castle, unusual in having four ramparts. Beyond it is the long expanse of Watergate Bay. Beneath the beach here, at Mawgan Porth, a very busy place in

summer, is an ancient settlement, dating from around AD 500, about the time of the Saxon conquest. The Cornish then lived in rectangular houses, the prototype of the later longhouses, and farmed, supplementing their diet with fish and shellfish.

Northward now is a superb stretch of coast to Porthcothan with the famed Bedruthan Steps set halfway. The Steps are named after a Cornish giant, but are actually granite stacks left behind by the erosion of softer, interleaving rock.

From Porthcothan, once notorious for smuggling when contraband was stored in cliff tunnels, the path runs easily on to Trevose Head – a lump of hard, igneous rock thrust out into the Atlantic. It continues right around it and on to Harlyn Bay, where there is a small museum of finds from the numerous local archaeological sites, from the Mesolithic to the Iron Age. From Harlyn Bay an easy walk by way of Stepper Point reaches the River Camel and Padstow.

Padstow is a fine harbour town whose May Day festivities include the famous 'Obby 'Orse. The 'Orse is a man dressed as a horse but with a ferocious mask, who is led through the streets. The festival is believed to be pagan in origin. From the town a ferry crosses the Camel, dropping the walker onto a path through Polzeath to Pentire Point. St Enodoc's church, a little way north of the landing stage, is fourteenth century and had to be reclaimed from the sand. It is named for a Celtic saint St Petroc, as is Trebetherick, who landed here from Ireland in the mid-sixth century. This area has always had strong connections with Ireland: a route frequented by Celtic saints and Irish pilgrims started here and led to the south Cornwall coast at Fowey. A new footpath, called 'The Saints' Way', following this route, has recently been opened.

Pentire means 'head of the land' and is another lump of hard rock projecting out into the sea. The coastal path does not visit 'The Rumps' at the headland's tip, but a visit is well worthwhile, as here there is one of the best cliff castles in Cornwall. There are three ramparts, built at different times from the first century BC to the first AD, though there is also evidence of occupation after the Roman conquest.

From Port Quin, a quiet place abandoned in the nineteenth century when the menfolk all died in a

Tintagel, famous as King Arthur's Castle, though actually dating from the twelfth century

storm – or so legend has it – there is a signed alternative, and longer, path which visits Kellan Head where there are the remains of an old antimony mine. The shorter route goes straight to Port Isaac, a pretty, typically Cornish fishing port, which grew up in the fourteenth century. Port Gaverne, on its east side was famous as a boat-building centre, making clinker-built rowing boats. Drivers often have difficulty in the village's narrow streets though one lane, Squeezibelly Alley, suggests that life is little easier for the walker.

The route north from Port Isaac to Tintagel is a little less inspiring, though Barrett's Zawn does have a collapsed tunnel – called Donkey Hole – a remnant of the slate trade, slate having been hauled through the tunnel from the Delabole quarry. Trebarwith Strand is popular with surfers, but, beware, the sand is submerged at high tide. This was historically useful when coal ships from South Wales dumped their cargoes at the base of the cliffs, so that the retreating tide left the coal handily placed.

Tintagel is a tourist trap, and is best avoided in summer unless you are a determined fan of King Arthur. It would be a shame to miss the castle though, so save your visit for low season. The Arthurian legends surrounding the site can be traced only to Tennyson's *Idylls of the King*, there being no supporting evidence for the castle's claim. In reality the castle is twelfth century and was once owned by the Black Prince, the first Duke of Cornwall, but reality cuts little ice with the believers – Tintagel, with its wild, atmospheric position *feels* right.

Between Tintagel and Boscastle are several interesting rock formations – Lye Rock, with the remains of a cliff castle, is a noted bird breeding site, while Elephant Rock stands on the beach at Rocky Valley. Nearby Bossiney Mound is said to cover King Arthur's Round Table. This section of the path

Tintagel Castle

receives little sun in winter, and it is often very wet and treacherous.

Boscastle is a small picturesque harbour built in the late sixteenth century to export slate and corn, and is now preserved from development by the National Trust. Pentargon, the next inlet after Boscastle, has a spectacular waterfall, while a little further on is the highest cliff in Cornwall, appropriately called High Cliff and 731 ft (223 m) above the sea. The cliff is an excellent viewpoint, particularly of The Strangles, the northward beach that was once notorious for shipwrecks. Also on a clear day, Lundy Island is visible.

The path runs above the beach past Cambeak and through some excellent National Trust property at Crackington Haven to an oakwood beyond Chipman Strand. This, England's most westerly oakwood, studs the path to Millook Haven. Widemouth Sand, where the first hotline from Downing Street to the White House came ashore, is then crossed to Bude.

Bude is a small resort, very popular with surfers.

While there, be sure to see the canal, which ends with its only lock – a sea lock – in Breakwater Road. The canal was built in the early nineteenth century to take sand to Launceston, 35 miles (56 km) away, bringing slates back for export. Launceston is 350 ft (105 m) above Bude, the lack of locks being overcome by a ramp where the wheeled canal tug boats were chainhauled up metal rails by water power. It was an extraordinary piece of engineering.

Northward to Sharpnose Point the beach can be walked, but take care if the tide is coming in as you near the jagged pinnacles of Sandy Mouth, as the cliffs here are very unstable and to try to escape up them is very dangerous. Duckpool, the last small cove before the headland, has a bridge, built with money from William IV, over a stream from the beautiful Coombe Valley.

There is a prominent landmark at Sharpnose Point - the US-owned satellite ground station. A little to the north and inland is Morwenstow, named after Morwenna, a Celtic saint, or so said its famous mid-nineteenth-century vicar, Robert Stephen Hawker, poet, practical joker, and true English eccentric. Hawker built his parsonage where he saw sheep sheltering from the weather – 'Where better for the shepherd of the flock?' he asked. The parsonage chimneys are shaped like the spires of the churches he had served. During wedding services he would toss the wedding-ring in the air to remind the groom of the lottery of marriage, and once excommunicated one of his 10 cats for catching and eating a mouse. He is also credited with the introduction of Harvest Festivals to the Church.

Beyond, Cornakey Cliff gives way to Marsland Cliff, and the path falls steeply to finish at Marsland Mouth, where a bridge over the stream takes the walker back into Devon.

The North Devon and Somerset Coastal Path

(OS sheets 190, 180, 181)

Marsland Mouth to Clovelly (14 mls, 23 km)

ONLY NARROW MARSLAND water separates Cornwall from Devon and the 'new' coastal path that starts beyond it begins without ceremony. The path is steep and tiring until Speke's Mill, where a spectacular waterfall drops 50 ft (15 m) down a steep, twisting gorge to the sea. The path then continues behind St Catherine's Tor, a hill with the sea on one side and a pastoral valley on the other. A chapel to the saint once stood here but has been long since lost to the sea, though the remnants of what was once the Swannery of Hartland Abbey can still be seen in the valley.

A short way north is Hartland Quay, whose story is told in the excellent little museum. The harbour was built following an Act of Parliament in 1566 sponsored by, among others, Raleigh, Drake and Hawkins, to provide a refuge on this hostile Devon shore. A thriving community of coastguards, fishermen and workers of the lime kilns developed around the quay until a storm in 1887 breached the harbour wall. With the arrival of the railway in Bideford, at almost the same time, it was considered uneconomic to repair it. It is hard to visualise an enclosed harbour here now, among the cliffs of layered and folded slate and sandstone.

Damehole, north of the quay, is a fine example of a dissected valley. Originally, the stream that flows down the valley to the north and into the sea would have carried on through Smoothlands and entered the sea at Damehole Point, but the comparatively weaker rocks have been eroded, leaving Smoothlands as a valley without a river.

On the climb towards Hartland Point the walker will realise why this part of Devon was known as a wrecking coast. Before the days of rail and road transport everything was carried by sea and this section of coast was one of the busiest. Most of the produce from the Welsh coal and steel industries, together with that from the factories of the Midlands, passed by on its way to the newly-opened markets of the Empire, and over 136 vessels were lost during the last 200 years before the introduction of steam engines. Sadder still is that there would have been few survivors after the boats had been tossed onto the local rocks. The Romans, no bad judges of a seascape, referred to the headland as the 'Promontory of Hercules'. The lighthouse here, built in 1874, has one of the most powerful lights on the British coast.

Around the sharp corner of the point the walker reaches Bideford Bay and the character of the coastline changes, as here the coast faces north and is, therefore, sheltered from the Atlantic swell and wind. The path pushes the walker right up to the cliff edge as it rounds Hartland RAF Station to Shipload Bay, a bay that is difficult to reach down a long, steep path, but very popular as it is one of the few sandy beaches in the area and is very sheltered. Beyond, the path continues in fine style, passing through the wooded valley of Brownsham to arrive at Mouth Mill with its old lime kiln and the spectacular Blackchurch Rock. Not surprisingly this inverted V of rock is much photographed, and is equally popular with rock climbers, the classic route 'Sacre Coeur' going up the steep seaward side. The bigger, but looser, main cliffs are less spectacular, but equally formidable.

Beyond the cove the walker enters the Clovelly Estate, passing Gallantry Bower, a cleft in the top of the cliff that gives spectacular views, and Angel Wings, a highly ornate carved seat with a shingle roof, that has also been well photographed. Beyond, a walk through the deer park brings the walker to Clovelly itself.

Clovelly is the West Country fishing village of everyone's imagination, the steep, cobbled streets – cobbled with pebbles from the beach – used by donkeys rather than cars, leading past beautiful cottages to a picture postcard harbour. The village was mentioned in the Domesday Book, but owes its present state to Christine Hamlyn, owner of the estate in the first third of this century. Lovely the village may be – and it undoubtedly is, despite the holiday crowds the overdone charm – it is a curious spot, a feudal village that charges the public to enter, and where residents live their lives as part of a tourist attraction.

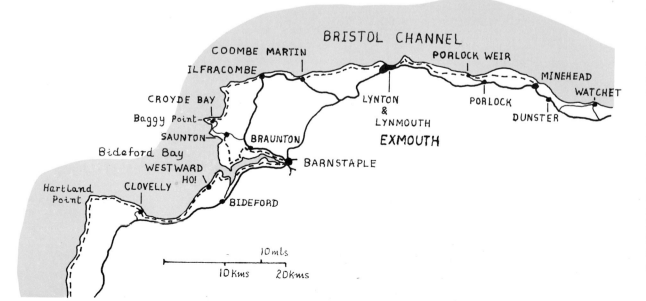

Clovelly

Hobby Drive to Barnstaple (21 mls, 34 km)

Hobby Drive follows on from Clovelly, a famous route through woodland which was actually built as a hobby by Sir James Hamlyn Williams (of the same family) during the Napoleonic Wars. The route was carved out of the hill as a means of giving winter work to poor fishermen and to occupy French prisoners of war. The drive is also a toll road, and in summer the walker often shares it with a great number of cars.

At the end of the drive, the coastal footpath takes a detour through Walland Cary Holiday Camp and down into Buck's Mill Mouth. This pretty hamlet has an interesting front, approached down a steep path. There are large overgrown lime kilns looking like a fort, and a small landing area from which a fishing fleet was once launched. The boats, herring yawls, were pulled up the beach and received only limited protection from a spit of rock called 'The Gore'. Legend has it that this is the start of the Devil's Causeway to Lundy which can be seen, often as a line of breaking surf, running north into the bay. Traditionally, the inhabitants of Buck's Mill are descended from the survivors of a wrecked Spanish

Galleon, although there is no record of such a wreck. An alternative tradition is that of the 'Braund Tribe', which has the villagers belonging to the same family, ruled over by the patriarchal Captain Braund. It is said that 'five generations of this race had set forth as fishermen and mariners, all the better for having no harbour'. It is a measure of the isolation of such local hamlets that legends like these grew up about their founding.

The eastern part of Bideford Bay is largely wooded and hopefully will remain so: the next valley, Peppercombe, has just been acquired by the National Trust, so that, at least, will remain an unspoilt valley of natural woodland, with no upgrading of the present track to a road. Closer to Westward Ho! – just after the pebbles start – be sure to visit a small waterfall, if only to see the bright red sandstone cliffs that appear for a short distance. Beyond, the hills are more rounded, though the way still involves the occasional steep climb. Greencliff has another, but smaller lime kiln, and from there the path is level into Westward Ho! passing Kipling's Tor, named for Rudyard Kipling who was a pupil in the village.

Westward Ho!, named after Charles Kingsley's Elizabethan adventure story, was created as a tourist resort in 1863 on the site of an old fishing village. The plan was to build villas and lodging houses using the beach and golf, the new import from Scotland, as the main attractions. Kingsley, who had been introduced to the area by the Rev. Robert Stephen Hawker, the eccentric vicar mentioned at the end of Cornish Coastal Path, was not a supporter of the scheme as he thought it would ruin the beauty of the village. It is difficult to fault his judgement. Kipling's old school, the United Services College, was housed in the large Victorian terrace overlooking the resort. He wrote about his stay here in his book *Stalky and Co.*

Many walkers catch a bus from the village around the Taw and Torridge estuaries to Braunton. This misses out 17 miles (27 km) of walking, but this stretch does not have quality of the rest of the route even though it does go past several interesting spots on the industrial section of the North Devon coast.

If the walker chooses not to take the bus, the path follows the pebble ridge around to the estuary's mouth, then goes up the estuary towards Appledore. This section is a taste of things to come as Northam Burrows, the dunes that back the beach, combine the functions of tourist attraction, golf course, nature

reserve and municipal rubbish tip.

Appledore is in many ways a typical North Devon village, pretty on the outside but having a base in the hard industries of shipbuilding, fishing and farming. The village was granted free port status by Elizabeth I for its help against the Spanish Armada, and acquired a reputation for being a tightly knit community of hardy people. In Bideford it was said that Appledore was the place where they ate the missionaries. At high tides in summer, a ferry crosses the Torridge to Instow, saving a walk of about 6 miles (10 km), to the magnificent, multi-arched, medieval bridge at Bideford.

From Bideford the railway line that once ran to Barnstaple, and now forms the basis of a linear country park, bridlepath and nature reserve, can be used to reach Instow. It does not correspond precisely with the coastal path, but by working between the two a reasonable route can be found all the way to Barnstaple. The front at Instow is worth walking, if only to see the cricket pitch that must be one of the most scenic in Devon. Northward, the Taw estuary is wonderfully wild, an excellent place to watch birds. Henry Williamson set *Tarka the Otter* around this river.

Otters still live on the Taw estuary where Tarka the Otter *was set*

Barnstaple is a fine old town, one of only four Devon boroughs mentioned in the Domesday Book. The church is excellent, with a timber-framed spire and a collection of seventeenth-century monuments. The castle mound is equally grand. Queen Anne's Walk in the town dates from the early seventeenth century. The Friday Pannier Market, when local farm

Saunton Down, the headland at the northern end of Bideford Bay

produce is sold, is a must for anyone wanting to capture the flavour of a Devon market town.

From Barnstaple the coastal path is not easy to follow. It goes down the Taw bank towards Braunton until it is stopped by the RAF station at Chivenor. Here it goes inland, regaining the river at Braunton, now quiet but which once competed with Appledore, Bideford and Barnstaple as a major port. The official path is not recommended from here, instead it is better to take a route down the estuary to Crow Point and then through the Braunton Burrows nature reserve to Saunton.

River Taw to Heddon's Mouth (37 mls, 59 km)

North now is Croyde, a small village surrounded by holiday camps and car parks. There is an excellent gem and shell museum here, and a beautiful bay, whose beach is covered with sunbathers in the season. The bay is also a haven for surfers, as it faces west, and the enclosing headlands concentrate the surf, producing excellent waves. Baggy Point, the headland to the north, is a mecca for rock climbers, and has numerous walks around its spectacular high cliffs. As the walker rounds Baggy Point the big sweep of Woolacombe Sand opens up with the path taking the down above it to Woolacombe village. Beyond is Barricane Beach, enclosed by rock buttresses and famous for the shells brought ashore by the tide.

The path then skirts the village of Mortehoe for Morte Point, another graveyard for shipping in the days of sail. Even today this area is treated warily, the lighthouse on nearby Bull Point being a welcome landmark for ships entering Bristol Channel. Walkers passing here in a mist must beware of the fog horn: it is very, very loud.

Lee, the first village beyond Bull Point, is a pretty place that belies its former reputation as a village of wreckers and smugglers. It is studded with fuchsias and set at the bottom of a beautiful wooded valley above a sheltered cove. To the east, the path is a well-made track into Ilfracombe, a Victorian resort seen to perfection from the Torrs Walk above its western edge. The harbour is a busy place, as might be expected in one of the very few ports along this coast that can be entered at lowish tides. Boats from it visit Lundy Island in the Bristol Channel, a National Trust property that takes its name from the Norse for puffin, and still has a sizeable breeding colony of the clown-like auks.

Legend has it that four French ships were sighted off the Ilfracombe coast in 1797 when all the town's garrison and menfolk were elsewhere. The town's womenfolk took their red petticoats, paraded on the seafront wearing them as scarlet jackets and succeeded in convincing the French that the town was well protected. The French, suitably disheartened, sailed away. Above the pier, on Lantern Hill, is the Chapel of St Nicholas built in the fourteenth century and from which a light has shone every night since then as a guide to sailors in the Channel.

From Ilfracombe the walker is faced with the worst section on the whole South West Peninsula Way – pathless main road for several miles into Watermouth Cove. To compensate, the cove is a scenic spot with a superb natural harbour and anchorage. There is limited public access to the bay although the coastal path crosses through it, and because it is in private hands the visitor must pay for entry to the sea caves. Watermouth Castle, built in the early nineteenth century, houses a museum that includes an exhibition on smuggling.

From Watermouth the path crosses a campsite and then joins the old coast road, a wonderfully leafy walk past old lime quarries. There is a path down to Broad Strand which is a quiet and peaceful beach. Efforts have been made to prevent the walker from having to risk life and limb on the main road, but the route down into Combe Martin is still more road than path.

Today, it is difficult to imagine the importance of Combe Martin's industrial past. Silver was mined here from 1293, the mines being especially successful during the reign of Elizabeth I. Mining stopped in the early nineteenth century, though there were several later attempts, all of which failed, to revive it. Now, there is almost no trace of the industry. The village boasts a collection of motor cycles, including that owned by Lawrence of Arabia, and also the 'Pack of Cards' Hotel, built by a seventeenth-century gambler George Lee, which has four floors for the four suits, each floor having 13 doors for the cards in the suit, and a total of 2 windows for the number of cards in the pack.

East of Combe Martin the walker enters the Exmoor National Park and is immediately rewarded with a few miles of wild heath and moorland that inclines steeply, but without big cliffs, into the Bristol Channel. The long climb from Combe Martin over Little Hangman to Great Hangman reaches 1,043 ft (313 m), the highest point on the whole South West

The cliff railway between Lynton and Lynmouth

Peninsula Way. The view from the top is, not surprisingly, superb, taking in the moors of Exmoor and the mountains of South Wales. Comparable splendour follows at Heddon's Mouth, where a wooded, craggy valley runs down from the famous Hunter's Inn. The ruins at the Mouth are old lime kilns.

Highveer Point to Minehead (25 mls, 40 km)

The path now goes over Highveer Point, then passes the site of a Roman fort, and reaches Woody Bay. The official path stays inland of this hamlet but the walker can follow the lane down to the beach to see the oak woods that give the bay its name, and also the ruined jetty, the carved-out bathing pool and some beautiful houses. In the early years of this century there was an attempt to develop the hamlet as a rival to Ilfracombe and other local resorts, but the attempt failed with its promotor, Col Lake, becoming bankrupt and then

Ilfracombe, one of the busiest ports on the Devon Coast

imprisoned. The cliffs of Wringapeak, on the western edge of the bay, has a famous seabird colony with guillemots, razorbills, shags, fulmars and many gulls.

Unfortunately, from Woody Bay the path follows another road all the way to the Valley of the Rocks, passing Lee Abbey, never an abbey despite the name, which is now a Christian holiday and conference centre. It is possible to find a route around the coast to avoid this road section, but the paths are neither marked nor obvious, and there is a need to cross private land, which cannot be recommended.

The Valley of the Rocks is a miniature Cheddar Gorge, complete with crags and tourists. The pinnacles and towers of limestone have fanciful names – the Devil's Cheesewring, Castle Rock and so on – though one spot, Mother Meldrum's Cave, recalls an eccentric inhabitant who Blackmore used as the model for the witch in *Lorna Doone*. The goat herd in the valley is famous, but elusive.

Beyond the valley the path leaves the road, taking the walker to the Lynton–Lynmouth Cliff Railway. This was opened in 1890 and is worked by waterpower and gravity. Each of the two cars has a 500 gallon (227 l.) water tank, which is filled at the top. The two cars are linked by a wire, and when the top car is filled it becomes heavier and descends, raising the lower car. At the bottom the tank is emptied into the sea. The railway rises 500 ft (150 m) on a track just over 850 ft (255 m) long – a very steep climb.

The seafront at Lynmouth is one of only two sites within the National Park where the visitor can drive down to the Sea Wall. In the Park Visitors' Centre on the front is a display on the epic rescue of the ship *Forest Hall* which was washed under Hurlstone Point on a stormy night in 1899. The lifeboat could not be launched at Porlock Weir, and local men got a line aboard from the shore to save the crew. A more tragic happening occured in August 1952 when the River Lyn, swollen by torrential rain, burst its bank, and flooded the village, knocking down houses and killing 34 people. On a happier note, though perhaps, not altogether happier, the poet Shelley came here to escape a pair of outraged parents after he had eloped with Mary Wollstonecraft, their 16-year-old daughter. The time he spent here enchanted him, and soon other poets, including Wordsworth and Coleridge, had 'found' the area too.

The route from Lynmouth follows the line of the very steep main road up Countisbury Hill. The cliffs here are among the highest in England, falling nearly 1,000 ft (305 m), but not as a single leap, into the Channel. From the hill crest the path goes around its last major headland, Foreland Point, continuing towards Porlock Weir through wonderfully wild country high over the sea. The path then drops down through an ornate stone gateway into the Glenthorpe Estate, one of the last sections of the coastal path to be negotiated, and one of the best. Here the walker crosses from Devon to Somerset. Excellent walking through more wooded country takes the walker on to Culbone, whose church is reputed to be the smallest in England, measuring 35 ft (10.5 m) long by 12 ft (3.6 m) wide and holding about 30 people. The church is over 800 years old and is believed to have been built on the site of an early Christian hermitage. In Culbone Woods beyond, the pits used by the local charcoal burners can still be seen. Later, the woods were harvested to supply the Bristol Channel shipbuilding industry.

Emerging from the woodland, the walker reaches Porlock Weir. Once a commercial port, now only small leisure craft use this tiny harbour. Porlock is famous for its hill of legendary steepness, and also for one of its inhabitants, the Man of Porlock, who interrupted Coleridge while he was working on 'Kubla Khan', causing the poet to lose his thread and so fail to finish the work – and all for some unremembered errand.

The pebble ridge here looks similar to that at Westward Ho!, but the beach is mainly stones. The coastal path runs behind the ridge through marshes and rich pasture to Bossington, a classic West Country village with thatched cottages, round chimneys and cream teas.

The last section of the coastal path has undergone several changes of route and has gradually become more maritime and less pastoral. The latest version takes the walker out towards the coastguard lookout at Hurlstone Point before climbing steeply up to Bossington Hill, then further onward and upward to Selworthy Beacon. The route drops slowly down tracks and paths through Moor Wood and into the town of Minehead.

Daniel Defoe maintained that Minehead had the safest harbour on the southern side of the Bristol Channel. Many of the cottages grouped around the quarry – where the coastal path officially starts and ends – are seventeenth century, though the town itself is much older, having been recorded in Saxon times. To reach the quay the path goes through the older and unspoilt Higher, Middle and Quay Towns, ignoring the more garish eastern end of the town that is dominated by the large Butlin's Holiday Camp.

Culbone Church near Porlock Weir

Lynmouth, where Exmoor meets the sea

The Bristol Channel, South Wales and the Gower

(OS sheets 181, 182, 172, 171, 170, 159, 158)

Minehead to the Severn Bridge (97 mls, 155 km)

FROM MINEHEAD the walker can reach Watchet by way of Warren Point and the shoreline around Blue Anchor Bay, though from Blue Anchor itself the B3191 must be followed to Watchet. A good alternative is to use the West Somerset Railway, letting a steam-hauled train take the strain.

Watchet is a fine old port one of whose sailors is believed to have been the model for Coleridge's Ancient Mariner. From the village the coast road must be followed to the A39 for West Quantoxhead, a road that in the summer is busy with holiday traffic. A

better idea might be to take a bus to Kilve, regaining the coast from there. Kilve Priory was founded in 1329 by Simon de Fureaux as a chantry chapel, but was destroyed by fire in 1850.

As Hinkley Point nuclear power station is reached the walker will notice ammonites all over the beach and in the shoreline rocks. The rock here is the same liassic limestone that yields the Lyme Regis fossils, the bed re-appearing at the other end of a fold. The station is passed by fenced footpath for Stolford, where the 'mud horse' can still occasionally be seen supporting a fisherman looking for shrimps. Steart is

The Old Wooden Lighthouse at Burnham-on-Sea

famous for its birdlife, especially ducks, geese and waders in winter. From it the walk goes inland following the river Parrett to Bridgwater a long and untidy detour. Regaining the shore is equally untidy, and it is best to take a bus to Highbridge or Burnham-on-Sea, from where the shoreline can be followed to Brean Down.

Burnham beach must be followed, if only to see the nineteenth century wooden lighthouse, now disused, that is built on stilts. Berrow has a fine old church, but a better one is St Bridget's at Brean, founded in the sixth century. However, the present building, seemingly out of place among the caravans, is thirteenth century. The beach here is expansive, but often choked with grey silt from the River Severn. Brean Down has a ruined nineteenth-century fort at its point, built to protect the Severn estuary from French invaders. One plan for a Severn tidal barrage has a dam wall from here to Lavernock Point in Wales.

Separating the Berrow Flats from Weston Bay, Brean Down points towards the island of Steep Holm and the South Wales Coast

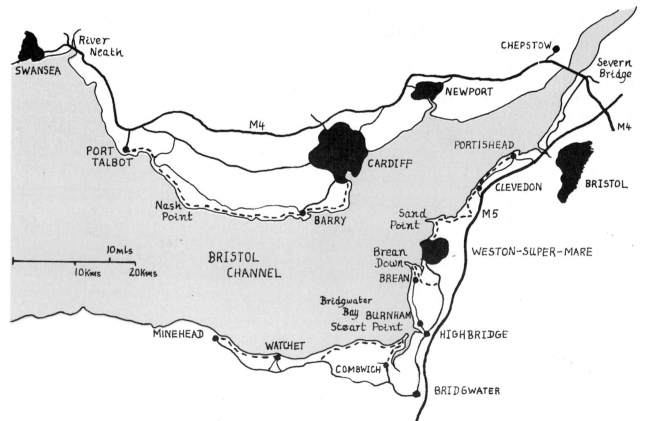

Berrow Church

Ahead lies Weston-Super-Mare which can be reached by ferry in the summer months or by a walk inland along the River Axe. Weston is a holiday resort with a pier in grand style and a sea beyond view on occasional low tides. From the town the shoreline can be followed to Sand Bay (is this the only British Sand Bay?), Sand Point and St Thomas' Head. From there the walker must go inland to cross the River Banwell at its sluice gates before heading back to the shore at Woodspring Bay. From the Bay, with its beautifully set Priory, the walker must head back inland to cross the River Yeo, reaching the shore again at Clevedon – an excellent old holiday resort – by way of country lanes. From Clevedon a

Brunel's Suspension Bridge, Newport

cliff walk leads to Portishead, a dormitory town for Bristol.

From Portishead the Avon and its docklands on both banks, block the way, and the walker must either go inland to the M5 bridge, or – and better – take a bus to Bristol where Brunel's suspension bridge can be crossed on the way to the restored *SS Great Britain*, also by Brunel. North of Bristol the Severn estuary is highly industrialised almost all the way to the Severn Bridge, and the walker should seriously consider a bus to Chepstow, if not to Newport or Cardiff. The bridge itself is worth the walk, however, if only for the view and the unnerving bounce every time a juggernaut goes by. The tide below the bridge has the second greatest rise and fall in the world.

Portskewett to Swansea (94 mls, 150 km)

A walk is possible from Portskewett to Newport passing stream mouths known locally as 'pills' – Caldicot Pill, West Pill, Collister Pill and Cold Harbour Pill. Newport should be visited if only for the transporter bridge, opened in 1906 and now one of only two surviving in Britain. The other we shall also pass is at Middlesborough. Beyond the River Ebbw, west of Newport, a sea wall can be followed to Cardiff, whose centre marks it out as a real capital. Here there is the castle – with a fine range of buildings, Roman, Norman and nineteenth century – the Civic Centre with the National Museum, the University and the Arms Park, all spaced out in best

Evening light over the islands of Steep Holm and Flat Holm. To the right is a sandbank off of Penarth, while to the left is the Monkstone Light

The Usk Transporter Bridge, Newport

capital city style. To the north of the city centre the cathedral of Llandaff houses the huge and once controversial Christ by Sir Jacob Epstein. Westwards is St Fagans, site of the Welsh Folk Museum.

The walker must round the Cardiff dockland area, once famous as Tiger Bay, to join the A4160 for Penarth, rejoining cliffs for the walk to Lavernock Point. Here the world's first wireless telegraph message was received from Marconi's transmitter on Flat Holm, the island in the Bristol Channel. St Mary's Well Bay beyond is a wild spot, not easily reached and frequently empty. Just offshore here is Sully Island which can be reached at low tide.

Rounding Sully Bay, Barry is reached. It is recorded that in 1880 there were only 17 houses here, and a population of 87. Then came the coal boom, and Barry's docks were soon the leading Welsh exporting harbour. The boom was short-lived, and today it is Barry Island that is famous, as one of the leading South Wales holiday resorts.

Westwards, cliff walking reaches Cold Knapp Point and Porthkerry Park en route for Aberthaw power station. Beyond, clifftop walking passes Summerhouse Point to reach St Donat's Bay. The castle here is fourteenth century, though the casual observer could be forgiven for believing it was a modern replica. It owes its appearance to William Randolph Hearst who

The Mumbles Lighthouse on the Gower Peninsula

restored it earlier this century. Beyond Nash Point and its lighthouse there are a series of small bays to Ogmore-by-Sea, from where, if the tide is out, the walker can cross the sands to Porthcawl, avoiding a walk inland to cross the river Ogmore. Porthcawl is a very pretty, holiday resort with a huge amusement complex. About a mile out to sea Tusker Rock can be seen, a well known danger spot in bad weather which has caused many shipwrecks. North from Porthcawl beyond Sker Point, are the Kenfig and Margam Sands. Kenfig is backed by dunes that form a nature reserve, while behind Margam Sands are the ruins of Margam Abbey. Beyond are the Port Talbot steelworks, so here the walker is forced inland for a bus to Swansea.

Mumbles to Amroth (98 mls, 157 km)

Swansea is a large, modern city, less spacious than Cardiff, but with a fine industrial and maritime museum. Access to the beach of Swansea Bay is easy, and the beach can be followed to The Mumbles. From the Mumbles Head lighthouse, beyond the lifeboat station, the view of Swansea Bay is magnificent. Even the steelworks seems to add, rather than detract, from the scene. Westward, there is a fine series of cliff-bound sandy bays. Brandy Cove, a particular favourite, is named from its use by smugglers. These bays are the first on the Gower, a superb piece of country, attached to South Wales as if an afterthought, and with limestone sea cliffs as good as any in Britain, and an excellent 'taster' for the more extensive cliffs of Old Pembrokeshire. The first really excellent cliff-scape is in Three Cliffs Bay, reached beyond Pwlldu Head. From the bay the clifftop or beach, on a falling tide, can be walked all the way to Rhossili. The walker passes the Oxwich

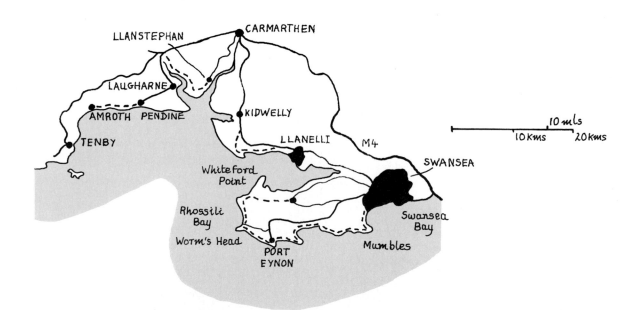

Smoke and steam rise from industrial Port Talbot on the eastern side of Swansea Bay

Burrows, a National Nature Reserve, and Oxwich Point for Port Eynon, a very pretty village in a small sheltered bay.

Beyond Port Eynon Point are the caves of Paviland, famous as the home of the Red Lady, a prehistoric skeleton discovered in the early nineteenth century and now known to be that of a man, the bones stained red with ochre. Here too is Culver Hole, a natural cliff filled in by a wall constructed with window-like openings. The date and reason for the construction are not known.

Excellent coastal walking follows to Mewslade and Fall Bays, and on to the cliff edge above Worms Head. This tent-like rock, named from the Old English for a sea serpent which from Rhossili Down it does resemble, is an island at hightide and an important sea bird breeding site. Take care when walking to the island, the rocks are slippery and sharp, and the going hazardous. Rhossili is a small village with a twelfth-century church and has a memorial to Petty Officer Edgar Evans, who was born in the parish and died during Captain Scott's ill-fated expedition to the South Pole in 1912.

Northward, the walker can take the beach of the magnificent Rhossili Bay, or take the path along Rhossili Down. The former allows a view of the remains of a couple of ships wrecked on the beach. The bay faces west, into the prevailing wind, and was much feared before the arrival of engines. Today, the same conditions make the bay a favourite among surfers. The down offers excellent views, especially to Worms Head, and also a close-up view of the hang-gliders using the same onshore winds. At the northern end of the bay another island, Burry Holms, can be reached at low tide. It was the site of a Celtic hermitage and, before that, an Iron Age hill-fort.

The walker touches Whiteford Sands, but cannot cross the dunes area of the nature reserve, and must go inland to Llanmadoc and on to Weobley Castle, built in the fourteenth century, but almost destroyed during the uprising of Owain Glyndwr, and now in ruins. The marshy Loughor estuary keeps the walker on the road to Crofty and beyond, and a bus is a worthwhile alternative, as another inland diversion is required soon to cross the River Tywi at Carmarthen. Only Pembrey will be missed by taking a bus, a 6-mile (9.5 km) stretch of sands now reclaimed from the MoD with a large country park and a marina.

Llanstephan, south of Carmarthen, and on the western bank of the Tywi, is a quiet little village with the ruins of a castle built by the de Clares in the twelfth century, and a healing well dedicated to St Anthony. But even from Llanstephan the walker must go inland, along quiet country lanes to Llanybri-Pont-Ddu to cross the bridge over the Dewi Fawr and Cynin rivers, returning along the A4066 and the River Taf to Laugharne.

Laugharne (pronounced Larne) has a massive castle, built originally by the Welsh prince Rhys ap Gruffydd, but converted into a mansion in Tudor times. Much smaller, but attracting far more visitors, is the boathouse where Dylan Thomas spent the last years of his life. The poet is now a cottage industry, but was not always so well liked by the townsfolk, who believed he had mocked them in *Under Milk Wood*, still his most famous work. In reality the play was already largely completed before Thomas arrived in Laugharne. In 1953 Thomas died during an American tour, a death attributed in large part to alcohol, but seeming to be equally due to self-critical fear, and he was buried in St Martin's churchyard, another place of pilgrimage. The boathouse, still as he left it, is open to the public.

South of the village East and West Marsh are MoD property, and the walker must use the A4066 to Pendine. The sands here were used by Sir Malcolm Cambell and Parry Thomas for attempts on the land speed record in the 1920s. Thomas was killed in 1927 when the chain snapped in his car, though a longer course – the sands are 6 miles (9.5 km) long – was already proving necessary.

From Pendine the walker can follow the shoreline, which offers easy walking on the sands or the cliffs, each equally good as the scenery is becoming increasingly picturesque, and remains so to Amroth and the start of the Pembrokeshire Coastal Path.

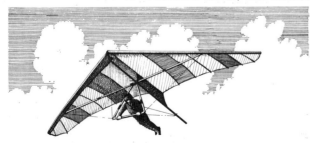

Hang-glider above Rhossili Down on the Gower Peninsula

Dylan Thomas's study, Laugharne

The Pembrokeshire Coastal Path

(OS sheets 158, 157, 145)

Amroth to St Govan's Head (24 mls, 38 km)

OUR NEXT 190 or so miles (300 km) – the actual length of the official path is open to question as several sections through urban areas which the walker must complete are not part of the official path – are straightforward. The path is not only well-signed – look for the Countryside Commission's acorn symbol – but keeps quite remarkably close to the high-water mark. The Pembrokeshire Coast was designated as Britain's fifth and smallest National Park, the path along its seaward edge becoming the third official long-distance path in 1970.

The path begins at a stream that marked the boundary between the old counties of Carmarthenshire and Pembrokeshire. Old Pembrokeshire's first village was Amroth, famous for a petrified forest perhaps 5,000 years old, which very low tides now reveal on the beach. Some strange, but interesting, fossils have been uncovered by the water, including hazel nuts and reindeer antlers. Further on, at Wiseman's Bridge, the memories are of later happenings: a full-scale rehearsal of the D-Day landings took place here in 1943 in front of Churchill, Eisenhower and Montgomery.

Path and minor road take the walker into Saundersfoot, a town built in the nineteenth century to export coal from the local anthracite mine. Today, the town is a popular resort, especially with sailors. Just beyond it the path reaches the beach and the Lady

The Tudor Merchant's House at Tenby

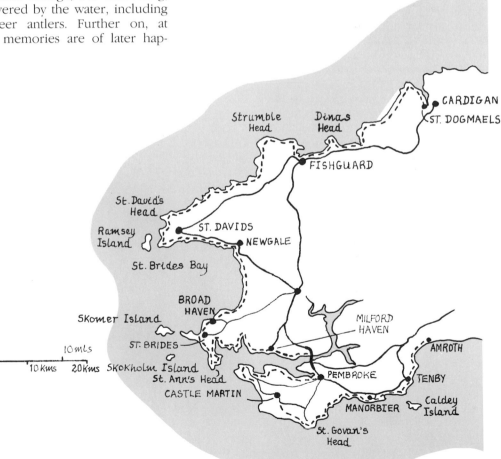

Cave anticline, a famous geological formation, which is an inverted V of folded sandstone. Ahead, Monkstone Point can be visited or bypassed to reach Tenby.

In Welsh the town is Dynbych-y-Pysgod, the small fort of the fishes, the addition of the fishes being to distinguish this town from Denbigh in North Wales. In the fourteenth century Tenby was an important herring port, having earlier been a Danish fishing village. By that time it was walled, and the walls were then strengthened at the time of the Armada. They also made the town important in the Civil War, when it was held for the King, but the town was later successfully sieged by Parliament when the attack included a bombardment from the sea.

Offshore from Tenby – or, to be precise, off Giltar Point south of the town – and reached from it, is Caldey Island. In Welsh this is Ynys Pyr, St Pyr's Island, named after the sixth-century Celtic saint who established a monastery here. Today, there is still a monastery, and Cistercian monks make chocolate and herbal perfumes for visitors, though only male visitors may enter the monastery itself.

The path hugs the coast westward from Giltar Point passing low cliffs to Lydstep Haven, a fine crescent bay. Lydstep Head, at the bay's southern end, is a major climbing area, the headland having some awesome sheets of rock, and the limestone itself is contorted into many beautiful shapes. The coastal path cuts off the headland, though it is easily reached, and heads for Skrinkle Haven, then inland of Old Castle Head to reach the coast again near King's Quoit, an evocatively sited Neolithic burial chamber. Beyond is Manorbier Bay, the village of Manorbier being easily reached eastward by lane as the bay is reached. The village is famous for its superb Norman castle, birthplace of Giraldus Cambrensis, Gerald of Wales, whose book on his journey through Wales in the late twelfth century is still an inspiration to travellers.

From Manorbier the path takes the walker easily forward, hugging the shore as it circles Swanlake Bay and the crescent beach in front of Freshwater East. This last bay is safe and well-sheltered, excellent for swimming. Trewent Point is passed, and once beyond it the view forward to Stackpole Head is excellent. The next headland, Greenala Point, is topped by an Iron Age hill-fort, but it is the Stackpole cliffs that hold the attention. Here, too, the limestone – we have just re-crossed the boundary between Old Red

Sandstone and limestone – has been energetically carved by the sea. There is a fine stack and several caves, one of which has collapsed to form a blowhole. Stackpole Quay, said to be Britain's smallest harbour, was built to serve a local quarry and was, almost literally, hewn out of the cliffs. The fossil hunter will also be happy here, as there are shells and corals in abundance.

From the quay the path takes an airy route above cliffs that are home to colonies of sea-birds. There are several blowholes at the cliff edge, and, beyond, the excellent Barafundle Bay. Griffith Lort's Hole is a huge cleft in the rock beside a natural arch known as Lattice Windows. Stakes in the ground on Stackpole Head and along the cliff to the west are used by rock climbers. **The path here passes through an MoD range and suspicious objects should not be touched.**

Inland from Broad Haven are the Bosherston Lily Ponds, almost 80 acres of old fish ponds now used by

St Govan's Chapel near Bosherston

ducks and waders. The ponds are another suggested site for the pool into which Bedivere threw Excalibur as King Arthur lay dying. Next is St Govan's Head, another rock climbing centre, named for the chapel buried among the rocks near the car-park. The chapel dates from the thirteenth century and commemorates Gavan, an Irish monk who had a hermitage cell on the site. Below the chapel is a well that is credited with healing powers. Legend has it that a silver bell was once hung in the chapel, but it was stolen by pirates. When their ship was sunk, the bell was rescued by sea-nymphs who placed it inside a rock near the wall. When the rock is struck it sounds like a bell.

St Govan's Chapel to Pembroke (30 mls, 48 km)

Beyond the chapel the coastal path passes through more of the MoD's range, the ground beside the path occasionally being littered with odd bits of metal. **Do not touch any of these objects**.

Stennis Ford is a long gash in the cliff that seems impressive until Huntsman's Leap is reached. Here the gash is so narrow that the base is rarely visited by the sun and seems cold and dark. The name derives from an old tale that a local huntsman jumped the cleft while out riding the chase one day. When he pulled up on the far side to look at what he had done, he promptly died of fright when he saw the chasm.

The coast westward is one long delight now, a succession of arches, stacks, blowholes and chasms. The quaintly named Bullslaughter Bay is passed, as is the superb hill-fort of The Caudron, to reach the Elegug Stacks and, beyond them, the Green Bridge of Wales. Between them the stacks and the bridge are a lesson in coastal erosion. The bridge is a natural arch formed by the meeting of two caves, one formed on each side of a finger of rock that aeons ago thrust out into the sea. When the caves joined they left an arch 80 ft (24 m) high and, at its narrowest, only 4 ft (1.2 m) wide. The stacks must once have been fingers connected to the main cliff and were probably arches too. Now they are home to thousands of sea-birds. Indeed, the name 'elegug' derives from the Welsh name for the guillemot, *heligog*.

Beyond the Green Bridge the official path heads inland to avoid the Castlemartin Range, 6,000 acres of

Folded cliff scenery and natural arches near the Green Bridge of Wales

headland owned by the MoD. In the strictly historical sense the army's presence here is a continuation of a noble tradition, the Castlemartin Yeomanry being the only regiment to have been awarded a battle honour for a battle on British soil, when they defeated a French force at Fishguard early in the Napoleonic Wars. History apart, the range restricts access to a beautiful stretch of coastline, the only saving graces being that limited access helps preserve the beauty, and parts of the cliff path are open at certain times. Read the notice boards carefully.

The inland route is straightforward, but un-inspiring and leads, by road, to the coast at Freshwater West. This beach is now popular with surfers, but was once a favourite for the collectors of laver bread, the edible seaweed. The path now traces a many-stiled route around to Angle headland, passing a fine rock arch and Sheep Island, that can be reached at low tide, to reach West Angle Bay. A short cut from here goes, by road, directly to Angle village, but the path should be followed, passing Thorn Island with a hotel reached only by boat, and Chapel Bay Fort, a mid-nineteenth-century fort built to protect this southern arm of Milford Haven. This fort, and that now occupied by the hotel, were part of a defence planned by Khartoum's General Gordon. The Angle headland has always been strategically important because of the Haven, the village of Angle itself having the remains of a castle, much older than the forts, but built for the same purpose.

Angle Bay is an excellent place for waders and ducks, but despite there being an 'official footpath' along its shore there is no path at all and the shore itself must be used to reach the BP tank farm. The tanks hold half-a-million gallons of oil. Beyond there are more oil tanks, all the way around Popton Point to the power station, a large oil-burning station. Beyond, the coastal path moves away from Milford Haven, crossing farmland to Pembroke.

Pembroke is a fine town with an array of old buildings and occasional stretches of the old town wall. It is dominated by the castle, an early Norman building exploiting a rock mass set above the Haven in fine style. The keep is a massive construction, 75 ft (22.5 m) high with walls 20 ft (6 m) thick, while the gatehouse is a marvel of defensive architecture. Beside it is the Henry VII tower where Henry Tudor was born in 1457. Heir to the Tudor dynasty, a small but remarkable lineage, Henry became King after defeating Richard III at Bosworth in 1485.

Pembroke Dock to Little Haven (41 mls, 66 km)

From Pembroke many walkers take a bus to Milford Haven to avoid a built-up section of the path. The continuous walking route crosses fields to Pembroke Dock, a town with an interesting history that suffers from an inelegant name. A different image would be conjured up by Paterchurch, the name of the village chosen as the site for a Royal Naval dockyard in 1814. Legend has the admiralty setting up the dock in response to the Milford Haven yard putting up its prices during the Napoleonic Wars. Whatever the truth, the dock became one of the world's leading shipyards. It closed suddenly in 1926 causing much local distress. Though re-opened briefly during the Second World War, to service Sunderland flying boats and the Atlantic Patrol, the dock and, therefore, the town have never recovered from the closure.

The path crosses Milford Haven by way of the Cleddau Bridge, going through Neyland – Brunel's preferred anchorage for his *Great Eastern* – and takes the coastal road, then field tracks to the town of Milford Haven. The town is a relatively new one, with a history based solely on seafaring, which has led to fluctuating prosperity. It rose and fell with whaling, with naval shipbuilding – as explained at Pembroke Dock – and with fishing. Today, it is prosperous again as one of Europe's largest oil ports. The original town was built by Sir William Hamilton whose wife, Emma, is famous as Lord Nelson's mistress. Nelson visited the town and is commemorated in and on several buildings. The most notable relic of the great man is a replica – the original that was here was removed to London – of a mast section from the French flagship at the Battle of the Nile. That ship, *L'Orient*, is the one on whose burning deck the poetically famous boy stood.

Beyond Milford Haven the path follows roads

Pembroke. The Norman Castle was the birthplace of Henry Tudor

Pembroke Castle

before returning to the coast. Pleasant country is reached again at Sandy Haven where a crossing, by stepping stones and causeway, can be made a couple of hours each side of low tide to avoid a 4-mile (6.5 km) road detour around the haven's head. Westward the many inlets of Milford Haven were indeed a haven, for smugglers. Dale, claimed to be the sunniest Welsh village, is a delightful place and from it more picturesque coast, with superb beaches, is followed to Mill Bay. Here Henry Tudor landed after his exile in Brittany, meeting 2,000 locals who were to stay with him on his lightning march to the crown at Bosworth. The original lighthouse on nearby St Ann's Head is said to have been built by Henry, perhaps on the site of a chapel dedicated to the saint herself.

From the lighthouse the path follows a short section of road before rejoining the cliff near the quaintly named Vomit Point. Offshore here is Skokholm Island, while ahead is the excellent sweep of Marloes Sands. The path runs behind the sands, but that misses the delights of the Three Chimneys – about one-third distance – vertical slabs of sandstone, and the cavitied lava near Matthew's Slade, about half-way along the sands. Gateholm Island at the end of the sands can be reached at low tides; it was the site of a Celtic village.

At The Anvil, the southern point of the next headland which is reached after a walk along an increasingly excellent section of cliff, Skomer Island is about 3/4 mile (1.2 km) away. The island is a National Nature Reserve, famous for its birdlife, most especially for Manx shearwaters. An estimated 100,000 pairs of these graceful, nocturnal birds nest in the island's burrows. In addition to the birds there is also a sizeable colony of grey seals. West from Skomer is Grassholm with Wales' only gannet colony and west again is The Smalls. The latter is a small rock with a lighthouse which was the scene of the tragedy that led to a requirement for three rather than two lighthouse keepers. In 1801 the keeper at the light died during a storm, and his partner, fearing he would be suspected of murder, made a makeshift coffin and tied it to the light. By the time a service boat came the survivor was half demented. Access to Skomer and Skokholm, which also has a colony of Manx shearwaters, is limited and camping is not allowed.

The boat for Skomer leaves from Martin's Haven, on the northern shore of the headland, a delightful

cove, popular with divers but with no beach. From Martin's Haven the path is straightforward, skirting Musselwick Sands to Tower Point and The Nab Head – where there was a Neolithic flint factory – then passing another Huntsman's Leap to reach St Brides Haven. St Bride, better known as Bridget of Kildare, was a fifth-century Irish abbess who never came to Wales, but whose followers carried her cult here. The old church does not stand on the site of the earliest chapel to the saint, that site having long since been lost to the sea. One interesting survival of the first site, however, is a pair of stone coffins set in the cliff near the ruined lime kiln.

St Bride gives her name not only to the beautiful Haven, but to the whole bay enclosed by the headland of Marloes and that of St David's, the path hugging the bay shore closely to Little Haven a former coal port. Beyond, the route lies on a steep road, and it is better to use the beach to reach Broad Haven.

Broad Haven to Pen Anglais (53 mls, 85 km)

North of Broad Haven there are some fine rock arches, the best being Haroldston Bridge just beyond Black Point with its Iron Age fort. Druidston Haven, a long, sandy beach popular with swimmers and surfers, is named for Alfred Drue, a Norman knight who was given land here for his services to Henry I. The beach finishes with a couple of small rock-arched havens before the larger, deeply-notched Nolton Haven is reached. The pretty village at the back was also once a coal port: the Trefrane Cliff colliery or, at least, the remains of it are passed a little way north.

Beyond it is better to walk along Newgale sands rather than along the park at the back of the beach to rejoin the cliffs at Newgale itself. This is just beyond Brandy Brook, the boundary between Wales and 'Little England beyond Wales' as English-speaking Pembrokeshire was – and is – sometimes called. Beyond Newgale, cliff scenery returns, with another good rock arch at Pwll March – the name being evidence immediately of our being back in Welsh Wales. Others follow on the fine walk section to Porthmynawyd, a small, pleasant cove.

Pen Dinas, an excellent viewpoint, is not visited by the official path, though it is easily reached. The official path heads straight for Solva, an inverted comma-shaped inlet understandably popular with sailors. The inlet's safe anchorage has always attracted

seafarers: once ships sailed to America from here, full of emigrants. There is no ferry or ford at Solva, so a detour through the village itself is necessary to reach the fine cliffs which are followed towards St David's. The city is a little way from the coast, but it is unlikely that many walkers will get this close without paying a visit. Despite being the Welsh patron saint, little is known about St David. It is probable that he was born locally and became a travelling preacher before returning here in the mid-sixth century to build a church. He died here in 601. Nothing remains of his original church, a Norman cathedral having been erected following pilgrimages by the early Norman kings, including the Conqueror himself in 1081. The cathedral – which turns a small Welsh village into a city – was an important pilgrimage centre, two visits here being the equivalent of one to Rome on the scale of indulgence. It stands in Cathedral Close, a walled enclave that also holds the Bishop's Palace.

Seals are frequently seen off the Pembrokeshire coast

Back on the coast the path reaches St Non, a possible birthplace for St David. The well here is said to have sprung as he was born, and was therefore considered sacred. The path moves around Porth Clais, an inlet smaller than, but as calm, as Solva and on to the headland at Penmaen Melyn, overlooking Ramsey Island. The island was a Celtic monastic site and can be reached by boat from Porthstinian further along the coast. St Justinian, after whom the island is named, was Ramsey's most famous monk. He was St

Looking north along the rugged northern edge of St David's Head

David's teacher, but his less resolute followers found him too strict and, legend has it, cut off his head. The saint picked up the severed head and walked across the water to the mainland to be buried at St David's church.

Around the headland from Porthstinian is Traeth Mawr, the sands of Whitesand Bay, from where St Patrick sailed to convert the Irish to Christianity. A chapel stands at his reputed departure point. The bay gives the best surfing in Wales, but is not always safe for swimming. At its northern end is St David's Head, topped by an Iron Age hill-fort. Astonishingly this headland was known to the Ancient Greeks who named it for the eight rocks, the Bishops and Clerks, that stand a few miles off it.

North from the headland is Pembroke's second important climbing area, though here the rock is gabbro rather than limestone. The cliff tops are excellent for flowers, which add a touch of colour to the walk to Abereiddy where there is a good beach of very dark sand. Nearby is the Blue Lagoon, a sea-filled quarry. Porthgain, the next village, was once a centre for quarrying and brickmaking, but is now a quieter place with a pretty harbour.

Beyond Porthgain is a magnificent piece of coastline, rugged and dramatic, but beautiful and quiet, stretching all the way to Strumble Head. The roads here lie well back from the cliffs, and there are few hamlets, so the whole section is unfrequented and unspoiled. Garn Fawr, inland from Pwll Deri where there is a youth hostel, is a fine viewpoint, the view extending to the mountains of Snowdonia and Wicklow. Strumble Head is a magnificent spot, and a good place to watch birds. From it our route turns east, following another fine section of rocky coastline to a memorial stone on Carregwastad Point. The stone commemorates the last invasion of Britain, in 1797, when a force of 1,400 Frenchmen, half of them convicts, led by a British-hating Irish American, William Tate, landed here. The force should have been one of three, but the other two – heading for Ireland and Newcastle – were damaged by bad weather and returned to France. Two ships landed the men at Carregwastad, and immediately left. The men captured a farm, raided the neighbourhood for food, got drunk on liquor salvaged by the locals from a recent wreck and were in no position to fight when confronted by the Yeomanry the following day. One legend has it that the final dispiriting straw was when the French saw Welsh women in their red cloaks and

tall hats, and thought they were Guardsmen.

To reach Fishguard the path cuts off Pen Anglais, the last headland before Fishguard Bay, but it is worth the walk out to see the 'penny loaves', regular 4-, 5- or 6-sided basalt columns, formed as the molten rock cooled – the same process that formed the Giant's Causeway.

Fishguard to St Dogmaels (26 mls, 42 km)

Fishguard is a pleasant, modern town built on the prosperity of its deep harbour and the sea-crossing to Rosslare in Ireland, though it is sandwiched between two older, fishing harbours. Goodwick, that we first enter, and Lower Town, are very picturesque. Fishguard has another commemorative stone to the Carregwastad invasion and Jemime Nicholas, famed for the capture of two Frenchmen with a pitchfork, is buried in the church.

Beyond Lower Town the path continues on the clifftop above some fine, wild coves that are mostly inaccessible, to Pwllgwaelod near Dinas Island. The island is so-called because Cwm Dewi and Cwm-yr-eglwys almost cut-off the headland of Dinas Head from the rest of Pembrokeshire. The walker can go round by way of the head, a beautiful, wild circuit, or can go along the cwms to save a couple of miles. This sheltered low-lying, marshy alternative is good for wildlife, especially flowers and butterflies.

On either route the ruins of the ancient church of St Brynach are reached. Built in the twelfth century and storm damaged to this parlous state in the mid-nineteenth, it is a fitting memorial to all seafarers who have died in storms at sea. The actual storm which wrecked the church, on 25 October 1859, also wrecked 114 ships on the Welsh coast, taking 459 lives. From the ruin the cliff path leads to Newport, a Norman village, though with ruins from far older peoples. Carreg Coctan Arthur is a Neolithic cromlech, while the ramparts of a defended Iron Age harbour stand beside the path.

Northward is a beautiful piece of coastline, a fitting finish to the path as it offers the last bit of true grandeur for many a mile. It starts with the lovely Newport Sands but reaches excellent coved and arched cliffs – choughs, the red-legged crows, can occasionally be seen here – and Pwll y Wrach, the Witch's Pool, a collapsed blowhole connected to the sea by a tunnel cave. From there to Cemaes Head the walker becomes increasingly further away from roads and villages, passing the delightful Ceibwr Bay, then

rising and dipping all the way to the head.

From the head the path turns south heading for the Teifi estuary and its finish, officially at Poppit Sands, but more sensibly at St Dogmaels. The village is named for a grandson of Ceredig, who gave Cardigan (Ceredigion) its name, who founded a monastic cell here in the fifth century. The Norman abbey was a rare foundation for the Order of Tiron, a branch of the Benedictines. The nearby church is much later, mid-nineteenth century, but contains a very old, fifth or sixth century, inscribed stone – the Sagranus Ogham. The stone is inscribed in both Latin and Ogham, the early Gaelic script, and was crucial to the deciphering of Ogham. The inscription suggests a memorial to Sagranus, son of Cunotamus.

Cardigan Bay and the Lleyn Peninsula

(OS sheets 145, 146, 135, 124, 123, 115)

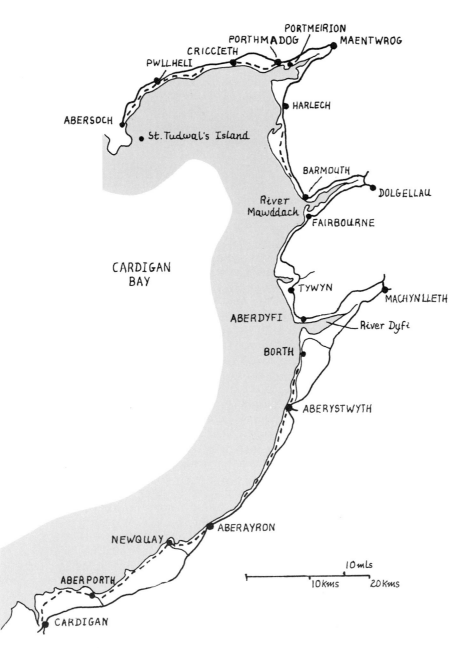

Cardigan to Borth (52 mls, 83 km)

THE LOSS OF a continuous coastal path is keenly felt when the walker leaves the Pembrokeshire National Park, not least because road, railway and caravan sites often limit coastal walking, especially around the spectacular Dyfi estuary. Indeed, there is much to be said for taking the Cambrian Coast Railway northward from Machynlleth. But there is hope – a Ceredigion Coastal Path is evolving.

Cardigan, across the Teifi from St Dogmaels, is entered over a splendid old bridge across the river. The castle here dates from the time of Richard I and was held by Rhys ap Gruffydd, Lord of South Wales. It was destroyed during the Civil War and today the ruins stand on private land. Over the hill is Gwbert-on-Sea, where dunes give way to cliffs. Nearby Cardigan Island is a nature reserve reached by boat from St Dogmaels. Wild Soay sheep share the island with sea-birds.

Steep lanes and paths lead to Traeth-y-Mwnt, the site of a battle against Flemish invaders in 1155. The church which adds to the enchantment of the hamlet, is thirteenth century.

A south-easterly track joins the line of lanes and paths towards Aberporth, but the RAF Rocket Testing Centre seals off the headland. Aberporth itself has a picturesque, north-facing horseshoe of sand and from it there is a fine cliff walk to Tresaith, a beautiful village where a waterfall drops to the beach. At low tide the beach walk to Traeth Penbryn is a must.

These two beaches form part of a designated Heritage Coast, and the standard is maintained to Llangranog which is reached by way of the Penbryn valley and the steep, airy tracks which lead past the transmitter mast and through the earthworks of Castell Bach.

Llangranog too has an excellent beach with rock masses rising from the sand, while the nearby headland of Yyns Lochtyn, owned by the National Trust, is a superb spot with wonderful views.

Ahead now the path takes the top of the steep Penmoelciliau cliff to Cwmtudu, another fine cove with caves in the cliffs. Here a coastal walk to New Quay starts by going over Craig Caerllan, also a

National Trust site, to a 'secret' cove with its own special island and another clifftop earthwork. Beyond, the walk reaches Bird Rock and New Quay Head, from where Snowdonia and the peaks of the Lleyn Peninsula can be seen.

Pretty steep-streeted New Quay vies with Laugharne for the distinction of being the original of the village in Dylan Thomas' *Under Milk Wood*. Though Thomas denied any specific location, the story *Quite Early One Morning*, from which the more famous work developed, was written while he lived in New Quay. The village is a popular spot: it faces east – unusual on a western coast – and so is sheltered from the prevailing wind. The popularity has brought the large caravan sites that spread eastwards and obstruct the route, but an enjoyable path skirts the twin bay of Little Quay.

Aberaeron, the favoured retreat of opera singer Sir Geraint Evans, is a gracious Regency town with an excellent aquarium. From it, a seaside path leads to Aberarth, but beyond that village the walker must take the main road to make significant progress. The coast is visited by a few paths, but the beaches are rough with big streams cutting across them, making walking very hard work.

Llansantffraid is eventually reached, a pleasant village with a slate-faced church, north-west from which is a sombre section of coast to Aberystwyth. This is country for the connoisseur, with paths winding up and down steep slopes above the cliff-line more like those encountered on the fells than on shores. The clay is treacherous to even a well-equipped walker and the subsequent loose shale is equally alarming, but there are rewards. The Monk's Cave, or 'Thunder Hole', lies in wildly distorted and layered cliffs, while Allt Wen plunges dizzily.

Arrival at Aberystwyth after such a wilderness comes as a shock. The town is a delight; a seaside resort with an array of fine 'sea front' houses; a ruined castle, once held by Owain Glyndwr, and destroyed in the Civil War; a mock-Gothic collection of university buildings near the tumbledown pier, a stark contrast to the new university complex on the hill; and the National Library of Wales, home of priceless treasures.

The last 'Great Little Train' to have been owned by British Rail runs inland to Devil's Bridge and, in season, a slow funicular climbs Constitution Hill, giving access to more miles of coastal path.

The walk to Clarach Bay is excellent, but the bay-

The National Library of Wales, Aberystwyth

cutting stream now approaches the shore through a vast holiday village. Onward is Wallog, where a shingle ridge, Sarn Cynfelin, runs out to sea. This ridge, mostly just below the surface, is a reputed site of the legendary land of Cantref-y-Gwaelod, a land lost due to the carelessness of the man set to watch for storms. The path north is exposed and precarious, and some may prefer to take the road into Borth. Either route offers spectacular views.

Borth is a strung-out village of no particular merit but in surroundings of quite unusual interest. To the east is the 'raised-bog' of Cors Fochno. A National Conservancy Council (NCC) permit is required to visit (obtainable from NCC (Wales), Penrhos Road, Bangor, (0248) 355141) and good local knowledge helps too as in places the peaty quagmires are 30 ft (9 m) deep. A very complete range of acidic bog plantlife is found here, including some very rare species. There is also a fine range of insects. To the north, the former island of Ynyslas is also a nature reserve, with estuary birds and many butterflies.

Ynyslas to Criccieth (75 mls, 120 km)

From Ynyslas the walker cannot take the ferry indicated on some OS maps across to Aberdyfi: it has long ceased to function. There is also no coastal path and the walker must take two trains, changing at Machynlleth, seat of Owain Glyndwr's first parliament. At least the lines stay close to the shore. The

trains run on part of the Cambrian Coast Railway, and many walkers may stay on board until Pwllheli, enjoying one of the best coastal railways in Britain.

Aberdyfi, on the other side of the beautiful Dyfi estuary, is another reputed site of the lost land of Cantref-y-Gwaelod. Here the bells can occasionally be heard from beneath the sea – or so the story goes.

From the town, which has a fine maritime museum, it is beach walking to Tywyn, the terminus for the Tal-y-llyn railway. The museum of the railway is also here. The church, dedicated to the sixth-century Breton saint Cadfan, is partly Norman and holds the curiously inscribed 'Saint's Stone'.

Walking is difficult north of Tywyn, the Dysynni river making a long inland detour inevitable, so it is best to take the train. At Fairbourne there is yet another 'Great Little Train' and a ferry to Barmouth, on the other side of the magnificent Mawddach estuary. The estuary is worth a day's exploration of its own. Those that do explore it should go as far as Penmaenpool, where a rickety wooden bridge crosses the river.

Barmouth's own wooden bridge can be used instead of the ferry to reach a town that clings to Dinas Olau rock, the National Trust's first ever acquisition in 1895. The beach here is excellent, and

Llangranog, a delightful village set on a steep sided gorge north of Aberporth

The Fairbourne Railway, with Barmouth across the Estuary

Glaslyn embankment, takes the walker into Porthmadog, a town whose name honours not only its founder, but the legendary Madog, said to have discovered America several centuries before Columbus. The town grew up where the slate quarry trains reached the cargo boats, though today the little trains carry tourists up and down the Vale of Festiniog.

Borth-y-Gest is Porthmadog's pretty 'resort' extension, just round the wooded headland. The beach can be followed to the majestic sweep of Black Rock Sands, the best of Welsh beaches. There are sea caves in the headland at its western end and beyond is Criccieth's bay. There are huge pebbles here, which make for heavy going to the town.

Criccieth is an unspoilt little resort with a superb castle, dominant on a steep promontory. The castle was built by the Welsh and is quite unlike its Edwardian counterparts even though it was captured by Edward within 20 years of completion. The scorch marks and splits are from a fire that raged when Owain Glyndwr seiged it in 1404.

The Lleyn Peninsula to Caernarfon (85 mls, 136 km)

The coastal walk next reaches the River Dwyfor at its reedy estuary where waterfowl and waders feed. The river must be followed some way upstream for a crossing at Llanystumdwy. This was 'home' to Manchester-born David Lloyd George who is buried in a simple grave beside the river. There is a Lloyd George Museum, and a memorial designed by Clough Williams-Ellis.

Only the rail traveller sees much of the next few miles of beach and then the Butlin's Holiday Camp has the monopoly. An inland route by way of Cabin Wood and the curious 'Wooded Way', a planted avenue extending to Afon Wen is possible, passing Butlin's and then on to a track for the Pen-y-Chain headland and Abererch Burrows. It is then possible to keep to the beach all the way to Pwllheli, the terminus of the Cambrian Coast Railway.

The town lies well back from the sea, connected by its harbour, 'The Salt-water Hollow', cradled behind a classic hooked sand-spit. A coastal tram-track once ran from here to Llanbedrog, but high seas washed it away in the 1920s. Nevertheless, it is usually safe to

Behind Porthmadog, set at the end of Maddocks' Cob, rise the mountains of Snowdonia

following it north the walker reaches Llanaber whose thirteenth-century church is said to be the best Early English style church in North Wales. Keeping north, the beach can be walked for miles, the walker only having to move inland for river crossings and high tides. An NCC permit is necessary for entry to the splendid Morfa Dyffryn Nature Reserve, which is in the dunes behind Dyffryn Ardudwy, though Mochras, Shell 'Island' has free access and is a popular picnic and collecting spot. Over 200 different varieties of shell have been found here. Patrick's Causeway, a sand bar that, legend has it, once stretched to Ireland, is sometimes visible here for up to half its 20 mile (32 km) length.

Northward, the sand-threatened village of Llandanwg is passed to reach Harlech. The sea once lapped the foot of the castle, but the vast dune range

of Morfa Harlech has now pushed it further away. This dune reserve also needs an NCC permit for entry. The castle, made famous by the song that commemorates a siege during the Wars of the Roses, is enormously impressive. It was the headquarters of Owain Glyndwr during his rebellion, the Welsh holding it for five years. From it the view of the Snowdonian peaks is magnificent.

There is no easy way across the Dwyryd estuary, so the Cambrian Coast Railway must be taken. But stop at Penrhyndeudraeth to visit Portmeirion. The architect Clough Williams-Ellis created this mock Italianate village in 1925, having been captivated by Portofino during a trip to Italy. There is nowhere else like it on Britain's coast, and it defies reasonable description. Go there, you will not be disappointed.

William Maddocks' Cob, the mile long (1.6 km)

go by way of the dunes, but be careful when rounding the seaward side of Carreg-y-Defaid.

Llanbedrog's seaward side is well-sheltered by its wooded headland, but do not go that way. Instead climb Mynydd Tir-y-Cwmwd, one of the best viewpoints on this section of the coast. There are many paths at the top, but be sure to locate the right way off westward, to reach a chalet park and Warren Beach, a National Trust property. The wonderful sands of the beach are followed to Abersoch.

Abersoch is glorious in situation and outlook: it has superb beaches and is alive with boats, a thoroughgoing success of a resort for the outdoor family. Off the headland beyond Machros are St Tudwal's Islands, one with the ruins of an 800 year old church. The islands are private, and landing is not allowed.

Porth Ceiriad is a fine sheltered bay with a sad history of boat tragedies, and a path through gorse reveals the site of more tragedies – Porth Neigwl, Hell's Mouth, a shipwrecking bay with a notorious undertow. The long, wild beach – popular with surfers despite the dangers – is sometimes disagreeably strewn with flotsam. There are not too many ways on or off it and the walker must not stay too long at the north-west end. Mynydd Rhiw ahead was the site of a neolithic 'axe factory', but the walker heads for the cliffs that conceal the next bay, Porth Ysgo. This is delightfully approached by a secret valley ablaze with wild flowers and studded with ruined mine buildings. The bay is among the best on the whole Lleyn.

Roads now lead to Aberdaron, an outpost of nationalism with international connections – 'Dick of Aberdaron', Richard Robert Jones, fluent in a dozen languages, was born here in 1788. It was also the embarkation point for medieval pilgrims to Bardsey Island. The town has a church that is perhaps 1,400 years old and there is also 'Y Gegin Fawr', the Big Kitchen, still a refreshment spot for travellers 700 years after being built as a pilgrim's rest-house.

To reach cliff-protected Porth Meudwy even at low tide, the walker must leave the beach and follow lanes which lead to Mynydd Mawr, the climax of this coast. Here, the fierce cliffs of Braich y Pwll mark the Land's End of Wales, near to St Mary's Well, where pilgrims not reaching Bardsey from Aberdaron, took a drink before their crossing. Bardsey Island, known as the Island of 20,000 Saints, so many are the holy men that are buried here, lies across a turbulent channel. The island has been a Christian sanctuary

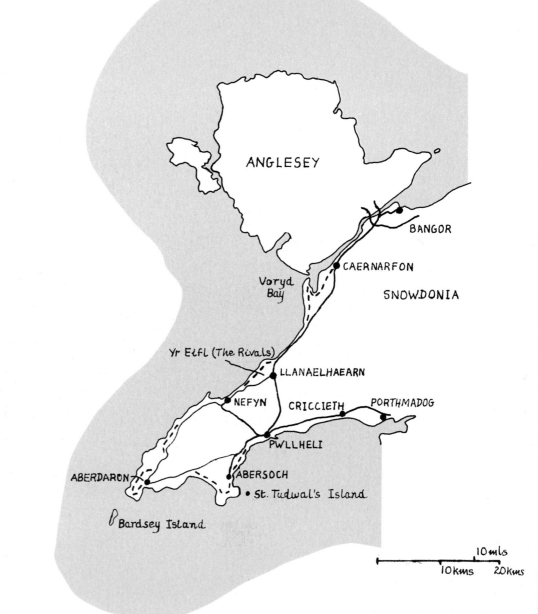

since the third century, but is today uninhabited apart from the lighthouse keepers and bird wardens. Landings are not encouraged.

The savage coast northwards is not continuously accessible. Porth Oer, reached down a steep, loose track, is famed for its Whistling Sands, the sand squeaking underfoot. Porth Iago, facing the afternoon

Clouds reflected in the waters of Voryd Bay to the west of Caernarfon. Beyond, the hills of the Lleyn Peninsula

sun, sheltering under Dinas Point and requiring a scramble down, is a beautiful, secluded bay.

A clifftop Right of Way has now been established from Porth Widlin to Porth Dinllaen and this opens up miles of perfect coastal walking. There is safe bathing and fine rockpools at Porth Colmon; Traeth Penllech is good for divers and surfers; and Porth Ysgaden has twin sheltered bays. Altogether this is a wonderful piece of coast.

Porth Dinllaen, a superb village, seemed destined to become the principal port for Ireland, but Holyhead was chosen by just one vote. So, instead of a busy port a few cottages snuggle under the hooked headland that offers excellent views over the twin sandy bays of Nefyn and to the three-pronged Yr Eifl.

The cliff path heads for Yr Eifl – anglicised to The Rivals, a name that maintains the sound, but ruins the meaning, Yr Eifl meaning The Fork – by way of Pistyll, whose seventh-century pilgrims' church, has a Celtic font. The most practical way is now over Bwlch yr Eifl, from where both the seaward western peak

and the remarkable Iron Age settlement of Tre'r Ceiri, on the eastern peak, can be visited. Each is well worth the effort.

Beyond the peaks is Trevor, where there are huge quarries and a little harbour that was once busy with the shipment of paving stones. Northward now the walker is forced onto paths and lanes for Clynnog-fawr, where the impressive fifteenth-century St Beuno's Church is the finest along this section of coast. Equally impressive is the Neolithic burial chamber beside the sea.

There is now no continuous path, and low-tide beach walking by Aberdesach is hampered by streams. Many walkers will be tempted to find the occasional bus that goes to Caernarfon, but they would miss Dinas Dinlle, a giant earthwork, and Voryd bay, a favourite haunt of waterfowl and waders. At the end of the shingle spit on the bay's western shore Anglesey is only yards away.

From the bay's eastern shore a fine walk along the shore of the Menai Strait takes the walker to

Caernarfon. Lost in the fields along the way is the remote Llanfaglan church, silent and untouched, with a Roman tombstone as door lintel.

Caernarfon has a long history. Twt Hill was the site of a Celtic fort and the Romans too had a fort here, *Segontium*, a little way south of the town. It is, however, the later fort, Edward I's castle, that now dominates the town. The huge castle, the best preserved of all the Edwardian castles, formed part of the town's defences, and a section of the town wall still remains intact. Caernarfon was the centre of English government in Wales, which is why the castle's living quarters are better than those else-where, and why Edward I proclaimed his son Prince of Wales here in 1301. Subsequent male heirs were also invested with that title here, most recently Prince Charles in 1969. Outside the castle, which has its own museum, the town also has a maritime museum.

From Caernarfon the Menai Strait cannot be realistically walked, and the walker must take a bus to Bangor.

Caernarfon Castle

Caernarfon. The castle is the best preserved of Edward I's 'Ring of Stone' castles

Anglesey

(OS sheet 114)

Most of Anglesey's coastal footpaths are generally clear and unobstructed, especially on the headlands. Some are not official rights of way, but their frequent use by sea-anglers and others is rarely, if ever, disputed. There are areas, Newborough Warren and Malltraeth Sands to name the obvious two, where access is possible, but the walking is difficult, and the walker is advised to visit rather than try for a complete circuit.

When the railway came to Anglesey, it was carried across the Menai Strait by the Britannia bridge built, in 1850, by Robert Stephenson, but this is not the bridge which exists today. Before a fire partially destroyed the bridge in the 1970, the trains ran over the Strait through elevated rectangular tubes. These tubes were pre-fabricated on shore and, before being hoisted into position on the bridge, were floated down the Strait on pontoons, under the direction of a full captain of the Royal Navy.

At about the same time, the names of two nearby villages were combined and the first call for the trains, to the delight of the passengers, was at Llanfairpwllgwyngyllgogerychwryrndrobwllllantysiliogogogoch. Today the name is regularly shortened to Llanfair PG.

South of the village the Marquis of Anglesey stands on a 100 ft (30 m) pillar above his home of Plas Newydd. The Marquis was second-in-command at Waterloo, where he lost his right leg, but he survived for 39 years on an early artificial limb of wood, metal and leather.

South again, the shore can be walked continuously to St Nidan's church near Brynsiencyn, a church founded in the sixth century, and on to Traeth Melynog near Newborough Warren.

The 'new borough' of the name was created when the villagers of a site to the north-east were moved to make way for Edward I's castle of Beaumaris. The site was fertile and the villagers cut the scrub cover, exposing the new village to the winds and the drifting sand. Marram grass had to be planted to stabilise the dunes, and those dunes form the basis of the nature reserve on the site. Llanddwyn Island can be reached from the beach at low tide. Here lived St Dwyn a fifth-century Celtic hermit. Legend has it that the saint was crossed in love before she came here, and she was revered as the patron saint of lovers. The island has the ruins of an abbey built on the site of Dwyn's hermitage.

From Newborough the walker is advised to take roads around Malltraeth Sands, reaching the coast again at Aberffraw. Nothing now remains to suggest that this small village was the site of the palace of the Princes of Gwynedd, that was the strongest kingdom in Wales before the final union with England. Legend has it, however, that an arch in the church was taken from the palace. The village pub is named the 'Prince Llywelyn', a memorial, perhaps, to Llywelyn the Last, who rode from here to his death at Builth Wells, who marks the close of the Gwynedd line.

From Aberffraw the clifftop can be followed, passing the magnificently set church of St Cwyfan, built in the sixth century and restored by the Victorians. This island church once stood on a peninsula, its present position bearing mute witness to the furious gales and tides that, on occasion, come roaring into the bay. They have already started to deal similarly with the causeway built across to the church, but it is still possible to cross dry-shod at low tide.

Back on the coast, Barclodiad y Gawres – the

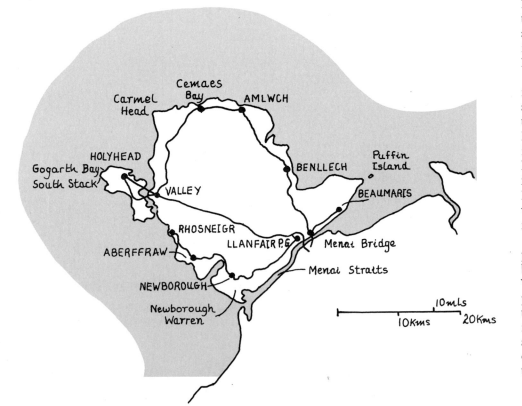

Rock Climber on the cliffs of Gogarth Bay

Giantess' Apronful – is a superbly set, strangely carved Neolithic burial chamber. From Rhosneigr, where the Wreckers of Cregyll lived, a gang remembered in a Welsh ballad written at the time of their execution in 1741, the walker passes RAF Valley, a huge site from where the Mountain Rescue helicopters fly. The walker must visit the village of Valley to cross on to Holy Island, whose cliffs are most spectacularly followed along the northern tip, near Gogarth Bay.

The cliffs here are one of the foremost rock climbing areas in Wales, and the southern end of the bay, near the lighthouse on South Stack, is a bird reserve. The RSPB have an observatory in Ellen's Tower, a summerhouse built for and named after the wife of an Anglesey MP of the mid-nineteenth century. Holyhead Mountain, above the bay, has, on its summit, the remains of a Celtic hill-fort and a Roman watchtower. Holyhead itself, in Welsh, Caer Gybi, *caer* from the Roman fort built here, *Gybi* from the Celtic St Cybi, is the principal ferry port for Ireland.

Back on the mainland, the northern Anglesey coast becomes increasingly good. Porth Swtan, 'The Bay of the Swedes', is believed to have been a favoured landing place in the days of the Viking invasions. The English name is the comparatively prosaic Church Bay. At Wylfa Heafd is Britain's largest 'Magnox', first generation, nuclear power station. The church of St Padrig on the headland of Cemaes Bay beyond is considerably older, having been founded, or so legend has it, by St Patrick in thanks for his having survived a shipwreck on the offshore island of Middle Mouse.

Amlwch now shows little sign now of the prosperity it knew in the early nineteenth century when the copper mines of Parys Mountain were in full production. At that time the mines on the nearby hill, topped by the ruin of an old windmill, were the largest and richest in Europe. Most of the ore was shipped from Amlwch, but the port fell into decline when the mines failed. Today, there has been a slight revival thanks to Shell's offshore oil terminal.

On Anglesey's eastern coast Moelfre is famous as the site of the wreck of the *Royal Charter* in 1859, a boat reputedly carrying a fortune in gold from the Australian gold mines. It was also the scene of a battle when men from ships of Henry II came ashore to pillage but were set upon and killed by locals. After the battle, a local bard maintained, the Menai Strait was choked with the bodies of dead Englishmen.

Beyond Benllech, a coastal path rounds Red Wharf Bay and heads for Puffin Island. On the island, the Welsh name is Ynys Seriol, are the scant remains of a cell started by St Seriol. The English name is for the once-large puffin colony, now much reduced by predation by man-introduced rats.

From Black Point, Anglesey's most easterly point, the walker follows lanes to Beaumaris. The castle, one of the most romantic of Edward I's castles, was built to secure the island, the Granary of Wales. It was from here, the name is 'fair marsh' in Norman French, that the villagers of Newborough were evicted. West again, more roads lead to Menai Bridge.

Before the bridge was built, the only way across to the island was either by ferry or by the hazardous crossing of the sands at low tide on foot. Thomas Telford's stately suspension design of 1826 was necessary because of an Admiralty constraint that a full-rigged ship, about 100 ft (30 m) high, had to be able to pass beneath.

North Wales and the Wirral

(OS sheets 115, 116, 117, 108)

Bangor to Llandudno (30 mls, 48 km)

BANGOR IS A cathedral city and the centre of the oldest diocese in Britain. As at St David's, the cathedral lies in a hollow sheltered from the sea, though unlike St David's, this low-crouching church fails, visually, to overcome the disadvantage of its site. Much mauling, in the name of restoration or rebuilding, has done little to improve the cathedral's appearance. Better are the main university buildings, built in fine Edwardian style on a ridge that overlooks the sea. We, too, go seaward, to Port Penrhyn, a harbour that served the huge Penrhyn slate quarries in Bethesda. The port stands within the park of the neo-Norman Penrhyn Castle, built with the wealth of the quarries, and with an interior that is often wonderfully tasteless.

From Aber Ogwen miles of the actual shoreline can be walked, the going being muddy and wet or rough and stony by turn. At one point the walker skirts Lavan Sands across which Anglesey was once, and perilously, approached.

Tucked into a deep valley of ancient oakwood with the famed fall at its head, Aber is announced by a sign that details the area's excellent bird-life. The village was a principal residence of Llywelyn Fawr – Llywelyn the Great – and the 'mwd' or grass mound on which the house stood is still visible.

From Aber several miles of shell-crunching lead to the seawall beyond which Llanfairfechan is heralded by a Gothic tower. The path follows the edge of a model yacht pond, one of Llanfairfechan's major features, passing a UDC metal plate, dated 1908, proclaiming 'the right of wheeling at a foot pace Bath Chairs drawn by hand or by Pony, Mule or Donkey. . . .'. Further on, on the seafront, unspoilt gables and bay windows face a spacious green. It is difficult to dislike the town.

Eastward, Penmaenmawr Mountain crowds the shore, making a coastal walk difficult. William Ewart Gladstone loved Penmaenmawr but even he would not love today's entry, which is nasty and noisy. The new elevated road will not help, as it roars its way over the once popular beach. All in all it is much better to take the ancient route over the back of the headlands, passing the so-called Druid's Circle, going above a prehistoric axe factory, over the famed Sychnant Pass and along the crest of Conwy Mountain, with its Iron Age hill-fort and Roman-Celtic name, Castell Caer Seion. This route offers fine views of sea and mountains, and an excellent entry into the walled town of Conwy.

The view to the estuary from the town will soon be interrupted by the amazing road tunnel, though it must be said that an earlier tunnel might have spared Conwy its multiple bridges. Much of the effect of Telford's suspension bridge is now lost, but even that, graceful as it is, intruded on the castle. There is an abbey church in Conwy, and fine old houses, including Aberconwy House dating from the fifteenth century and Plas Mawr from the sixteenth, and though the quay is not quite what it was, modern development has largely spared one of the best Welsh coastal towns.

The castle was designed by James of St George for Edward I as one of his 'Ring of Stone' castles, and perfectly combines beauty and utility. The castle was supposed to be siege-proof as it was capable of being restocked from the sea, but Edward himself was besieged there in 1294 when the river flooded and stayed high all over Christmas. Eventually the water receded and Christmas was celebrated late, festivities including the execution of several Welsh bards.

Llandudno, across the River Conwy and reached via Deganwy with its scanty castle ruin – Edward I realised the importance of the river and moved across it – is a super-league seaside resort, its 'back door' looking out to Snowdonia. Alice (in Wonderland) Liddell live nearby and the story may well have evolved here. As if to confirm the Lewis Carroll connection there is a statue of the White Rabbit.

Great Ormes Head to Chester (51 mls (82 km)

Great Ormes Head, almost 700 ft (210 m) high, has an anticlockwise Marine Drive but the walker can wander widely over the limestone upland where wild

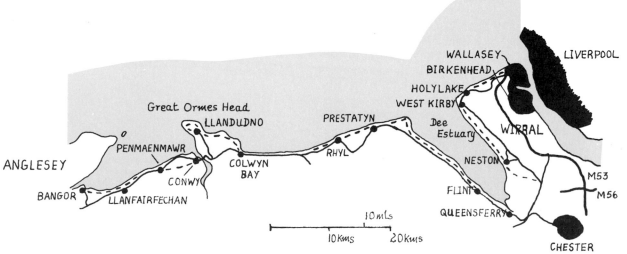

Thomas Telford's bridge over the Menai Straits

The Beach at Llandudno

goats also roam, above cliffs alive with cormorants, razorbills and gulls. Access is by cabin-lift or a rumbling tramway from Happy Valley. The nearby pier is a centre for sea cruises.

The town itself still retains the atmosphere evoked in Arnold Bennett's *The Card*, curving elegantly round the perfectly proportioned bay, though it fades out in an unfinished way before reaching Little Ormes Head. Here, our next objective, there are tremendous sea cliffs 200 ft (60 m) shorter than those of the Great Orme, but more imposing, exciting footpaths reaching the best view points.

After Little Orme, descending to neat, bungalowed Penrhyn Bay seems an anticlimax but the tiny, ancient chapel of St Trillo and remains of Conwy Abbey's fishing weir make Rhos a good stopping point. Beyond, Colwyn Bay's delights are hidden from the shoreline by the railway and new road, but the sands offer a good stretch of unhindered walking, by-passing the resort.

The beach walking ends at the lime quarry chutes serving transport vessels off Llanddulas. There is no way for walkers here, and they must climb by Penmaen Point over the Lysfaen and Rhyd-y-Foel hills, with views over the mock-Gothic Gwyrich Castle (now an entertainment centre), to reach Abergele.

Abergele is slightly removed from the coast, and has a church that has been oddly despoiled over the centuries from archers to schoolboys. There is a seaside extension, Pensarn, from where the embankment can be followed almost to Rhyl, skirting the teeming 'caravan city' of Towyn. Here, many will feel, the coast reaches its nadir, the superb G.E. Street church, with an amazing wedge-shaped tower emphasizing the scrappy look of most of the rest. We leave the beach at the clustered breakwaters of Kinmel Bay, entering Rhyl by the Voryd Bridge to follow mills of traditional 'prom' to Prestatyn.

Much of Rhyl is now run down: it has lost its pavilion and its pier, the funfairs being an inadequate replacement despite the monorail, palms, and artificial waves. Yet the beach is spacious and looking westward at sunset, with miles of coastline curving below the Carneddau range of the Snowdonia National Park, all the town's sins could be gladly forgiven.

Prestatyn, at the other end of the 'prom', is another seaside resort, better known to the walker as the start, or finish, of the Offa's Dyke Long Distance Footpath. The dyke itself in fact, never reached this spot. Offa fought to decide the dyke's line from the Clwydians to the shore but died in a battle, probably at Rhuddleau a couple of miles to the south-west.

The Prestatyn sands extend to Point of Ayr, but seafront signs warn of deep water at hightide, when a path across the golf course must be used. The Right of Way ends at Presthaven Camp, and the walker is not allowed to walk through this caravanerama, but instead must follow upland ways by Gronant and Talacre Abbey, then the straight lane to the Point. Here there are dunes, an old lighthouse, and an active colliery with undersea workings. Bird watchers are frequent, especially when winter brings wildfowl and waders.

The railway, roads and a security-patrolled industrial estate seal off miles of coastline around Mostyn Dock, the walker being forced inland, onto hills with excellent sea views. It is best is to go by Llanasa, where Emlyn Williams' schooldays coloured his later writing; Whitford with a memorial to Thomas Pennant (1726-98), one of the best Welsh travel writers who lived here in a house called Downing; regaining the coast at Llanerch-y-Mor. This is a strange place, with the rusting *Duke of Lancaster* lying high and dry by the creek, but open as a 'fun ship', a craft centre in the old mill, and an open market miles from anywhere.

East of the creek an uninviting cinder track leads to the shore, but soon another collection of industrial buildings forces the walker inland again to discover Basingwark Abbey, beautiful sited and blissfully calm. Giraldus Cambriensis came here in AD 118 during his recruiting campaign for the Third Crusade. From the abbey paths across the Greenfield Valley Country Park reach one of the 'Seven Wonders of Wales', the healing Well of St Winefride. Vengefully beheaded by the lustful Caradoc and miraculously restored to life by her uncle, St Beuno, the seventh century St Winefride aroused great devotion, a devotion which persisted long into post-Reformation times. The spring which appeared where she fell is contained in a star-shaped pool in a chapel rebuilt by Lady Margaret Beaufort, mother of Henry VII.

Beyond the factory, back on the shore there are coastal paths to Bagillt and on to Flint. Although the 1840 town hall is now the only striking town-centre building, Flint was the first of Edward I's castles. The castle now rises from green marshes clear of the tide, though once it, like Conwy, could be serviced from the sea. It is unlike Edward's other castles in plan; the keep being detached from the square layout. The site is wonderfully atmospheric, and has a fine history with melancholic associations with Edward II and Richard II. Shakespeare has the latter surrendering to Henry Bolingbroke here, though historians place that event at Conwy. The castle was ruined during the Civil War.

A continuation along the Rive Dee to Chester, once, but long ago, Chester was England's second port, now it is famous for its walls and rows, and a return by way of Shotwick, Puddington and Burton to Neston is possible. It is a little to the south of Shotwick that the walker enters England. Instead of this, many route walkers will choose to bypass the Dee and the danger area that lies north of it to make straight for Neston, birthplace of Lady Hamilton, Nelson's mistress.

Ness to Wallasey (28 mls, 45 km)

A good place to re-start the walk is at Ness, a little south of Neston where the Liverpool University Botanic Gardens are sited. Open daily, Ness has wonderful displays, outstanding amongst which are

Evening over the Dee Estuary and Hoylake

Eastgate Street, Chester

the heather, azalea and other ericaceous collections, while the mountain ash section is unique in its extent.

Close by, the edge of the Dee marshes, controlled by the Dee Wildfowlers, and the industrial desolation – slag heaps, crumbling brickworks and the disused Neston Quarry – offer a memorable contrast.

Soon after Neston Quay the walker is at Parkgate, the town trying hard to look seaside-y with its well-defined 'front' and the local specialities of shrimps and ice cream much in evidence. What is more the sea, elusive since we arrived back in England, has only departed in living memory and still returns briefly several times a year.

A path by way of the golf course leads to Heswall from where the old railway has been tranformed into the Wirral Way, a linear country park that leads delightfully to Caldy and West Kirby, passing the informative Thurstaston Visitors' Centre. Wirral's supreme outlook is from Caldy Hill, the view taking in the hills and sea from Cumbria to Snowdonia as well as the estuary itself.

West Kirby has a busy shopping area and an enjoyable walk between the Marine Lake and the tidal water. There is more sand than we have seen for

some time and from Dee Lane slipway there is the ONLY safe approach to the Hilbre Islands. For the full visit a permit from the leisure department in Riversdale Road is needed. The department also supplies a map of the route that must be followed. The nearest island can be reached three hours after high tide and a way can then be made on the seaward side of the middle island to Great Hilbre itself. The islands must be left three hours before the next high tide, but some decide to sit out a tide. This should be pre-arranged and word left locally. The whole expedition is not to be undertaken lightly, but the rewards – the population of waders is excellent, over 200 bird species have been noted, flowers include the two-flowered narcissus, and seals are frequently seen – are considerable.

There is a further reserve, where the rare natterjack toad is protected, behind the dunes on the sandy walk from West Kirby to Hoylake. Hoylake once had an enclosed anchorage, the Hoyle Lake, amid the sand banks, but this vanished when the Dee changed course and with it went the town's importance as a harbour for Liverpool. Now primarily a golfing centre, the town rather turns its back on the sea, giving the promenade a deserted appearance.

From the town the sea wall can be followed for many miles, with the sea wide open and wild to the west and the set-back blocks of suburban housing to the east seemingly totally unrelated. The right to coastal access here is now more assured with the establishment of the new North Wirral Coastal Park whose landmarks include the 1763 Leasowe Light-house set on its foundation of salt-petrified cotton bales washed up from a wreck. Leasowe Castle, also known as Mockbeggar Hall, giving the name to Mockbeggar Wharf, was a sixteenth-century residence of the Earls of Derby, but it has been added to and 'improved', particularly in the nineteenth century. The resulting stylistic jumble is now a hotel.

As New Brighton is approached, a dual carriageway joins the seawall walk. Here there is brash entertainment, a seedy and battered main street and a dour offshore fort on the polluted beach where 'No Bathing' warnings dominate the once pleasant sands. This is a resort in seemingly terminal decline. The view of Liverpool's docks, also declined, at least industrially, and the city skyline is still a unique feature, present throughout the long promenade southward through Wallasey. The name derives from *Wallawey*, Welshman's Island.

On the approach to Wallasey Pool, the waterway that almost makes an island of north-east Wirral, is a Mersey ferry. It is possible to make a route along the Mersey, going through Birkenhead, with the ruins of a twelfth-century priory, Wirral's oldest building, the optimistically named Port Sunlight, which has a fine art gallery; and on to Eastham Ferry. Beyond is the Manchester Ship Canal and progress becomes hopeless. But no matter whether the walker takes his ferry at Wallasey or Eastham, there is no better way to enter Liverpool than by ferry across the Mersey.

The Isle of Man

(OS sheet 95)

IT WOULD BE rather trite to describe the Isle of Man as a walkers' paradise, but the three legs on the island's coat of arms do seem rather appropriate. In 1986, to commemorate Manx Heritage Year, a long-distance footpath was established, which enables a complete circuit of the Manx coast to be walked. The path is called 'Raad ny Foillan', the Road of the Gull's, and it is way-marked by signs with the silhouette of a gull. It will be obvious why a sea-bird gave the path its name, but it could equally well have been named after many another bird, even the national bird, the Manx shearwater, reported to be nesting again in small numbers on the Calf of Man, after becoming extinct locally. Around the 70-mile (112 km) coast line, a river comes down to the sea every 3 miles (5 km) on average. Usually, the river flows through a deep, narrow glen. These glens are a special feature which distinguish the Manx coastline; 17 of them (not all on the coast) have been designated as National Glens, and they enjoy the same protection as that given to a national park on the mainland.

The island's hills lie generally north-east to south-west, and their slopes are gentler to the east, so the most spectacular cliff scenery is to be found on the south-western side, between Peel and Spanish Head. Here, too, is one of the best examples of a glen, Glenmaye, best seen by a walker heading south from Peel Castle. On the way the walker traverses the clifftop above Traie Cabbag, Cabbage Beach, reputedly named from the day when a cargo of the vegetable covered the beach after a shipwreck! Glenmaye is a cool, sheltered, wooded haven in which there are several waterfalls. It is hard to imagine that the sea is only 10 minutes walk away.

Peel, where this coastal section began, is a beautiful old fishing port, dominated by the castle that stands on St Patrick's Isle, an island in name only. Inside the fourteenth-century castle are the ruins of the thirteenth-century cathedral of St German.

Beyond Glenmaye the coastal path reaches its highest point on top of Cronk-ny-Array-Laa — say 'kronk-neary-lay' and you will be fairly close. The name means 'The Hill of the Morning Watch', and dates from feudal times, when every Manxman had to stand his stint of "watch and ward" against possible invasion. Naturally, it is an excellent vantage point, and it provides a superb view of the coast to the north.

The walk section finishes at the huge cliffs of Spanish Head, beyond Port Erin with its fine railway museum. Across Calf Sound is Calf of Man, an uninhabited island with excellent bird colonies.

By far the easiest walking is to be found on the island's southern shore, especially on the approach to Castletown from the west, where much of the coastal way consists of a surfaced path along an artificial causeway around the bay. Castletown has a maze of winding lanes, and Castle Rushen, a fine medieval building on the site of a Viking stronghold.

On its south-eastern side the island is more urbane and residential, and some visitors might prefer to take the delightful Manx Electric Railway from Douglas to Ramsey. The railway stops at Groudle Glen, another fine glen that can be followed to the beach, and at Laxey, where there is the most famous island tourist attraction. The Laxey waterwheel is the world's largest, with a diameter of 72½ feet (21.75 m). It was built in 1854 to provide power for the lead mines on Snaefell, and is also known as the 'Lady Isabella', having been named after the wife of the island's Lt Governor of the time.

The railway traveller misses Dhoon Glen, a spectacular glen with two 60 ft (18 m) waterfalls, and Maughold Head, an excellent viewpoint, each of which is almost too good to miss, before arriving at Ramsey, a centre for yachting and with a good beach.

The margins of the northern plain, which lies to

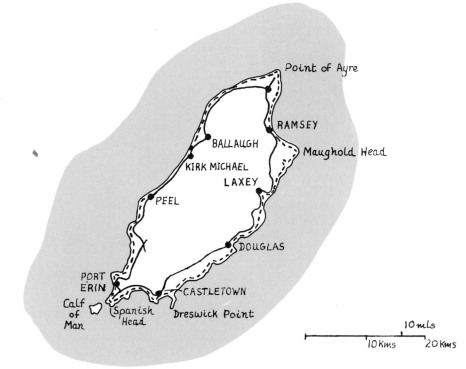

Point of Ayre

RAMSEY

Maughold Head

BALLAUGH

KIRK MICHAEL

LAXEY

PEEL

DOUGLAS

PORT ERIN

CASTLETOWN

Calf of Man

Spanish Head

Dreswick Point

10 mls

10 Kms   20 Kms

the north of the Ramsey to Kirk Michael Road, are not as dramatic, but no less attractive. Broad beaches flank flat farm land, which finally gives way to The Ayres. This is an area of sand-dunes, part of which is a nature reserve, where many rarities, insects, birds and plants, can be found. Terminating all of this is the red and white striped exclamation mark of the Point of Ayre lighthouse.

At a village with the elegant name of The Cronk near Ballaugh, about 8 miles (13 km) along the northern coast from the Point of Ayre is the twelfth-century church of St Mary de Ballaugh. Ballaugh itself is, for many, more famous for its bridge, a landmark on the TT course. Nearby, the Curraghs Wildlife Park has both Manx cats and the four-horned Manx (Loghtan) sheep.

South of Kirk Michael is Glen Mooer with a superb waterfall, the *Spooyt Vane* or white spout. Here, too, is *Cabbal Pheric*, Patrick's Chapel, the remains of a chapel and a ninth-century hermit's cell.

The World's largest Waterwheel at Laxey

Lancashire and Cumbria

(OS sheets 108, 102, 97, 96, 89, 85)

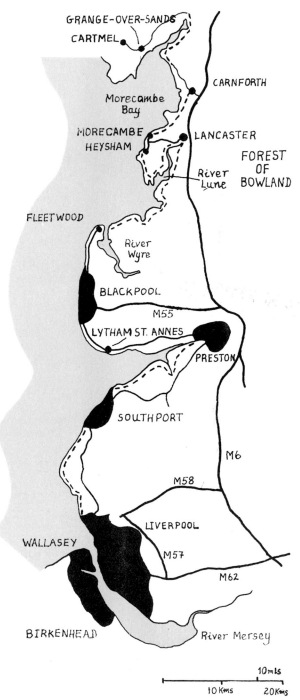

Liverpool to Lancaster (85 mls, 136 km)

THIS MILD, LARGELY low lying coastline is punctuated with opposites, from huge industrial and dockland complexes to isolated estuarine wildernesses, from tinsel town resorts to vast lonely stretches of sand. Overall, it is one of the most underwalked areas of the British coast.

Liverpool, with its unique dialect is probably more renowned for exporting the Mersey beat and football, despite its 7 miles (11 km) of dockfront. It took over from Chester as a port in the eighteenth century when the Dee silted up, and though now much of the docklands has fallen into disuse, it remains a major port. It has some fine and interesting buildings, especially the new cathedral and the Royal Liver building with its two Liverbird statues. However, it is not a place for the walker to linger, nor is it an enjoyable exit, so it is best to take a train to Crosby

Liverpool's Royal Liver Building

where the city's rich merchants built their Regency terraces. Now take the wide sands and dunes that skirt the golf course and head towards the Formby dunes over the river Alt. The vast dune systems between Formby and Ainsdale are a National Nature Reserve, a home to sand lizards, natterjack toads and many scarce plants.

The shore now curves in towards the Ribble estuary at Southport, a busy resort which retains much of its elegant Victorian architecture, especially along Lord Street, with its glass and wrought iron arcades and shopping verandas. The sand here is firm enough to land a plane on and at low tide the pier is left high and dry. The long promenade road, past the marine lake, meets the Ribble estuary at Fiddler's Ferry. A seawall takes the walker out overlooking Banks Marsh used by large numbers of knot and bartailed godwit as moulting grounds between August and October and by thousands of pink-footed geese. An embankment takes you around the twisting creeks and over the river Douglas at Tartleton then back out along the inner estuary salt marsh as the Ribble narrows and enters Preston.

Preston was the birthplace of Richard Arkwright of spinning-frame fame, and used to have many huge cotton mills. Lack of reasonable access from the town means a bus to Freckleton from where the walker can skirt the edge of Warton marsh to reach Lytham. On the front a white windmill, built in 1805, overlooks the estuary, with fine views to Southport pier across the Ribble. North, beyond Lytham St Anne's with its golf course, its firm sands and fine flower-decked dunes is Blackpool.

Blackpool is a classic holiday resort dominated by its tower and renowned for the golden mile, its landladies and the illuminations. In mid-season it is a brash place, boisterous youths mingling uneasily with families and pensioners. The coming of the railway in 1846 opened the holiday-maker flood gates, the town attracting droves of Lancashire cotton mill workers. The replica of the Eiffel Tower, built in 1894 and 518½ ft (155.5m) tall, offers superb views, but really comes into its own when the illuminations are lit, from September to late October, when it appears as a

Blackpool Tower

huge flashing beacon.

For peace and serenity you can follow the beach but it is a rare treat to take the tram along the 7 miles (11 km) of track which follows the prom right into Fleetwood. Fleetwood, called the Grimbsy of the west coast, is bounded by the sea on three sides. The Cod Wars somewhat devastated its fleet though it still has trawlers fishing the Irish Sea.

The summer walker can take the passenger ferry across the mouth of the Wyre to Knott End-on-Sea, but the winter walker has a detour along the estuary to Shard Bridge and then along the east facing salt marsh and sea bank, which holds a surprising variety of plants, to Knott End. The Lune estuary, where at low tide the sea is some 3 or more miles (5 km) out, offers fine views across Morecambe Bay and the Lune to the Lake District. A marvellous sea bank takes you along the estuary, topped by the ruins of Cockersand Abbey built in 1190 and past the lighthouse towards Glasson, where the Lancaster canal reaches the sea. Glasson is a neat and busy yachting and sailing centre and from it a nature trail along a disused railway line takes you over the river Conder and into Lancaster. Lancaster is a good place to stop over before tackling Morecambe Bay.

According to Defoe in 1725 'The town is ancient, it lies, as it were, in its own ruins and has little to recommend it but a decayed castle'. Ignore this. The Norman castle is a triumph of strategic fortification built on a crag of millstone grit overlooking the Lune.

At the town we cross the Lune following a minor road to Overton and Sunderland Point where the road gets regularly flooded by high tides. From the shingle of Sunderland Point a good path leads towards Heysham with its grey cube nuclear power stations. Better views arrive at Chapel Hill, overlooking the narrow ancient streets of Old Heysham. The ruins of St Patrick's Chapel lie on the hill edge alongside a curious grave – a solid lump of sandstone has coffin shapes carved into the rock. Originally covered with stone slabs these now lie open and water filled. From the hill descend to the long promenade which takes you into Morecambe.

Morecombe to Gutterby Spa (79 mls, 126 km)

Known as the 'Lungs of Lancashire', Morecambe's fresh sea air has cleansed the smoke-filled lungs of Northern mill workers since the 1900s. Beyond the amusements and the pier, the promenade takes the walker out to Hest Bank and the vast sweep of Morecambe Bay, a mecca for bird watchers. The wide sands here hold between 10,000 and 15,000 birds on high spring tides. Oystercatchers, dunlin, knot, sanderling, ringed plover, turnstone, redshank and bar-tailed godwit can all be seen in large numbers in and around the bay.

In the nineteenth century horse-drawn carts used to cross the sands of Morecambe Bay to Cartmel 9 miles (14.5 km) away. Sheltered by the Furness peninsula, the flat sands are built up from silt deposited by the rivers Wyre, Lune, Keer, Kent and Leven. The rivers are constantly changing the channels they take through the bay to the sea and the whole bay of some 150 square miles (388 sq.m) is riddled with quicksands. It is still possible on a few days each year to walk across the bay at low tide, but you must have an official guide, known as a King's guide, to lead you. Otherwise, follow the salt marsh towards Carnforth where the walker must join the road past Warton Crag. Near this there is an unusual rock formation, the 'Bride's Chair' where a newly-wed girl should sit if she is to have a baby! The nearby RSPB reserve at Leighton Moss is still home to bitterns, bearded tits and marsh harriers. Fed by streams from the surrounding limestone hills it is also a beautiful place at dawn and dusk, the best times to catch a glimpse of an elusive otter.

Rejoining the coast at Jenny Brown's Point, the walk to Arnside is one of the jewels of the west coast, with wooded limestone crags, bounding the shore.

Yew, ash, whitebeam, hazel and spindle mix with typical carboniferous limestone plants – herb paris, green hellebore, solomon's seal and columbine, harebell, thrift, rock rose, sea campion, thyme and bloody cranesbill. The views, across the Kent Channel to Humphrey Head and down to the Kent viaduct at Arnside, are equally good.

Arnside is a good centre for exploring the area, and from it the best way forward is a short, one stop, train ride over the Kent viaduct to Grange-over-Sands, a Victorian resort lying in the shelter of wooded slopes and with stunning views south across the bay. Just along the coast rises 172 ft (51.5 m) Humphrey Head with the only real cliffs between north Wales and St Bees Head. It is here that the last wolf in England is said to have been killed. Descending from the headland, the walker reaches the Leven estuary, with more sand flats and salt marsh. Again here the train is best, the ride crossing the Leven viaduct from Cartmel to Ulverston.

Ulverston is dominated by Hoad Hill, a 435 ft (130.5 m) mound topped by a lighthouse-shaped tower. Named after a Saxon landowner, called 'Ulph' the town was burned down twice by Robert the Bruce's men. From it, in the eighteenth century, coaches used to carry mail across Morecambe Bay, saving miles of rough roads around the estuaries. The shore offers good walking to Aldingham which has lost many houses to the sea over the centuries and whose twelfth-century church now has its graveyard almost at the water's edge. From there a road hugs the shore and at Rampside the long shingle spits of Roa and Foulney Island claw out into the bay. Foulney, nearly 2 miles (3 km) long and in parts only a few yards wide, holds colonies of breeding terns. Out in the middle of the channel between here and Walney Island lies Piel Island and the scraggy remains of its twelfth-century castle.

But to reach Walney Isle the walker needs to go through Barrow-in-Furness, a town that grew up around Furness Abbey – founded by Cistercian monks in 1127. The town became an iron and steel town and an important shipbuilding centre in the eighteenth century. It is now a centre for building nuclear-powered submarines. Walney Island is a 12 mile (19 km) long strip of sand, shingle and dune only a quarter of a mile (0.4 km) wide in places, sheltering a salt marsh at its southern tip. The spit at

Blackpool with its Tower, piers and Golden Mile

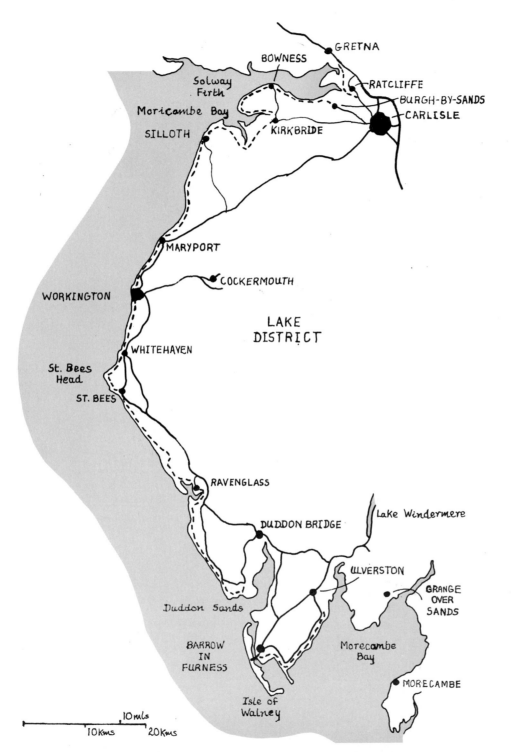

The ruins of Furness Abbey in Southern Cumbria

this end holds one of the largest colonies of herring and lesser black-backed gulls in Europe and has breeding eider duck at the southernmost limit of their range.

Southward, Blackpool Tower can be seen, 12 miles (19 km) away across the bay. From here we again have a choice – a long detour around Duddon estuary or a magnificent train ride from Barrow to Millom, overlooking marshes and estuary all the way.

It is from Millom that the walker begins to walk the Cumbrian coast in earnest. A 12-mile (19 km) sweep of firm sand backed by dunes reaching 70 ft (21 m) in places, leads you to the Esk estuary at Ravenglass. At Silecroft low clay cliffs begin to rise and the horizon is dominated by the looming shape of Black Combe that brings the Lake District fells almost down to the beach. At Gutterby Spa the beach becomes shingly and boulder-strewn as the cliffs fall away.

Ravenglass to Rockcliffe Marsh (87 mls, 139 km)

At Ravenglass the beautiful River Esk winds its way to the shore, together with the Mite and Irt which have twisted and cut their respective ways through the Lakeland hills to an estuary sheltered by sand dune spits on either side. If time permits take a return trip

St Bees Head, the extreme western tip of Cumbria

'Ratty', the Ravenglass and Eskdale Railway

on the steam Ravenglass and Eskdale railway, through these beautiful wooded valleys. The 'Ratty' was built to bring iron ore down the valley in 1875: the museum at Ravenglass tells its distinguished history.

From Ravenglass there is again a choice, a 2 mile (3.2 km) train ride to Drigg or getting your feet wet. If you decide to dip your feet you will not fail to see and hear, on Drigg dunes, the largest colony of black-headed gulls in Britain. Akin to an infant school playground riot, especially at the end of May when hatching begins, the birds benefit the plants by depositing huge quantities of guano, and many rare and unusual plants thrive on this exclusive diet. Few people explore this coastline, between Drigg and Nethertown, understandable perhaps as you hurriedly pass the nuclear complex at Sellafield – Windscale, as it was known, before someone tried to disguise its existence.

Beyond the site is St Bees Head, a beautiful spot where the Cumbrian coast reaches its highest and westernmost point. Cumbria sticks out into the Irish sea because the Lake District is built from the hardest, least weatherable and highest rocks in England. Here on the coast though, as the path gently dips and then climbs, low cliffs of sandstone gradually become more prominent, rock that is softer

and more easily weathered. The village of St Bees lies in the valley of Pow Beck and St Bega, a seventh-century Irish princess, is said to have founded a nunnery here. St Bees Head rises sharply from a fine beach, its beautiful umber cliffs, wave-sculpted below and weather-ridged above, rise to 300 ft (90 m) and support the largest sea-bird colony on the west coast of England. Razorbill, guillemot, kittiwake, fulmars and puffins breed here, together with England's only – and small – mainland colony of black guillemots. On clear days the Isle of Man can be seen from here and at your feet on the close turf of the clifftops flowers abound – birdsfoot trefoil, sheepsbit, thyme, harebell heather, gorse and tormentil.

Before reaching the lighthouse at North Head descend to Fleswick bay, where a stream cuts narrowly through the rock to form a small gorge, down to the unusual red shingle beach and sandstone rock pools. Beyond the head is Whitehaven, a centre for exporting Cumbrian coal, its own coal mines stretching 4 miles (6.5 km) out under the sea. In 1730 it was a major port, but as Liverpool grew so it declined, though its sturdy sombre harbour is still active with fishing boats. Next is Workington where steel and coal have combined to make a typical Victorian industrial town. The local carboniferous rocks are rich in iron ore, which helped make the area 'an isolated outlier of industrial Britain'. Beyond the town along the shingle beach lies the last of the industrial outliers, Maryport. Developed originally by the Romans and called Alauna, a fort was built here to stop seaborne northern raiders turning Hadrian's Wall. As industry developed in the eighteenth century so the town grew, with a typical gridiron layout.

The Allerdale ramble takes the walker out over Alauna fort and down to the shore which is followed sometimes muddily, round into Silloth, with views across into Scotland that are magnificent and best seen at dusk. Silloth, lying at the southern edge of the Solway, has been a popular holiday resort for over 100 years. A walk out to Skinburness and Grune Point on an evening in late summer shows the Solway at its tranquil best, though Skinburness itself was wiped out in a flood in 1303.

Our walk now wends its way lazily around the creeks and saltmarshes of Moricambe Bay, where the rivers Waver and Wampool have deposited their silts, forming a vast wild track of salting sheltered by the shingle bank of Grune Point. Newton Arlosh across the base of the bay was founded by monks from the

nearby Holme Cultram Abbey to house victims of a flood in 1303. The fourteenth-century St John's Chapel has a squat fortified tower with stone walls 5 foot (1.5 m) thick and narrow slits for windows, and a peel tower to protect the locals from Scottish raiders.

Having skirted Moricambe Bay, a road follows the coast alongside Cardurnock Flats as the Solway narrows towards Bowness. On its way it is flanked by saltmarshes bisected with creeks and channels and huge mud-flats which in winter attract vast numbers of pink-footed and barnacle geese. A small headland, Herdhill Scar, projects into the Firth here, a memory of a railway viaduct which used to cross to Annan in Scotland until it was destroyed in 1935 by incensed Presbytarians. The Scots used the bridge to cross over to England on their 'dry' Sundays for a drink!

On the flat coast at Bowness lies the end of Hadrian's Wall, though as it was only a turf embankment here little remains to be seen. In the church at Bowness are bells stolen from Scotland in retaliation for a Scottish raid when raiders stole the local bells, but lost them half way across the Firth.

The estuary widens again where the waters of the rivers Esk and Eden meet, and the mud-flats spread out once more from the saltmarsh. At Burgh by Sands another heavily fortified fourteenth-century church lies on the line of Hadrian's Wall and is built with stone from the Roman defences. Out on the marshes a monument pinpoints the spot where Edward I died in 1307 whilst leading his troops across the estuary. The huge marsh is cut in two by the River Eden as it makes numerous twists into Carlisle. Founded by the Romans around AD 78 and used as a base for wall building, Carlisle has a sandstone castle with a huge keep built in 1092, and a small sandstone cathedral dating from 1123. Being only 8 miles (13 km) from the Scottish border the town changed hands many times in the trial of strength between the English and the Scots. Defoe described it very well, in 1725, 'the city is strong, but small, the buildings old, but the streets fair; the great church is a venerable old pile'!

The opposite bank of the Eden leads us twisting again back out to the marsh opposite the monument to Edward I. Here, between the Eden and the Esk, Rockcliffe Marsh can be skirted along an embankment. The marsh is a lonely and exposed place, but still a beautiful spot to leave England for Scotland.

The Solway Firth which separates England and Scotland

From the Solway to the Clyde

(OS sheets 85, 84, 83, 82, 76, 70, 63)

Gretna to New Abbey (44mls, 70km)

GRETNA'S RUNAWAY MARRIAGE industry in legendary. In 1754 the notorious 'Fleet' marriages in London were outlawed and amorous couples, whose intended unions were frowned upon by their parents, fled to Scotland where a man and woman needed only to exchange their vows before a person of standing, in the presence of two witnesses, to be legally married. Trade boomed to the extent that there were several 'Marriage Houses' and a number of roving 'Priests' who would conduct marriages indoors or out. The procedure was slowed by an Act of 1856 requiring three weeks' residency in Scotland as a prelude to marriage, and virtually eliminated in 1940 when the law was changed so that marriages could be conducted only by church ministers or registrars. However, in 1970 the residential qualification was replaced by fifteen days' postal notice to the Registrar, and couples are once more free to make day trips to Gretna to be married. The Old Blacksmith's Shop at Springfield which incorporates a horse-drawn carriage museum, offers mock marriages for those not wanting, or needing, the real thing.

From Gretna it is possible to follow the Solway shore all the way to Annan, the easiest section being along the former Loch and Dornock Fisheries road where old nets can be seen staked out on the flats at low tide. Solway salmon are a delicacy available at practically every fish shop along the coast. A disused railway runs southwards from Annan and an embankment, a twin to that near Bowness on the far shore, noses out to sea before ending abruptly.

Annan would be a peaceful town without the A75, a continuation, perhaps, of the curse put on the town by St Malachy O'Moore in 1140 because of the general unchristian behaviour of the locals. Certainly for several centuries after the curse it was a place of 'perpetuall thrift, greif & slauchter' with 'Inglishmen thair perpetuall ennymes'. The town hall is the most imposing building with a top-heavy tower.

A huge sign outside Annan indicates the start of the Solway Coast Heritage Trail, the motorist's alternative to the lorry-loaded A75. Our walk is less well signed as it follows the River Annan to the sea, then follows roads, tracks and stretches of saltmarsh to Ruthwell.

A small village of low houses, Ruthwell is set back from the marsh. In a modest little house is the Savings Bank Museum, commemorating the establishment of the world's first savings bank by the Rev. Henry Duncan in 1810, while Ruthwell church, holds a magnificent seventh-century Runic Cross. On the nearby Dumfries road is the Brow Well, where Robert Burns sought a cure for an illness in 1796. Sadly the cure failed, and the poet died a few days later in Dumfries. His house and haunts, where he spent his last few years, may be visited in the town.

The loops of the Lochar Water force the road inland and were it not for Caerlaverock Castle the temptation would be to move straight on to Dumfries, walking opportunites being few. The castle has a unique triangular design, with each corner protected by massive drum towers and surrounded by a water-filled moat in what was already a natural defensive site. Despite that, its position meant that it changed hands regularly, until its final seige in 1640 when it stood for 13 weeks against the Covenanters. Nearby, the Wildfowl Trust has established a reserve, the main wintering ground from September to April for the entire Spitzbergen population of barnacle geese. The reserve supports other grazing geese, ducks, swans and a variety of waders. A large colony of natterjack toads is also in residence.

Although Dumfries lies far from the Solway it is at the tidal limit of the River Nith and the lowest bridging point. The Old Bridge House is a museum portraying the bygone life of the Royal Burgh, while the prominent white windmill tower houses a fine museum and is capped by a camera obscura for

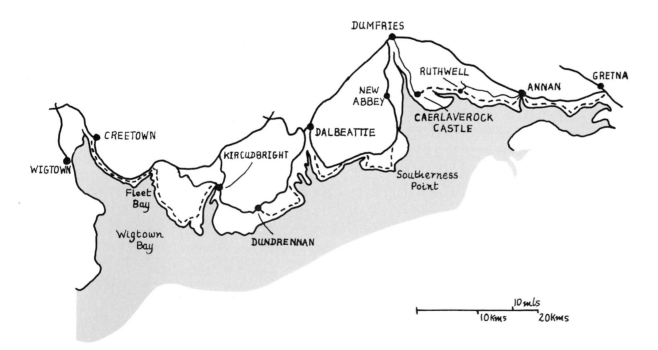

Evening over the sandbanks where the River Cree flows into Wigtown Bay

Cumbrian coast, offers fine views seaward. In addition, take time to visit the gardens of Arbigland, an estate that includes the birthplace of John Paul Jones, born in 1747, who became founder of the American Navy. A descent from Criffel can be made towards Caulkerbush, cutting out the flat coastal plain and the main road.

Entry to the Rough Firth is best achieved by following a cliff path from Sandyhills to Rockcliffe and Kippford. The National Trust for Scotland own part of the coast as well as the Rough Island bird reserve noted for its nesting terns. The long promontory of Moyl thrusts itself out into the sea, though access from Kippford is difficult due to the muddy trench of the Urr Water at low tide. If a boatman cannot be persuaded to ferry the walker across, then it is a long journey round by road via Dalbeattie and Palnackie. An approach from Palnackie does, however, offer the opportunity of studying the fifteenth-century tower at Old Orchardton. With a wary eye on the tides the walk down the Moyl peninsula can be extended to Hestan Island, and given enough time it is also possible to walk across the sands of Auchencairn Bay – the peninsula of Torr Point can be

used as a stepping stone for added interest. Back on dry land Balcary Point can be rounded on a cliff path leading to Rascarrel Bay. Progress along the coast from Rascarrel Bay, possible only as far as the firing range, is dependent on the tides.

Historians are undecided as to whether Mary Queen of Scots fled Scotland from Port Mary or nearby Abbey Burn Foot. Either way, her last few steps on Scottish soil, in 1568, were from Dundrennan Abbey, a twelfth-century Cistercian foundation, to the shore. Our route moves inland to Dundrennan, bypassing the firing range for Kirkcudbright.

Kirkcudbright (pronounced Ker-koo-bree) offers an interesting town trail, while the Stewartry Museum covers the history of the area. The Selkirk Arms celebrates the visit of Robert Burns and the writing of the 'Selkirk Grace' which is recited by exiled Scots the world over each Burns Night. A walk round the wooded promontory of St Mary's Isle fails to reveal anything of the Priory – Sancta Maria de Trayel – which gave the place its name but was subsequently dismantled to build the castle at Kirkcudbright. John Paul Jones landed here in 1778 and kidnapped the

Caerlaverock Castle

studying the town and surrounding countryside.

Southwards to the Solway the road is set back from the sea. New Abbey village has grown alongside the thirteenth-century 'Sweetheart' Abbey, 'Sweetheart' because of the devotion of Devorgilla, to her husband John Balliol, the ill-fated puppet-king of Scotland. His embalmed heart was her 'sweet silent companion' after his death and she founded the abbey in his memory. She has also given her name to a fifteenth-century bridge in Dumfries.

Criffel to Isle of Whithorn (94 mls, 150 km)
The lack of a coastal path on the next section coast is sad, though the climb of Criffel, a coastal mountain which has been in view since we reached the

Barnacle Geese, which winter at Caerlaverock

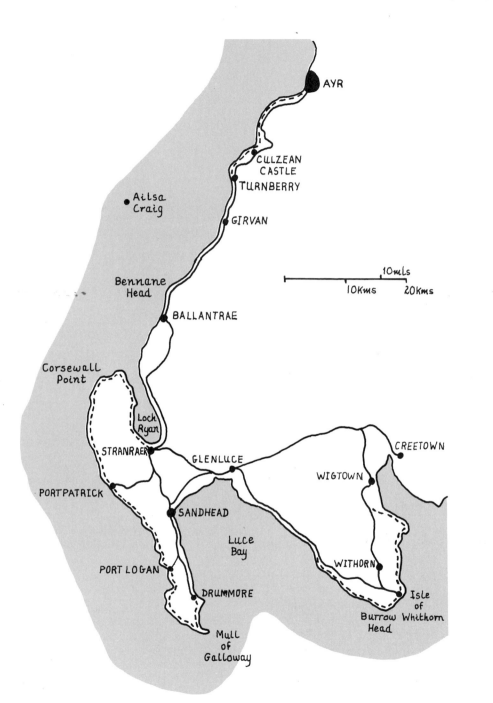

Earl of Selkirk, though he later had to release him as no one was inclined to pay the ransom.

On the western side of Kirkcudbright Bay a path through Senwick Wood can be used to reach Ross Bay and the peninsula of Meikle Ross overlooking the island of Little Ross, though from here the coastline towards the Fleet estuary does not lend itself to walking. Go inland instead, using tracks and minor roads to reach Kirkandrews, from where Sandgreen can be reached by sand at low tide. A tour of the Islands of Fleet may also be included. From Sandgreen a long track can be followed through the Fleet Forest to reach Gatehouse of Fleet, a town of great character founded on the cotton trade in the eighteenth century. In the Murray Arms Hotel here, Robert Burns wrote Scotland's unofficial anthem 'Scots Wha Hae'.

The coastline to Creetown is rocky in parts and as there are no continuous paths access is restricted to a low-tide shore walk. A short way from Ravenshall, down on the shore, is Dick Hatteraick's Cave. Sir Walter Scott wrote about it first, though subsequent writers have differed about whether it was used as a hideout for smugglers – Dick is said to have been one – or a store for contraband goods. Built into the cave are a series of stone pigeon holes. The cave is difficult to locate, even more difficult to enter, and notoriously difficult to leave. The aid of a rope and at least one person on the outside is essential for any exploration of the innards. Once Creetown is reached a visit to the Gem Rock museum is a must, and the town is also home to a fine array of craftsmen.

The road between Creetown, Newton Stewart and Wigtown can hardly be classed as coastal and is best covered at speed. Youth hostellers, deprived of accommodation since Carlisle, will no doubt sample a night at the Old School House at Minnigaff. Be warned that the hostel stamp reads: 'Come to sunny Minnigaff. . .and watch it rain'. Wigtown is a surprisingly small former county town, arranged around an impressively large square. On the saltmarsh a lonely marker indicates the spot where two women were tied down and drowned by the incoming side for being Covenanters.

Crossing the tidal River Bladnock – near Scotland's most southerly distillery – the Baldoon Sands are reached and a shoreline trek eventually picks up a fishery road on a delightfully wooded and rocky shore. The road leads to Garlieston, a port built in 1746, from where the shoreline can be followed.

Burrow Head to Ballantrae (116 mls, 186 km)

From Rigg Bay it is necessary to return to the road and the opportunity should be taken to move inland to Whithorn where St Ninian established Scotland's first Christian church in the fifth century. It was known as Candida Casa – the White House. The hymn 'Ninian of Galloway' records how 'Softly the Christian morn dawned o'er the lone Whithorn' and in time there was a cathedral, priory and pilgrimages, though these were banned by the Scottish parliament in 1581. Major excavations alongside the priory have revealed important discoveries which are housed in a nearby museum. A large collection of early stone crosses is also on display. The pilgrimage has now been revived on an annual basis and St Ninian's Cave, said to have been the saint's retreat, is well signposted from the roadside. A better way to visit the cave is to walk to it from the Isle of Whithorn, travelling round Burrow Head, a rocky headland, rich in bird life that, at 18 miles (28 km), is closer to the Isle of Man than any other point on the mainland. St Ninian's Cave is plain to see from the beach, though it was recently almost buried by a landslip. Visitors traditionally leave a makeshift cross, or scratch a cross on a pebble and set it in a niche.

It is now possible to walk along the shore, turning inland to Montreith where a bronze otter on Point of Lag is a memorial to Gavin Maxwell. The otter is a reference to his book *Ring of Bright Water* though it is another book, *House of Elrig*, which records his childhood on The Machars.

From Montreith it is best to make the entire circuit of Luce Bay by road all the way to the Mull of Galloway as walking is otherwise limited largely to an unpleasantly bouldery beach, and even that ends at a firing range that cannot be traversed. There are a number of things to see on the road: the tumbled ruin of Chapel Finian – St Finian was a scholar at Whithorn; a large Cistercian abbey; and a small motor museum at Glenluce. Ardwell Garden, shielded by trees and surrounded by sea, has a range of exotic plants, while the Logan Botanic Garden is an out-station of Edinburgh's Royal Botanic Garden.

Drummore is the last village on the way to the Mull of Galloway, and proclaims itself to be Scotland's most southerly village. Beyond is the Mull, as far south as Workington, Penrith, Bishop Auckland and Hartlepool. The sea can be reached safely at East and West Tarbet; two bays which almost bite the Mull from the mainland and a walk can be easily made

The Lighthouse at Portpatrick, Galloway

around the cliff line. The cliffs are home to kittiwakes, fulmars, razorbills, the occasional puffin and a great number of gulls, while the jagged Scares in the middle of Luce Bay house a large gannetry. On clear days a magnificent view extends to the Galloway hills, the Lake District fells, the Isle of Man and the Antrim coast of Northern Ireland.

Abutting the North Channel the Rhins of Galloway feature aggressive cliffs and numerous little bays, and magnificent coastal scenery stretches for miles between the Mull of Galloway and the mouth of Loch Ryan. The problem facing the walker on this section is yet again, access. Farm pastures, each walled or fenced, run to the very edge of the cliff, and where there are no pastures there is gorse and bramble. These difficulties mean the coastline can only be visited piecemeal using access from the farms, or the

supply roads to the lighthouses of Crammag Head, Black Head and Corsewall Point. By virtue of its difficult nature this is coast for the connoisseur, revealing its splendours only to those willing to pay in blood for the privilege.

Easier pickings are available at a couple of points however. Port Logan is a charming little village and nearby is a remarkable fish pond, constructed in 1800. The pond is connected to Port Logan Bay and allows fish a one-way entry. Further north, Portpatrick is a larger village which was once the premier port for Ireland. Legends of St Patrick abound here – he leapt across from Ireland, leaving an imprint of his foot on a rock on the shore, was beheaded by the

Looking north over the Isle of Whithorn, with Wigtown Bay to the right and the hills of Galloway beyond

natives, but nonchalantly picked up the severed head and swam back to Ireland! Northwards from Portpatrick a coastal path has been beaten through to Black Head where steps and other aids set the Southern Upland Way on its first few miles to the North Sea at Cockburnspath. Although a raised beach can be at least a partial aid to walking round the coast to Loch Ryan, the Southern Upland Way is by far the easier way to reach Stranraer.

Loch Ryan is the first of Scotland's true sea lochs. Its mouth is narrower than its head and its deep waters make it a more suitable site for a harbour than Portpatrick which was replaced as the premier Irish port by Stranraer, from where a ferry still connects with Larne in Northern Ireland. There is a museum in the town and an old castle, built around 1520, that became a seat of the Clan Kennedy. The Solway Coast Heritage Trail ends here, though a publicised, but unsigned, continuation reaches Troon by way of the main A77, with variations.

There is no good walking route around Loch Ryan, apart from a short pathway at the end of the promenade at Stranraer. It is better to take the road straight to Ballantrae, from where Ailsa Craig, a dozen miles (19 km) out to sea, dominates the seascape. The Kennedy Castle of Ardstinchar, small and ruinous, stands on a rock overlooking the village.

The Carrick Coast to Ayr (35 mls, 56 km)

The Carrick coastline – as a sidelight, the Prince of Wales is Earl of Carrick – from Ballantrae to Ayr features several small villages, ruined castles and larger-than-life characters, such as 'Souter Johnnie' a local cobbler immortalised in Robert Burns' poem 'Tam O'Shanter' and Sir John Cathcart. However, the road's closeness to the sea leaves little scope for walking, though from Ballantrae itself the beach provides the best means of early progress. The River Stinchar and the sea have worked the beach material into a bar – on which terns breed – which diverts the river mouth. The beach ends at rocky Bennane Head where a small monument records: 'Henry Ewing Torbet (Snib) of Bennane Cave 1912–1983. Respected and independent'. 'Snib' was formerly a bank manager, but turned his back on the easy life and moved into the cave across the road. Local folk remember him with affection, though after his death the cave was sealed to stop any further inhabitants. A narrow path from the small car-park here leads to a quiet cove where, tucked behind a headland, is a narrow,

evil slit of a cave, once the home of Sawney Bean and his family in the seventeenth century. It is said that the family captured travellers on the lonely coast-path and ate them. One man, who had to watch his wife being eaten, managed to escape and alerted the authorities. A force was sent against the family, who were subsequently executed at Edinburgh. There is considerable doubt about whether Sawney Bean really was a cannibal, but the cave is real enough, and its sinister depths penetrate far into the headland – further than you would want to go alone.

Nearby is Games Loup, a place where Sir John Cathcart of Carleton Castle above Lendalfoot, used to push his newly-wed brides to their deaths. He only married wealthy women and killed seven for their fortunes. His eighth wife, a cannier lass, managed to push him first. Lendalfoot is a small settlement on a raised beach. Several cottage gardens contain huge, marooned sea-stacks, bringing a new dimension to the idea of a 'rockery' or the phrase 'making a feature of it'.

From Lendalfoot it is best to take the road straight to Girvan, to go inland a short way and to walk over Grey Hill for a wider view of the surrounding countryside. A descent can then be made via Ardmillan Castle, the ruins of which are lost in a caravan site.

Girvan is a popular resort with a mile of golden sand and a neat harbour that is the starting point for trips to Ailsa Craig. In the centre of town is a curious tower known as the Stumpy Tower, or just plain Stumpy. Once the old jail house, Stumpy had first a steeple, then a clock added in later years. Again it is best to follow the road straight to Turnberry past a large factory that processes seaweed, extracting alginates to form a gel-base for certain food and industrial products.

Turnberry golf course is world famous, certainly better known then small, ruined Turnberry Castle, birthplace of Robert the Bruce in 1274. Bruce landed at the castle from Arran to begin his guerilla campaign to gain the Scottish throne. There is a track across the golf course which can be used to visit the castle.

From Turnberry, tides permitting, it is possible to walk round Turnberry Point to the village of Maidens, from where there is easy access to Culzean (pronounced Cullane) Country Park and Culzean Castle. The castle crowns a cliff line and looks impressive, despite having been built in the eighteenth century as

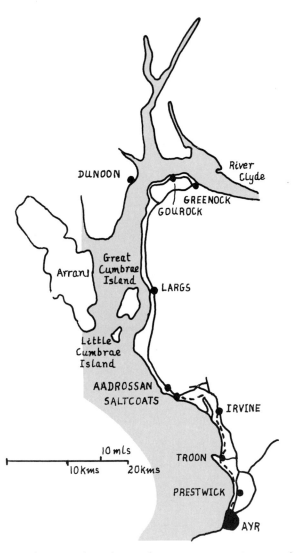

a residence rather than a fortress. It was given to the National Trust for Scotland in 1945, and is the gem of the Carrick coast. It even features on the Royal Bank of Scotland's £5 note!

It would be a popular move if the disused railway line along the coast from Culzean to Ayr were to be tidied up to provide a walkway, but in the absence of such a scheme, it is still possible to link various paths, tracks and rocky beaches to form a walker's route from Culzean to Dunure, then round the Heads of

Swan Lake in the Culzean Country Park. Beyond, Culzean Castle stands on the shore of Culzean Bay

Ayr to reach Ayr itself. The only major attraction of the coast that would be omitted by such a walk would be Croy Brae, or the Electric Brae. An optical illusion on the brae makes an uphill road into a downhill road and vice versa, a phenomenon best tested by bicycle rather than on foot.

Above the tidy harbour of Dunure is a mouldering pile, yet another Kennedy castle – Ardmillan and Culzean were Kennedy too. In an effort to obtain control of the lands of Crossraguel Abbey, the Kennedy earl roasted the Abbot on a spit in the Black Vault of this castle. Once round Heads of Ayr, a Butlin's camp and another Kennedy castle are passed on the way to Ayr.

Alloway, a charming old village that appears on maps as a mere suburb of Ayr, brings the walker back into Burns' Country. The poet was born here in 1759 in a building which is now the Burns Cottage and Museum. There is a lofty Grecian-style monument and a hi-tech Land o' Burns Centre; a signposted Burns Heritage Trail which starts from Dumfries, charting the birth, life, work and death of the poet; and Alloway's thirteenth-century Brig o' Doon

features in Burns' writings. Continuing, the youth hostel at Ayr, set in one of the town's fine old buildings, stamps cards with the opening line of 'Auld Lang Syne'; there is a Tam o'Shanter Museum full of Burnsiana, the Auld Kirk of Ayr where Burns was baptised, and yet another Auld Brig, built in the fifteenth century, which Burns immortalised. Burns aside, Ayr is a bonny town, well worth exploring.

The Kyle Coast to Gourock (48 mls, 77 km)

Beyond Ayr the Kyle coastline does not have a coastal path and apart from Prestwick's promenade, progress to Troon has to be made by following the beach. Prestwick, with its international airport, is a town with an ancient past, being the oldest recorded burgh in Scotland. The town's older features include a well-preserved Mercat Cross and a well, behind St Ninian's church, which was visited by Robert the Bruce searching, and finding, a cure for an unidentified illness. Moving on to Troon we find another world famous golf course. We also find a beach walk that eventually reaches an impasse at the mouth of the River Garnock which requires a detour into Irvine.

Irvine is a new town and, as is usual, the best thing about it is the old town it was built around. Here olde worlde Hill Street plunges straight into a modern shopping precinct. Irvine, too, has Burns associations, its Burns club is one of the oldest in the world and maintains a museum. The poet's workplace and lodgings in the atmospheric Glasgow Vennel can also be visited. As a change, the Scottish Maritime Museum with a fine, if bewildering, collection is based on Irvine's harbourside.

The inland detour around the tidal Garnock reaches as far as Eglinton Castle and Country Park and Kilwinning Abbey, returning to the coast by road through the towns of Stevenston, Saltcoats and Ardrossan which jointly celebrate their history in a museum housed in an old church at Saltcoats. Ardrossan is the ferryport for Arran, which can itself be used as a stepping stone to the Kintyre coast in the summer months.

The last decent stretch of coastal walking is some miles north now, at Portencross, best reached by road. There, a striking fifteenth-century keep and a few houses stand by a tiny harbour. Nearby is a cannon from a ship of the Armada wrecked by a local witch, or so it is said. Walking along the coastal track northward, the ivy-clad cliffs nearby hide a profound deterioration in the landscape further along. The Hunterston nuclear power station rises above the scene, while a scruffy fish farm blocks out the seaward view. A sewerage outfall adds flavour to the air. Further along is an iron ore terminal and a construction yard, both built out on the Hunterston Sands. Hunterston House, on whose estates all this has taken place, looks oddly out of place.

Beyond, the remainder of the coast to Gourock is best covered at speed by road, but do visit the Kelburn Country Centre, near Fairlie. Nearby, Largs was the scene of the repulsion of a Viking force in 1263, an event which signalled the end of Viking domination in Scotland. Also at Largs is the ferry link to Great Cumbrae Island with its Cathedral of the Isles. At Wemyss Bay near Skelmorlie another ferry departs for Bute. In time, Gourock is reached, a small town which has been practically absorbed by Greenock to its detriment, though it still preserves something of its own character. From there a ferry crosses the Clyde to the rougher Highland coasts.

Brig o'Doon, immortalised by Robert Burns

Culzean Castle, one of the gems of the Carrick Coast

Arran

(OS sheet 69)

DESPITE THE DAILY influx of mainland visitors from Ardrossan, Brodick remains a relatively unspoiled little town. The town is well set below Goat Fell and has a fine fifteenth-century castle which houses some rare furniture and artwork. The castle gardens are equally good. Also in the town is Arran's Heritage Museum, well worth a visit. From the pier, roads and paths across the South Corrygills to Clauchlands Point provide a better introduction to Arran's glorious scenery than the ankle-wrenching rocks of the shoreline.

Across the water Holy Island – holy because St Laerian lived here, in a cave with Runic inscriptions – protects Lamlash Bay, a sheltered haven for small craft. The impressive Hamilton Terrace properties were once let out to summer visitors while the occupants retired to their 'back houses'. Less happy times are commemorated in a monument to the 86 people who emigrated to Canada in 1829 when they were evicted during the Clearances.

Back on the main island, Kingseress Point offers one of the best views of Goat Fell, while behind Whitings Bay, further south, a pretty wooded path leads up Glenashdale burn to fine waterfalls. Kildonan, near the island's southern tip, is unforgettable in September when lines of golden stocks border the whitewashed farmhouses and sandy beach. The beach is also home to mink which can occasionally be seen searching the rock pools for food. Numerous dykes point seawards here: molten lava from the island's central volcanic complex was forced through the surrounding rocks, and, exposed by erosion, these 'dykes' of harder rock stand out like walls running down the beach.

The southern coast, with caves, ancient standing stones, a chambered cairn and an Iron Age enclosure is mainly pastoral, the hedgerows brilliant with flowers in spring. There are various access points but for continuous walking, some quite rough, it is necessary to take to the beach.

From the tiny harbour at Blackwaterfoot a sandy walk out to the basaltic cliffs at Brumadoon leads on to King's Cave where some say Robert the Bruce hid and watched the spider. Others say the cave is named for Fingal, the mythical Celtic King.

For about 14 miles (22.5 km) now the main road, using the raised beach where earliest man settled, hugs the shoreline. As it is much quieter than most English lanes it can be recommended to the walker. From Pirnmill – 'pirns' were birch spools – and Thundergay, paths lead up into eagle country, with fine views of Kintyre. Catacol has a unique line of fishermen's cottages, 'the twelve apostles', each with a different window designed for identification from the sea. Some of the world's oldest rocks, contorted and veined with quartz, appear along this stretch of coast. Indeed, the time span represented by Arran's rock formations makes the island a geological treasury.

Lochranza, where Bruce landed in 1306, now receives the Kintyre ferry (summer only). The 400-year-old ruined castle is severe but evocative. Purple thistles grow at the head of the loch, beyond which a

The Kirk and Manse, Sannox

clear path winds up the hill and over to Laggan with long views of Glen Chalmadale where herds of red deer roam. This is a remote and demanding walk, but there is a handy cave en route, well-known as a 'howff' or shelter.

Southward, the road is regained and it again controls coastline walking. Sannox has a fascinating old church, while at Corrie there is a tiny harbour the remains of limestone workings and charming cottages. 'Corrie Capers' in early August includes the ceremonial burning of a Viking ship, in memory of a fleet anchoring off shore in 1263. Just to the south of the village some of the oldest dwellings on the island form a delightful cluster.

South again new red sandstone, artistically sculpted by the sea, is vividly exposed at Carlo. Agates from these formations can occasionally be found on Brodick beach.

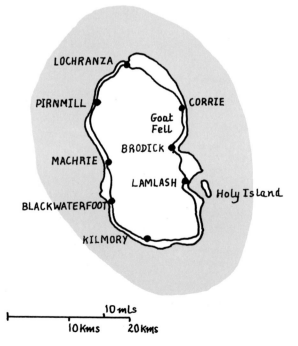

Towards the Islands

(OS sheets 63, 62, 55, 49, 40, 47, 33)

Dunoon to Southend (193mls, 309km)

THE WEST SCOTTISH coastline from Dunoon to Cape Wrath encompasses some of the most dramatic and breathtaking scenery that Britain has to offer, and it is rich in history, fauna and flora.

In parts it is a coastline not to be trifled with, especially in the more isolated regions, such as Knoydart, Torridon, and the far north-west. Here the walker should be fully equipped, and also able to use map and compass.

Once Dunoon is reached the walker soon faces the unfortunate fact that this part of the coast is not entirely suited to serious walking as the shortage of available level land means that the roads tend to hug the coastline. Not until the walker is half-way up Loch Striven's east coast will the road yield to the shore.

But we must start at Dunoon. Here Mary Campbell was born, the nursemaid who Robert Burns fell in love with, and who inspired some of his best poetry. Her statue gazes across the Clyde from the bottom of Castle Hill, named for the castle, now just a pile of rubble, at its top. Here, in the mid-seventeenth century, the Campbells murdered many hundreds of their Lamont prisoners.

North of the town is Holy Loch, reputedly named for a shipload of earth sent from the Holy Land to Glasgow for the foundations of the cathedral. The ship sank in the Loch, with the loss of the shipment. Today, much of the Loch is off-limits to walkers because of the presence of the United States Navy. South of Dunoon is Morag's Fairy Glen, a delightful spot with fine waterfalls.

Loch Striven was used in the 1970s to mothball supertankers during the oil depression. Its northern reaches offer the only reasonable walking in the district, and even so the walking is not of the very best, and many will settle for a general overview of the area – and a pleasant walk – by climbing Cnoc Breamanach. From the summit the view extends over the fjord-like Lochs Striven and Riddon (also known as Loch Ruel) and the Kyles and Isle of Bute.

Better walking starts again at Tighnabruich, 'the house on the bank', the English translation giving a fair indication of the terrain that the walker faces. The village's houses and cottages really are 'on the bank', being spread up the hillside away from the water.

Southward, the road must be followed at first until Ardlamont Point is reached. Then, beyond the bays of Kilbride and Asgog the 'artificial' village of Portavadie comes into view. This is a modern village, originally built as accommodation for an oil rig construction site. Now an attempt is being made to develop it as a timeshare village.

From the village the walker can make better progress up the eastern shore of Loch Fyne, the loch famous for its kippers. Otter Ferry does not take its name from the animal, but from the Oitir sandbank, oitir, confusingly, meaning sandbank.

From Otter Ferry the walker has little choice but to follow the road, albeit a minor road, right round the head of the loch. Clachan is passed at the loch's head to reach Inveraray, the ancestral home of the Clan Campbell. Inverary Castle was built, as was most of the town, at the time of the Jacobite rising, in 1745, when the Campbells fought with the English king against Prince Charles. Today it is one of the finest

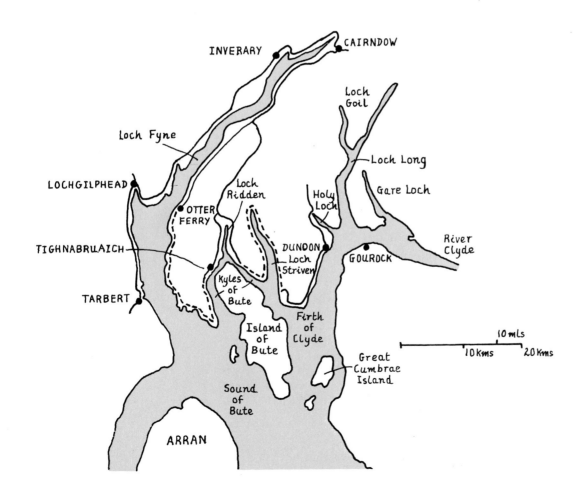

'houses' in Scotland for the richness of its interior, with tapestries and paintings in panelled rooms. There is also a fine armoury with over 1,000 swords.

South of the town, at Auchindrain, the visitor can see how the clansmen lived, for here, at the Farm Museum, is a stone and turf crofting cottage that survived the Clearances. The contrast between the lairdly splendour and the subsistence farming is stark indeed.

South again, on the way to Lochgilphead, are the gardens of Crarae, a mix of ancient wild highland and exotic, imported plants. Lochgilphead, the major town of the district, lies at the eastern end of the Crinan Canal that cut off Kintyre, joining Loch Fyne to the Sound of Jura. The canal is still in use today by small tramp steamers and yachts.

The road is followed down to Tarbert, once the chief port of the local herring industry. From Tarbert the walk south to Skipness is excellent, passing mainly through deciduous woodland. Skipness Castle is reached, a huge thirteenth-century building, beyond which a minor road is followed to Skipness village. From here, in summer, a ferry service is available to Lochranza on the island of Arran. Unfortunately, the same minor road has to be followed almost all of the way to the Mull of Kintyre. One delightful exception is the shore path from Grogport to Carradale.

Southward, the ruins of Saddell Abbey lie among the trees of Saddell Forest. Southend, at the tip of Kintyre, is only 15 miles (24 km) from Ireland and is one of the reputed landing spots of St Columba in the sixth century. In the caves near Keil Point are two rock-cut footprints, known as St Columba's Footsteps, but they are more likely to be pre-Celtic.

Mull of Kintyre to Loch nan Uamh (418 mls, 669 km)

North of the Mull the walker is forced inland by the RAF base at Machrihanish, and is well advised beyond that to catch a bus back to Tarbert and the eastern side of Loch Caolisport. The western side of Caolisport is accessible, however, and a wild place it is, one to be savoured. At Kilmory, around from the Point of Knap, the ruined chapel contains a superb collection of carved Celtic grave slabs, while outside stands McMillan's Cross, a 12-foot (3.6 m) carved medieval cross.

The Island of Danna, on the west coast of Loch Sween, can be reached, and the Sound of Jura

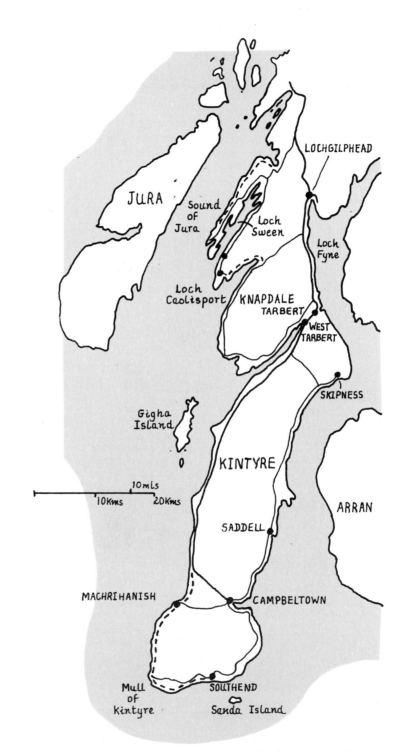

Sunset over Mull seen from Loch Feochan

followed to Crinan and Duntrune Castle beyond. Northward, the shore of Loch Craignish can be followed, but the walker is recommended to head straight for Oban, pausing only to walk the northern shore of Loch Melfort in order to reach Clachan Bridge.

The bridge joins the mainland to Seil Island, and since Seil Sound is part of the Atlantic Ocean, the bridge technically spans the ocean. Not surprisingly it is known as the Bridge over the Atlantic.

Oban is a curious, but likeable, place with its half-completed Colosseum – known as McCaig's Tower and financed by John McCaig in the late nineteenth century in part to provide work for local people, in part as a museum. The town also has an odd-looking railway station. Dunollie Castle, to the north of the town, is an ancient MacDougall fortress.

From Oban there is some merit in crossing to the Island of Mull, regaining the mainland near Lochaline or Kilchoan, as Loch Linnhe's shore is dominated by a road. Some excellent country would be missed however: Dunstaffnage Castle, where the Stone of Destiny was kept until the mid-nineteenth century when it was moved to Scone, and where Flora Macdonald was imprisoned on her way to the Tower of London; the Falls of Lora, where Loch Etive reaches the sea, not real falls but a fine set of rapids; Loch Creran, with its brilliant aquarium; Castle Stalker, one of the romantic of all Scottish castles; and South Ballachulish, with its monuments to the killing of Colin Campbell and the unjust hanging of James Stewart, a place of pilgrimage for readers of Robert Louis Stevenson's *Kidnapped*.

Ballachulish stands at the northern end of Appin, land of the Stewarts and of the Red Fox and other legends in Jacobite history. It is also a gateway to the infamous Glen Coe, scene of the killing of members of the Clan Macdonald by government troops under Captain Robert Campbell in 1692.

The old ferry at Ballachulish has been replaced by a bridge that has been described as an escapee from a Second World War film. Over it is Fort William, nestling under Ben Nevis, Britain's highest peak.

From there the road again hugs the shoreline, going west to the head of Loch Eil, then along that loch's southern shore to Loch Linnhe, and down that loch's western side. It is not until the road branches inland at Loch a Choire that the walker finds solitude. From here around to Lochaline there is freedom from roads and traffic, and superb views over Loch

McCaig's Tower, Oban

Linnhe and the Sound of Mull. The coast is, however, very hard going.

Lochaline is a pretty town, famous for its ruined Church of the Keil, which has a medieval gravestone inscribed with a kilted man, the earliest known representation. From the town it is road again to west of Drimnin, from where the walker is allowed back to the shore for the exposed and arduous following of Loch Sunart to Strontian.

The old mining town of Strontian gave its name to strontium a metal originally used in fireworks, but now more usually associated with nuclear power. Mine workings dating back to the Napoleonic Wars can be found in the hills above the town.

Unfortunately, for much of the southern edge of Ardnamurchan, a less rugged piece of country than many hereabouts, the road again hugs the shore, but Ben Hiant can be crossed to Mingary Castle, a thirteenth-century ruin, and from there the Point of Ardnamurchan, the Point of the Great Sea, can be reached. Here the walker is over 20 miles (32 km)

west of Land's End.

North now to Ardtoe, at the mouth of Kentra Bay, there is beautiful walking along the shore of the Atlantic Ocean. From Ardtoe the walker enters Moidart, passing the fire-destroyed Castle Tioram for Glenuig.

Across the Sound of Arisaig from Glenuig, on the Ardnish peninsula reached by road to Lochailort, is the bothy of Peanmeanach. It was here that a former Church of Scotland minister, the Rev. Geoff Shaw, wanted to establish a college, but when he died so did his dream.

Westward is Loch nan Uamh, where Prince Charles landed in the summer of 1745 on a campaign that was to lead not to the throne, but to Culloden and fugitive retreat. It was from here he also left for exile in France, in September of 1746. A cairn at the loch's head commemorates the events.

The Point of Ardnamurchan with Eilean Carrach beyond

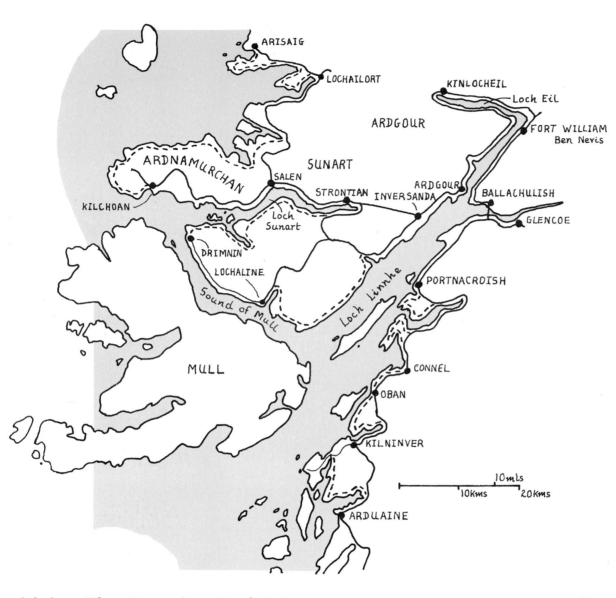

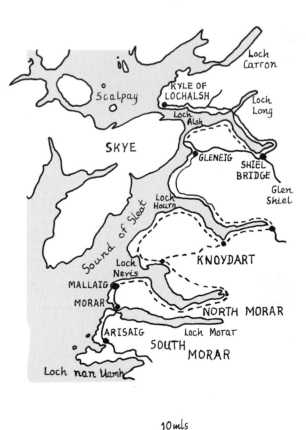

Knoydart, to the north, is the last great wilderness of the Highlands, a land sandwiched between Loch Nevis, the loch of hell, and Loch Hourn, the loch of heaven. The road-free peninsula is a walker's paradise, and it is difficult not to suggest that after the walker has reached Inverie a route across the peninsula to Barrisdale Bay, where there is a bunkhouse, be taken.

Inverie is reached from Sourlis by following the coast past Atlantic oarsman and sailor Tom McClean's outdoor centre at Camusory. A more enjoyable walk, though not wholly coastal, is to head over the Mam Meadail, after crossing the new bridge at Carnoch. Inverie can also be reached by ferry from Mallaig.

Whether the walker reaches Barrisdale Bay by way

Eilean Donan Castle

Arisaig to Eilean Donan (100mls, 160 km)

From Arisaig beyond to Mallaig, the road lies along the shore. A good alternative is to take the train along the West Highland line, one of Britain's finest railways. Mallaig itself is a bustling port, and from it the walker should climb Carn a Ghobhair for what is often described as the finest view in the Highlands, taking in Skye and Rhum, Morar and Knoydart.

From Mallaig the walker can follow the coast to Tarbert via Mallaigvaig, but a more scenic route is to go by way of Loch Eiregoraidh, the loch of the

sheltered place, then eastward for the coast at Stoul. The advantage of this route is that it commands the high ground and offers wonderful views of the Western Isles. From Stoul the coast is followed to Tarbet, where there is the most isolated post office in Britain.

From Tarbet the path continues by the coast past the ruins of Ardnamurach, and Camusaneighin to the bothy of Sourlis at the head of Loch Nevis, a bothy with craggy mountains on three sides offering a sense of complete and peaceful isolation.

of the heart of Knoydart, or around the coast, the shore is now followed to Kinlochhourn, a tough, isolated, beautiful walk section, with no habitation except for solitary crofts. Paths abound in parts, while elsewhere they are non-existent.

The northern shore of Loch Hourn is similar country – surely Loch Hourn must be the most spectacular and beautiful of all Scotland's sea lochs?

A road, of sorts, is reached beyond Sgurr Mor, and is best followed to Glenelg, where there is a ferry for Skye. Along Gleann Beag, to the south, are the brochs of Dun Telve and Dun Trodden, two of the best preserved in Scotland. The latter seems to be offering a house name for all ex-coastal walkers.

Northward, apart from the immediate shore of the Kyle Rhea, and the southern shore of Loch Alsh, there is a road all the way to Kyle of Lochalsh, and many walkers will take a ferry to Skye, returning to the mainland by ferry to Kyle itself. The major disadvantage of such a plan is that it misses Eilean Donan, as

Eilean Donan Castle, Loch Duich

seen on the lid of many a shortbread tin and postcard. The original castle on this island at the junctions of Lochs Alsh, Duich and Long, was built in the thirteenth century, but was ruined by two naval frigates in 1719 when it was held by Spanish troops for the Old Pretender. Only this century has it been restored to its magnificent glory. This is one of the great sites of Scotland.

Ben Nevis and Fort William from Corpach

Road bridge linking Ardelve and Dornie across the mouth of Loch Long

The Outer Hebrides

(OS sheets 8, 13, 14, 18, 22, 31)

THE ISLAND CHAIN of Lewis, Harris and Uist forms a barrier to the Atlantic weather, protecting the Scottish mainland at the expense of its weather-swept self. The islands are, nonetheless, fascinating places, their coasts easily followed, even if the following does involve some rugged terrain and takes the walker to some wild, isolated country, where Gaelic is still spoken and the signs are bi-lingual. The Sabbath is strictly observed here, with no ferry sailings and no shops or bars open.

Lewis is famous for the stone circle of Callanish, one of Britain's foremost archaeological sites. The stones here, which rival Stonehenge in many respects, are wonderfully sited, and have the advantage of being accessible. Nearby Doune Carloway is an Iron Age fort, an evocative site commanding magnificent views. Northward, there is an excellent crofting museum at Shawbost and another to island life in the Black House at Arnol, on the way to Butt of Lewis, which is the most northerly point of the island group. Here there is a restored twelfth-century chapel to St Moluog, a sixth century companion of St Columba. Stornoway, the island's capital, is a fine town, and the centre for the making of Harris Tweed.

Harris itself is not a separate island, North Harris being the southern tip of Lewis, though South Harris is joined only by a neck of land at Tarbert. Harris offers a more dramatic landscape, with rugged hills and a barren moor. A road links all the coastal sites, though walking is possible, visiting Rodel at the southern tip, where the sixteenth-century church is the finest on the island group.

Southward, the islands of North and South Uist and Benbecula are joined by road. The coast here is less easily followed on the western side, and made difficult by jagged inlets on the east, though the 'Machair', the flat coastal plain, does offer straightforward, if tedious, walking. The Machair has been likened to an extended golf course – in parts it is a golf course – and is, in many places, overrun with rabbits.

On the western tip of North Uist is the Balranald nature reserve, a site for waterfowl and waders,

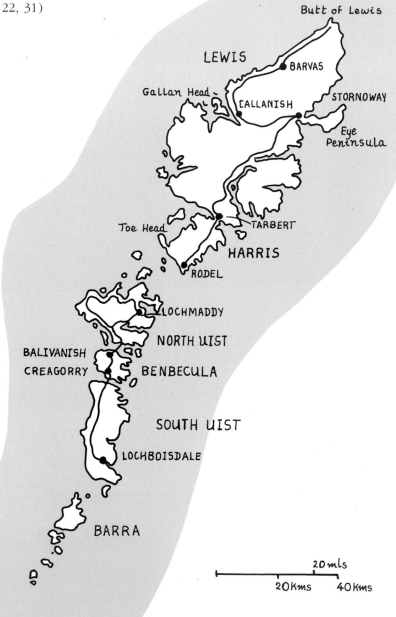

The Stone Circle at Callanish on the Isle of Lewis

where red-necked phalarope occasionally nest. Benbecula holds the island's airport, and here, too, is Prince Charlie's Cave where the Prince hid while waiting for Flora Macdonald who took him, as her maid, over the seas to Skye, escape and exile. Flora herself was born on South Uist, though nothing now remains of her home, while to the south the next island is Eriskay where Prince Charles landed in 1745. The grounding of the whisky-carrying *Politicia* here in 1941 gave Sir Compton Mackenzie his idea for *Whisky Galore*.

The Inner Hebrides

(OS sheets 39, 46, 47, 48, 49)

RHUM, JUST SOUTH of Skye, can only be visited with permission as it is the scene of the attempted re-establishment of the white-tailed or sea eagle. All lovers of wild country and wild things will wish the project success.

To the south are Eigg and Muck, the former famous for the singing sands at Camas Sgiotaig – quartzite crystals that squeak when walked on – the latter for its tranquillity. South again are Coll and Tiree. Coll is a low, heathery island, except for the eastern coastline which has a line of rugged cliffs. It can be easily walked, the walker crossing the inflow stream to Loch Breachacha, Struthan nan Ceann, the stream of heads. Here the McCleans defeated the Duarts and such was the slaughter that the stream was blocked by the heads of men from Clan Duart.

Tiree is a more cheerful place, though so battered by winds that its people are said to lean at all times. It is a low-lying island with none of the grandeur that takes the walker to other remote sites.

Mull, further south again, has its own scenic character: successive lava flows from the volcanic complex around Ben More having given the land a tiered profile.

The island's capital, Tobermory, features brightly painted houses curving round a sheltered bay in which lies the Spanish galleon *Florida*, sunk in 1588, and yet to yield its reputed treasure. The wooded shores offer forest walks southward, though the road runs so close to the shore and is so quiet that it can be used to explore the coast as far as Craignure where the Oban ferry berths. The impressive Duart castle on the point south-east of the town was built in the thirteenth century and is open to the public in the summer. Southward, the coast can be followed again, the best section being around Loch Buie.

Another fine walk follows the shores of the rugged Ardmeanach peninsula, passing McCulloch's Tree, where 50 million years ago a conifer was engulfed by a lava flow, and has now been exposed in the cliff face. This is an arduous walk, and the tree is accessible only at low tide.

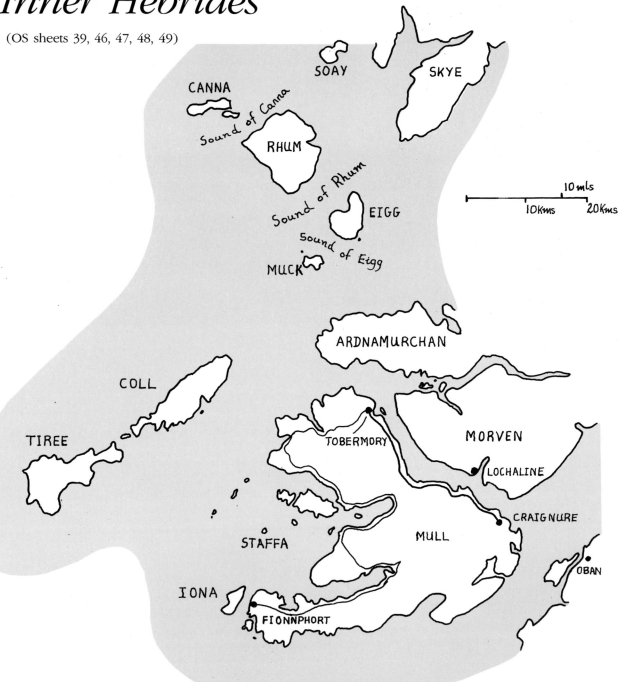

Stone Cross on the Isle of Iona

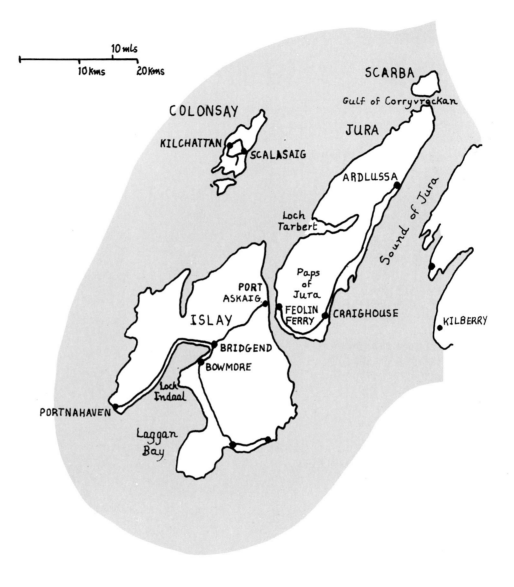

Every visitor to Mull should cross to Iona, another reputed landfall of St Columba on his voyage from Ireland in 563. Iona is reached by passenger ferry from Fionnphort, and its abbey, carved crosses, and the Graves of the Kings are for quiet exploration, as are the white sandy beaches and rocky coves of the shoreline. For a final treat, climb the peak of Dun I for a stunning view of both Iona and the other Hebridean islands.

The last group of islands comprises Colonsay, Jurä and Islay. Colonsay, linked for three hours at low tide to Oromsay, offers fine walking, being both rugged and accessible. It has an astonishing array of prehistoric sites, but do visit as well Kiloran Bay, a fine, well-protected beach.

Jura, by contrast, is rugged beyond the capacity of all but the most experienced walkers. It is an almost uninhabited, vaguely hostile island. Those who venture onto the island should go north, beyond Barnhill, where George Orwell wrote *1984*, to see the Gulf of Corryvreckan, a narrow channel – separating Jura from Scarba, which is another rugged remote island – famous for its vicious tidal race.

Islay is the most southerly of the Hebrides, its green fields, white cottages and low hills offering a strong contrast to Jura. The coastline is very varied. The longest beach stretches over 4 miles (6.4 km) along Laggan Bay, north of Port Ellen, and along it walkers can stride to their hearts' content, keeping their eyes open only for the headless horseman said to ride it. By contrast there are impressive cliffs at the Mull of Oa, also near Port Ellen. Bowmore, the island's 'capital' has a distillery museum, Islay being famous for its rich, peaty whisky. To the west there are attractive bays at Kilchoman and Saligo, while the north coast is more remote, with celebrated examples of raised beaches and a nature reserve, at Loch Gruinart, which is a wintering area for white-fronted and barnacle geese.

111

Skye

(OS sheets 23, 32, 33)

SKYE, 'THE WINGED ISLE', is rugged in both plan and profile. Great peninsulas separated by sea lochs present an extensive coastline, along which the walker is never far from views of the 3,000ft (900 m) Cuillin ridge. It is the western side of the island that is the most exciting, a weather-swept, mountainous coast, mostly away from the road. By contrast, on the eastern side the road clings to the shore.

At the southern end of the island, at Armadale where the ferry from Mallaig docks, the Museum of the Isles is housed in a nineteenth-century castle, and tells the history of the Macdonald Clan. From Armadale the walker heads past Ardvasar and Calligarry for the Aird of Sleat from where a landrover track and footpath lead to the Point of Sleat, the extreme tip of the island.

From the point north to Torrin at the head of Loch Slapin there is difficult and exposed walking until, at Torrin, the road is met. The former township of Boreraig on its secluded slope overlooking Loch Eishort is reached, a poignant place today, with its clustered walls of cottages whose inhabitants were cleared from the land in the nineteenth century to make way for sheep. Much older is the promontory fort. From Boreaig the path follows the coast westwards slanting upward through a gap in the coastal crags and over to Suisnish, passing under the high bluff of Carn Dearg. From the shepherd's bothy here a track winds north above Loch Slapin to the main road.

Of the entire coastline the next section is by far the most difficult, especially in the region of Lochs Scavaig and Coruisk. From Elgol a well-trodden path heads for the bothy at Camasunary from where the path heads for Loch Coruisk. The path crosses the south face of Sgurr na Stri giving more rock climbing than walking, especially at the 'Bad Step'. In 1968 the Territorial Army, at the request of the police, announced that it was going to blast a footpath through this rocky slab in order to ease rescues. This announcement caused such an outcry that the plan was very quickly shelved.

It must be stressed that the whole sec- tion around Loch Scavaig at Loch Coruisk is for the mountaineer and climber rather than the walker, a point most especially true in wet weather, when the Cuillin gabbro becomes very greasy and slippery. Please be careful.

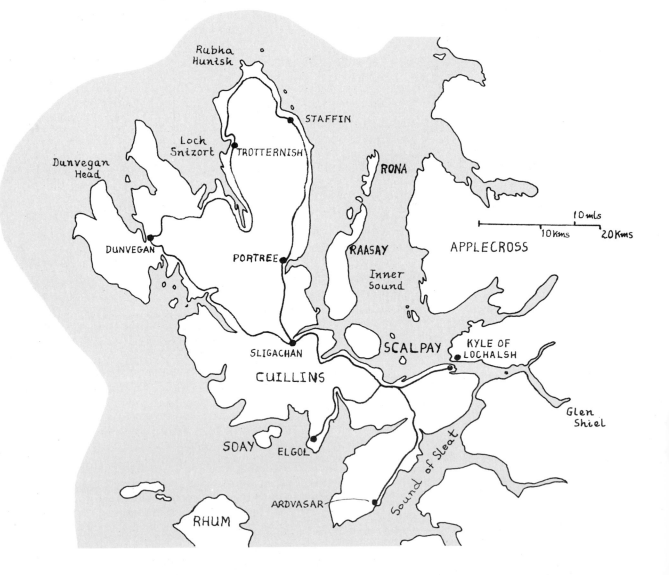

over 900 years old. There is only one certain occasion when it was used in battle: in 1578 some Macdonalds burned the church at Trumpon, on the Waternish peninsula, killing all the worshippers except one old woman who raced over the hills to Dunregan. The flag was taken to Trumpon where the outraged MacLeods slaughtered the Macdonalds to a man.

Borreraig, nearby has a piping centre at the home of the McCrimmons, the ancient pipers to the McCleods and near the centre there is a memorial to them. Close to the extreme northerly tip of Skye is the Skye Cottage Museum, devoted to the history of the island's crofting, which was set up near to the spot where Flora Macdonald landed with Prince Charles after their trip from the Outer Hebrides.

Southwards, the Old Man of Storr, a 150 ft (45 m) sea stack, and yet another Prince Charles' Cave are passed on the way to Portree, the island's capital, near which Vriskaig Point, a headland, must be visited.

The Cuillins from Torren

It is not until Gars-Bheinn has been rounded and the Allt Coire nan Laogh crossed that the land becomes suitable for the walker again. At Loch na H-Airde the remains of a Viking settlement can be found, with fields still identifiable, and a canal from the sea to the loch still in existence. From the site an excellent footpath leads to Glen Brittle.

Northward, the walking can be dangerous in bad weather, except for the Loch Eynort side, the cliffs being among the highest on the island. Sandy Talisker Bay offers a welcome break, and the walker must eventually take to the road to reach Drynoch.

Ahead now the island is dominated by two flat-topped peaks, McLeod's Tables. Legend has it that a local McLeod chief, Alister Crotach, while visiting Edinburgh, was rather put out by the comments of a Lowland Earl who wagered that 'nowhere in Skye have you seen a room so big, and spacious, nor a roof so high, nor a table so rich, nor a candelabra so brilliant as in this Palace of Holyrood'.

In reply Crotach invited the lowlander to Skye for a banquet which took place on the smaller of the two peaks. The banquet took place at sunset, with 50 torch bearing clansmen standing in a circle around 50 square yards (42 sq m) of the peak that was covered with meat and wines. The banquet finally finished in the wee small hours under a starry starry sky. Crotach, as legend has it, turned to the Earl and said, 'I ask you to agree with me, Sir, that my room is loftier than Holyrood's, this table greater than any to be found in the cities, and my clansmen more splendid than any candelabra.'

The coast from Loch Bracadale round to Galtrigill via Glendale and Dunvegan Head offers serious exposed walking along clifftops, and close attention should be paid to local weather reports.

Dunvegan Castle is home to the MacLeods. The castle contains a lock of Prince Charles' hair and the Fairy Flag, legendary battle flag of the Clan MacLeod. Though said to have been given to the Clan by a fairy it is likely that it was actually taken from the Norwegian king Harald Hardrada, which means it is

North Scotland

(OS sheets 32, 24, 19, 15, 9, 10, 11, 12)

Kyle of Lochalsh to Loch Broom (188 mls, 300 km)

KYLE OF LOCHALSH is not only a ferry port for Skye, but a terminus for another of the great rail journeys of Britain. Using the train does get the visitor to Strathcarron better than any attempt at a

coastal path, and even the northern shore of Loch Carron offers only limited walking, to the west of Strome Castle. The only real miss, if the train were taken, would be a section north from Kyle itself, around Erbusaig Bay, if tides allow, and on to Plockton, a delightful and most picturesque village.

Loch Kishorn offers the walker a glimpse of the new Highlands, Black Gold – oil – for here is an oil rig construction site, albeit at present much run down from its heyday. A beautiful, though slightly difficult, walk starts from the end of the construction site, hugging the coast round to Toscaig where the road is once again met. On this section the walker can enjoy the beauty and tranquillity of the Applecross peninsula.

In the seventh century St Maelrubha established a sanctuary for fugitives at Applecross, and it still feels as though both village and peninsula offer an escape from the pressures of the real world. Only in the last 20 years has a road existed around the northern end of the peninsula, joining the village to Shieldaig, and even that seems to have done little to intrude on the peacefulness. Inland, the Applecross Forest is a wilderness of peaty moorland, small lochans, and streams. Two hills that are well worth climbing for their views are Sgurr a Chaorachain and Beinn Bhan, both accessible from the car-park at Bealach-Na-Ba, the Pass of the Cattle, which is the highest pass in Britain crossed by a road.

The 'new' road takes the walker round the coast to Shieldaig, but it is worthwhile stopping off occasionally for a sight of the numerous caves and natural arches that abound on the shore of the Inner Sound and Loch Torridon.

From Sheildaig the A896 is best followed to Torridon village nestling under Ben Damh. The views on this section, across Upper Loch Torridon to the mountains of the Torridon Forest, Beinn Alligin, Liathach, and Beinn Eighe are magnificent, some of the most sumptuous backdrops on the entire coastline, and they offer some of the most awe-inspiring sunsets of any spot in Britain.

A road follows the northern shore of Upper Loch Torridon, connecting Torridon to Lower Diabaig by an epic of engineering, the road twisting and turning, rising and falling like a big dipper. Only after Alligin Shuas, reached by a turning off the Diabeg road – and before the major switchbacks – is it possible to reach the shore away from tarmac, and then only briefly. From Lower Diabaig there is a well-trodden path to Red Point. The path, beautifully placed between the sea and the hills of Wester Ross, passes a youth hostel at Craig, one of few that can be reached only on foot.

Unfortunately, the road is rejoined again at Red Point, but it is a fine road, passing through some excellent birch and oak woods. The views are magnificent, Loch Gairloch being very picturesque, and Skye rising across the Minch. From Rubha Reidh, where the road ends – although it is a private road from Melvaig – the Hebrides can be seen. On the last section to the lighthouse the cliffs are spectacularly worked into a succession of small coves.

From Rubha Reidh to the hydrographic survey pillar at the opposite end of the peninsula between Loch Gairloch and Loch Ewe, there is a beautiful walk even after the road is joined. Near Poolewe, at the head of Loch Ewe, are the Inverewe Gardens. Here Osgood McKenzie spent half a century, from around 1865, transforming a barren peninsula into a superb garden with plants from all over the world. What McKenzie realised was that although Poolewe was at the same latitude as Canada's Labrador Bay the warming influence of the Gulf Stream could be used to assist growth, and to keep alive plants usually found only in more southerly regions. Today the site, which covers over 2,000 acres and which no visitor should miss, is owned by the National Trust for Scotland.

From the jetty at Tournaig farm, a little north of Poolewe, a delightful clifftop walk reaches Aultbea, with superb views of Loch Ewe all the way. After a road section to Mellon Charles the clifftop can be

Strome Castle and Castle Bay on the northern shore of Loch Carron

Golden Eagles are regularly seen in Northern Scotland

school is run by the villagers themselves. However, many walkers will cut across the peninsula to the ferry which can be met at Allt na h-Airbhe which crosses Loch Broom for Ullapool.

Ullapool to Cape Wrath (130 mls, 208 km)

Ullapool's gridiron streets suggest a well-planned town, and that is the case, the town having been built in the late eighteenth century as a station for the local herring industry. From above, the town, jutting out into Scotland's largest sea loch, a real fjord, looks truly Scandinavian.

walked again, passing the ruins of the old village of Slaggan, rounding Rubha na lice Uaine, or, less romantically, Greenstone Point, to meet the road again at Opinan.

Southward, a ruined church occupies a site on which, it is said, once stood a church built by St Columba. The walker is now in Gruinard Bay with Gruinard Island just offshore. Due to experiments in germ warfare during the Second World War the island was infected with anthrax and so landings are prohibited. Tests are carried out annually, and it is hoped that soon the island will become safe. Let us hope so; Gruinard Island is a sad loss, too good to be a permanent memorial to lunacy.

The walker can round Stattic Point, but there is a road on the southern shore of little Loch Broom. To the west here is An Teallach, 'The Forge', one of Scotland's finest peaks. From Dundonnell progress can be made up the northern shore of the loch, a path existing northward towards Cailleach Head from Badrallach and to Scoraig, where an independent

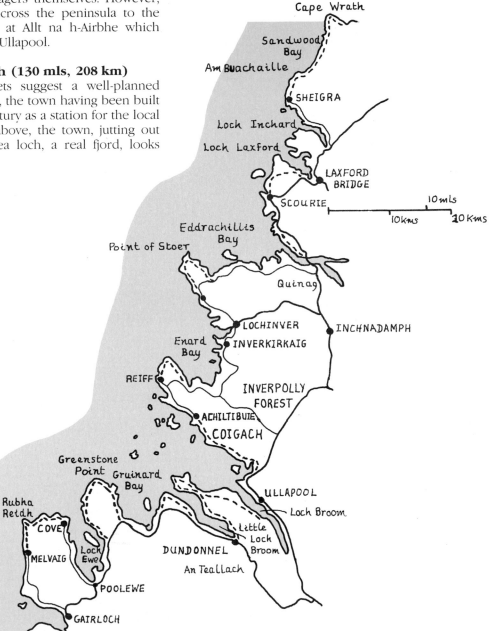

The sea stack of Am Buachaille, the shepherd, with a mist-shrouded Sandwood Bay beyond

Northwards from Ullapool is an area offering backdrops of Hollywood magnitude, lochs and lochans by the score, hills such as Coigach and Suilven rising out of the moor, yet with a coastline offering excellent, but at times difficult, walking.

First is the peninsula of Rubha Mhor, Coigach Point, which ends at Rubha Coigach, named after Coigach, the hill that dominates the area. It is reached by a path leaving Blughasary just south of Strath-kanaird. The path leads to the road for Achiltibuie and, offshore, the Summer Isles, a favourite diving spot. The road ends at Reiff, but the point can be rounded to Achnahaird Bay, where there is a campsite. From the Brae of Achnahaird a road goes to the fishing port of Lochinver, though the shoreline of Enard Bay can be followed with difficulty. At Rubh Phollaidh such a traverse can be very tricky, and should be treated with caution. Check both the map and local tides.

Inland from here is the Inverpolly National Nature Reserve, second only to the Cairngorms in size, and covering some magnificent country. Stac Pollaidh is one of Britain's most instantly recognisable peaks. From Inverkirkaig, Suilven, another fine peak, can be climbed.

From Stoer, a road runs out to the lighthouse from where a path passes the Old Man of Stoer, a sea stack 220 ft (66 m) high and first climbed in 1966, to reach the Point of Stoer. Beyond are a natural arch and a Pictish broch before Clashnessie Bay is rounded to Culkein.

From Culkein the deeply incut Eddrachillis Bay can be followed, but it is better to follow the road to Unapool. Inland from here are the falls of Eas Coul Aluin, at 650 ft (195 m) Britain's highest, but by no means the easiest to reach. Northward the 'new' bridge over Locha Chairn Bhain reaches Kylestrome, from where the loch's northern shore can be followed to the road for Scourie. The view inland is dominated by the twin peaks of Arkle and Foinavon. Were the racehorses named after these peaks?

Offshore is Handa Island, an RSPB reserve which can be visited from Tarbet. North of Tarbet is Loch Laxford where there is a seal colony. The loch must be passed by going inland, and it is difficult to recommend an alternative to a dash up the road to Rhiconich. From Rhiconich follow the minor road to Oldshoremore, and on to one of the very best sections of the west coast which runs north to Cape Wrath.

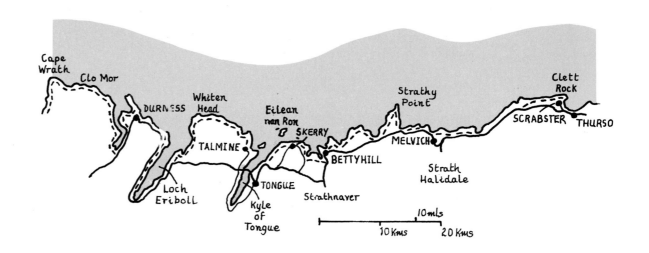

The cliffs rise to over 400 ft (120 m) early on and the walker must look down on the beautiful sea stack of Am Buachaille, the shepherd, although the stack is well seen, in profile, from Sandwood, the fabulous sweep of sand beyond the small inland loch. The bothy at the loch is certainly not the Hilton of the North, in fact it has neither floors, doors, or windows,

The Sea Stack of Am Buachaille in Sandwood Bay

and is haunted by the ghost of a shipwrecked sailor. However, it does offer dry shelter and the opportunity for a fire, if one gathers driftwood from the bay.

Northward from the end of the bay is a very rugged 6 miles (9.5 km) of walking, but it is magnificent country, especially at the cliff-protected Keisgaig Bay, where there is also a shelter. Ahead now, the lighthouse at Cape Wrath is a beacon for the walker.

Cape Wrath, a grim bulwark against Atlantic storms stands 523 ft (157 m) high and is the most north-westerly point on the British mainland. The name derives from the Norse *hvraf*, meaning a turning point. The lighthouse on the headland was built in 1827 and is accessible only by walkers or by way of the ferry and minibus service from the Kyle of Durness, along 11 miles (18 km) of narrow road over wild moorland. This moorland, the Parbh, is the largest uninhabited piece of land in Britain, over 100 square miles (259 sq km).

Clo Mor to Scrabster (112 mls, 179 km)
Going eastward from the lighthouse, the walker reaches the sandstone cliffs of Clo Mor, the highest sheer cliffs on mainland Britain at 920 ft (276 m). This section of cliff is, not surprisingly, a great bird

A rainbow rises from the sea near Armadale Bay

sanctuary. From Clo Mor east to Cleit Dhubh and Port Odhar the clifftop is MoD property, and if it is in use the lane to the ferry must be followed. Either way, Daal Cottage is reached, *daal* from the Norwegian little valley, from where Beinn an Amair can be climbed for tremendous views of the Kyle of Durness, Balnakeil Bay and Faraid Head.

The River Dionard is crossed by the bridge built by the 59 commando Royal Engineers in 1986, and the eastern side of the Kyle of Durness is followed to Balnakeil Bay. Balnakeil village has the ruins of a church built in 1619. Inside, there is a monument to Rob Dunn, a famous Celtic bard, which has sides each inscribed in a different language. There is also a skull and crossbones by a niche in the south wall which commemorates Donald MacLeod, a notorious local thief and murderer, who reputedly paid a high price for the privilege. Inland, is the Balnakeil Craft Village, set up in 1964 by Sutherland Council in a former radar station. At the village craftsmen from all over the world exhibit their work.

Ahead now are Faraid Head and Aodann Mhorr, with Durness beyond. **This is not a walk for poor weather as the cliffs are very exposed and unprotected.**

From Durness the beautiful sands of Sango Bay take the walker to the Cave of Smoo. This enormous cavern, the name is from the Norse *smjuga*, a cleft, has an arch 130 ft (39 m) wide and 33 ft (10 m) high. It contains three caverns; the first two accessible by footbridge, the third only accessible to experienced potholers. From the main cave, by the light of a powerful torch, the waterfall of the moorland stream of Allt Smoo can be seen.

Beyond the cave the walker reaches Loch Eriboll, one of the most breathtakingly beautiful lochs in Scotland and seen to perfection from this north-western corner, from where Ben Hope, the most northerly Munro, rises behind it. The loch was used by the Royal Navy during the two World Wars, the island at its centre having been used as a target for crews training for the attack on the Tirpitz.

The walker must then take to the main road to follow the loch's western arm. Just before the island is reached, search among the bracken for the souterrain, an underground room reached by steps that is believed to have been an Iron Age food store.

From the head of Loch Eriboll the walker follows the road on the eastern shore at first, before heading directly for An Ceann Geal or Whiten Head as it is

less romantically known. Eastward from the head the cliffs can be followed to Talmine. Just offshore here are the Rabbit Islands and at low tide it is possible to walk to them across the sands. From Talmine the road is followed to the Kyle of Tongue on the far side of which is the village of Tongue.

In Tongue the seventeenth-century church is worth a visit to see the 'Lairds Loft', a gallery where the family of the Mackay clan chief would sit for services. The ruins of Castle Varrich on the nearby hill are said to stand on Viking foundations, though what we see is a former Mackay stronghold of the fourteenth century. From the ruins there is a fine view over the Kyle of Tongue.

On the eastern side of Tongue Bay the road is followed until the walker can head for Carn An Fheidh, from the top of which the views are very impressive. Offshore, the uninhabited island of Eilean nan Ron Seal Island, has several rock arches that are equally impressive. There are a couple of hamlets now before Airdtorrisdale, and if the tide is out, it is a lovely walk around Torrisdale Bay. If the tide is in, a walk inland is necessary to reach the bridge over the River Borgie, passing Invernaver to cross over the River Naver for Bettyhill. The village here was named for Elizabeth, Countess of Sutherland, and one wonders whether the irony was lost on the inhabitants who were, largely, crofting families evicted by her husband during the Clearances.

Eastward, the rugged coast is followed to Farr Point and on to Armadale Bay, a delighful square-cut bay. Ahead now, an equally rugged coastal walk reaches the magnificent Strathy Point. The lighthouse here was built in 1958 and can be visited; the view from it extends westward to Cape Wrath and eastward to Dunnet Head. There are colonies of skuas and gannets at the point. On the eastern side of the River Strathy, be sure to see the cottages of Strathy itself, some of which are still turf-roofed.

Melvich Bay, another square incut, has, at its back, Bighouse, the home of a head of Clan Mackay. Ahead is the Dounreay Experimental Reactor Establishment, Britain's centre for research into fast reactors, and the walker must go inland to avoid it, heading for the village of Reay and taking the main road. The coast is regained from the Bridge of Forss for a walk to Holborn Head and Clett Rock, a stubby sea stack that is home to many gull colonies. Around the corner is Scrabster renowned among fishermen for its safe harbour, and from which there is a ferry to the Orkneys.

The Experimental Reactor Establishment, Dounreay

Dunnet Head, mainland Britain's most northerly point

Orkney

(OS sheets 5, 6, 7)

IT IS SAID that while the Shetlander is a fisherman with a croft, the Orcadian is a farmer with a boat. Although the two island groups are of similar size and share a Viking heritage, the softer sandstone rocks of Orkney form a generally low-lying and fertile archipelago, with herds of beef and dairy cattle, and dappled with tempting trout lochs. Coastal walkers are welcome, notwithstanding the Norse udal law which extends ownership of land down to low water mark, in contrast to the high water limit applicable on the Scottish mainland.

The mountainous Isle of Hoy is an exception to the general Orcadian description, with Britain's highest perpendicular cliffs at St Johns Head which tower 1,020 ft (306 m) above the sea, and the famous sea stack known as the Old Man of Hoy. The lonely bay of Rackwick on Hoy has been inspirational to the composer Sir Peter Maxwell Davies, whose works feature in the annual St Magnus Festival in Kirkwall, Orkney's capital. The island's coast is comfortably walked, but do go inland to see The Dwarfie Stone, a unique pair of rock-cut chambers, possibly 4,000 years old.

A historic feature of Kirkwall, on the largest island, known as Mainland, is St Magnus' Cathedral, begun in the twelfth century. Kirkwall also has two palaces; the Bishop's palace from the twelfth century and the Earl's palace from the sixteenth century. On the western side of the island is Stromness, whose older houses rise from piers built out into the sea for the convenience of the traders who lived there. Stromness was the watering point for ships of the Hudson's Bay Company, many of whose personnel were Orcadians, and for the Scottish whaling fleets of the nineteenth century, Greenland-bound.

Far older settlements are revealed by Orkney's unparalleled range of archaeological sites, which include the Ring of Brodgar, the Standing Stones of Stenness, the chambered cairn of Maeshowe with its more recent Runic graffiti, and the settlement at Skara Brae. These sites are between 3,000 and 4,000 years old.

The walker of Mainland's coast gets an excellent

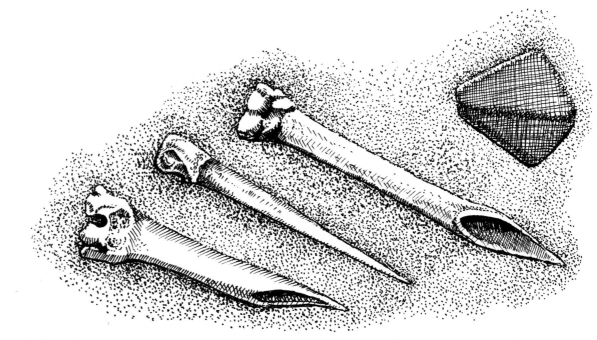

Bone Tools from Skara Brae (above)

The Stone Age Village at Skara Brae (left)

view of Scapa Flow, anchorage of the British fleet in the two World Wars and resting place of the scuttled German fleet of the First World War. Today, the Flow is home to a major North Sea oil terminal, and is a mecca for divers. There is a rich natural environment too: seals abound, and there are no fewer than nine RSPB Reserves.

Two Heritage Walks have been established on Orkney, one at Westness on Rousay, the other on the Isle of Eday, both interpreting man's influence on the landscape. Rousay has a number of fine ancient sites: a Norse cemetery and the remains of a Viking ship buried have been found among the Stone Age monuments.

Further north the smaller islands can also be comfortably walked. Westray has the fine, if stark, ruin of Noltland Castle, built in the sixteenth century by Gilbert Balfour, who some believe helped in the murder of Lord Darnley, Mary Queen of Scots' husband. Papa Westray, off Westray's northern coast, is named for the *Papae*, the Gaelic priesthood. It can be reached by the world's quickest air route – 2 minutes from Westray.

North Ronaldsay is the northernmost Orcadian island, with a fine broch at its southern tip. On the island the walker can follow a wall that encircles the whole island, built to keep sheep off the pastures. The sheep, confined to the shore, have learned to survive on seaweed.

Shetland

(OS sheets 1, 2, 3, 4)

Over 70 miles (91 km) in extent, and on the same latitude as the southern tip of Greenland, Shetland's more than 100 islands are quite distinctly different from anywhere else in Britain. Their Viking heritage is celebrated with the festival of 'Up Helly Aa' when, on the last Tuesday in January, Lerwick resounds to the tramp of bearded men with battleaxes and horned helmets, and a replica longship burns on the seafront.

Shetland was under Norwegian rule until 1469, and its placenames echo their Norse origins. Here are *wicks*, bays; *voes*, sea lochs; and *fields*, hills, and what bird-watcher could possibly ignore the sign for Nesting?

With no point further than 3 miles (5 km) from the sea, walking here is like traversing the back of a whale. The winds blow cool and the treeless landscape offers little shelter, woolly sweaters being the rule for visitors, residents, and of course, the islands' hardy sheep. Between hills and sea the better land is crofted, and though the coastline itself is often rocky or cliff-girt, and remote from roads, there is little to restrict considerate exploration except the terrain itself and obvious developments such as the Sullom Voe oil terminal.

Near Sumburgh airport, at the southern tip, lies Jarlshof, a settlement named by Sir Walter Scott and with remains from the Stone Age to the age of Vikings, over 3000 years of history. One of the most interesting features of this fascinating site is an earthhouse, the underground passage and chamber of which can be explored with a torch provided by the custodian. Here, too, there is a broch.

Northward from the airport no one should miss taking the ferry to the uninhabited isle of Mousa, where the broch is one of the best preserved examples of its kind. The massive, circular tower can be climbed by stone stairs within the wall. Mousa offers seals, eider ducks and, for the quietest of wanderers, the occasional otter, for whom the rich unpolluted waters of Shetland's coastline have a particular attraction.

North, but this time on the west coast, is Scalloway,

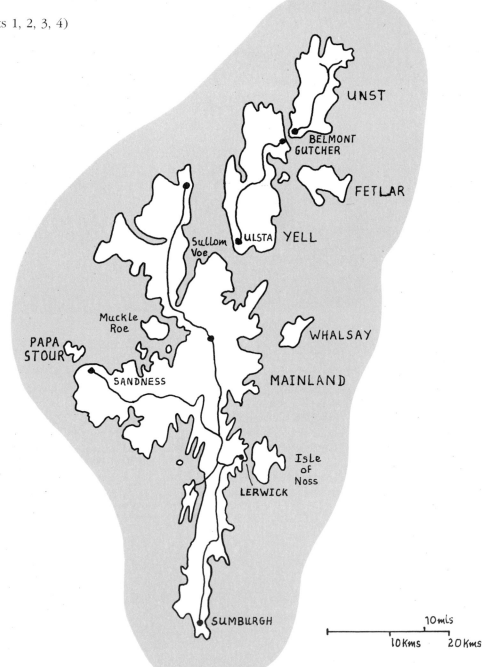

once the capital of Shetland and named for the *skali*, or hall, now long vanished. The ruined castle dates from the early seventeenth century when Scottish law was imposed on the islands. North again few visitors will want to miss Sullom Voe, a magnificent glacially-formed fjord, now the site of Europe's largest oil terminal.

For the enthusiastic long-distance walker, a circuit of the island of Yell is described in a booklet by P.N. Guy. The full route is a surprising 100 miles (160 km), but it can be tackled in shorter sections to suit the walker's ambition. Yell is Shetland's second largest island, and is the starting point for visits to Unst and Fetlar. Unst, Britian's most northerly island, has a large population of Shetland ponies and, at Hermaness, a National Nature Reserve with a large gannet colony.

Fetlar is famous for the Snowy Owl, Britain's only

Snowy Owl

site for the bird whose appearance in 1967 caused the whole island to be declared a bird reserve. Sadly, the owls no longer breed, though individuals are still occasionally seen. The bird-watcher lives in hope.

The climax of a visit to Shetland could well be a trip to Noss, a trip best kept for a calm day with good visibility. A circuit of the island on foot takes in the magnificent 600 ft (180 m) cliffs of the Noup of Noss with its colonies of gannets, razorbills, guillemots and kittiwakes. Should the clifftop seems a little airy, a diversion inland can bring its own, but less expected, hazards, for this is the land of the bonxie, or great skua, whose defensive tactic is to dive-bomb the intruder from behind, an approach best countered with a raised arm or stick. Access to Noss, which is a National Nature Reserve, is by inflatable dinghy across Noss Sound.

Pentland Firth to Moray Firth

(OS sheets 12, 11, 17, 21, 26, 27)

Thurso to Dornoch Firth (141 mls, 225 km)

THURSO IS REACHED by following the beach from Scrabster. Though the harbour, overlooked by the ruin of a seventeenth-century castle, was once important to the town, Thurso is a modern town, having developed since the building of the reactor site at Dounreay. At Pennyland Farm there is a memorial plaque to Sir William Smith founder of the 'Boys Brigade' who was born there.

East from the town the going is easy and the cliffs small. Harold Tower is passed, built in the eighteenth century over the burial place of the Sinclairs of Ulbster. The Harold of the name, the Earl of Orkney, was buried here after the Battle of Claredon in 1196. Castletown, the next village, was famous for its paving slabs, exported through Thurso's harbour, but the old quarry is now disused. Beyond is the superb beach of Dunnet Bay, and then Dunnet Head, the most northerly point of the British mainland. The cliffs are 300 ft (90 m) high and sheer, and topped by a lighthouse. With its views – Cape Wrath can be seen on a clear day, as well as the Orkneys – and fine scenery, this is an excellent extremity.

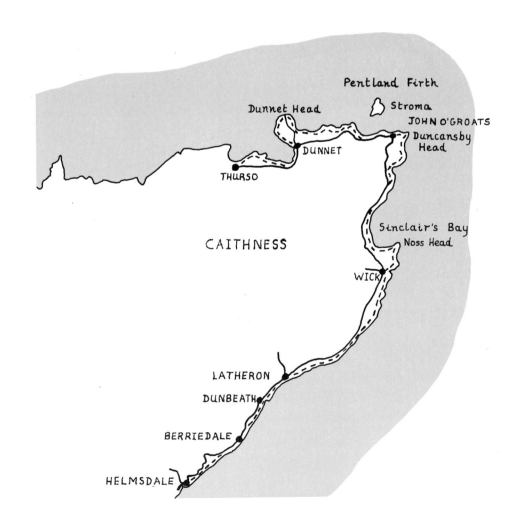

Red Deer often come down to the shore during hard winters

Dunbeath Castle with the hills of Caithness beyond

The walker can follow the eastern side of the headland all the way to the Castle of Mey, the Queen Mother's favourite Scottish home. The castle was built at the end of the sixteenth century and was once owned by the Earl of Caithness. It is tree-screened, the trees being most of the population of Caithness trees, or so it seems.

Eastward, easy ground takes the walker to Canisbay Kirk at Kirkstyle. a fifteenth-century church that is the resting place of Jan de Groot, the founder of John o'Groats, who died in 1568. de Groot was a Dutchman commissioned by James IV to start a ferry service to the Orkneys. The church is used by the Queen Mother when she is staying at the Castle of Mey. John o'Groats itself, a little further on, is the famous spot, the opposite end of the country from Land's End, though it can lay little claim to anything other than being the most north-easterly village. But it has the first and last house, hotel, gift shop, signpost, and so on. In summer there is a ferry from here to the Orkneys, the boat crossing the Pentland Firth, stormy waters connecting the Atlantic Ocean to the North Sea, where the incoming current can reach speeds of 12 miles (19 km) per hour, the fastest current around the British coast.

From John o'Groats the walker heads for Duncansby Head via Cannick Bay. Duncansby Head is the most north-easterly point of the British mainland and is a magnificent, dramatic piece of coastline with superb sea bird colonies, particularly auks. Here if the visitor is patient he may see hooded crows robbing puffin burrows of their eggs.

Southward from the lighthouse the walker is treated to an array of superb natural features, most obviously the amazing conical Stacks of Duncansby. Beyond the village of Skirza are the white sands of Freswick Bay, the longest sandy beach in Caithness. At its southern end the walker returns to cliffs, passing Castle Girnigoe, an imposing ruin, once the seat of the Sinclair Earls of Caithness. The castle is believed to date from the fifteenth to seventeenth century. The walking is now straightforward, rounding Noss Point to Wick.

Wick has a Viking name, from *vik* an inlet, and has, to the south, one of the oldest castles in Scotland, the twelfth-century castle of Old Wick. The town was once a large fishing town but now services the many oil rigs offshore.

Southward, the Old Castle is passed on the way to Whaligoe, a fishing harbour built in the eighteenth

North Scotland is the last home of the Wild Cat

and nineteenth centuries. There are 365 steps cut into the steep cliffs to give access to the village's sheltered cove where the fish catch was unloaded. The village women then carried the fish in baskets up the steps and on to the market in Wick.

The fine coast can be followed from the village through Lybster, where there is still crab fishing, to Latheron, a small, pretty fishing village and Dunbeath which has a restored fifteenth-century castle. The castle is still lived in and is not open to the public. It was once owned by the Earls of Caithness, as was that at Berriedale to the south. Here too are trees, the first for many miles.

Occasionally in this area the walker is forced onto the main road that sits close to the shore, for instance at Berriedale itself where the river must be crossed, but usually the clifftop can be walked, with fine positions and views. At Badbea is the site of a crofting community driven off during the Clearances. A fine broch is passed at Ousdale, and the walker reaches Ord of Caithness, a viewpoint over 700 ft (210 m) above the sea. In 1513 the Earl of Caithness led 300 green-clad local men over the Ord to the Battle of Flodden. Only one survived the battle in which over 10,000 Scots were slaughtered. Today, no local will cross the Ord on a Monday wearing green.

South of Helmsdale the railway holds the cliff, and the walker can take a ride to Brora, although that means missing the broch at Kintradwell to the north of the village. Another, to the south, is not as well preserved, but beyond that is Dunrobin Castle, one of the landmarks of this section of coast. This former seat of the Dukes of Sutherland is sixteenth century

The beautiful cliffs of Badbea, south of Berriedale

and has the air of a French château – with a strong Scottish influence. The mix is due, in large part, to the addition of the pinnacles in the early years of this century. The castle is still inhabited, an unbroken occupation over at least seven centuries on the same site, and is not open to the public. The gardens – a refreshing change as gardens are not a feature of this section of coast – can be visited, and there is a small museum.

Golspie, beyond the castle, stands beneath Beinn A'Bhragaidh on the summit of which there is a monument to the first Duke of Sutherland. He is facing out to sea because, it is said, he was so cruel to the local crofters that when he died they turned the monument to prove he had lost his control over the people.

South of Golspie is Loch Fleet, a sheltered inlet, but one that forces the walker onto the road, using it to cross The Mound, the road embankment built by Thomas Telford in 1815. Along the southern edge of Loch Fleet the walker reaches the ruins of the fourteenth century Skelbo Castle. South now, low-lying shore is followed to Dornoch, a small town with, it is claimed, the third oldest golf course in Britain. In the centre of the town is the thirteenth-century cathedral with beautiful stained glass windows. There is also a stone on the spot where one of the last 'witches' to be burned in Scotland was burnt in 1722 for changing her daughter into a pony.

Bonar Bridge to Inverness (117 mIs, 187 km)

The shore can be followed to Dornoch Point and Meikle Ferry, where there is no ferry, but the walker is forced onto the road soon after to round the Dornoch Firth. The bridge at Bonar Bridge was also designed by Thomas Telford.

On the southern side of the Firth the route is mainly on the road. There is a Pictish stone at Edderton commemorating a battle between the Picts and the Vikings. Tain was first granted a Royal Charter in 1066 and is thought to be the oldest burgh in Scotland. The now ruined fourteenth century St Duthus Chapel was built to house the remains of St Duthus, born here in AD 1000, brought back from Ireland in 1253. Many years later the town was the administrative centre for the Clearances.

From Tain a minor road is followed along the southern edge of the RAF base at Morrish More. To the north there is a bombing range and at times the area can be quite noisy. The walker regains the coast

Dunrobin Castle, Golspie

at the small village of Inver, following it all the way to Tarbat Ness. The cliffs here are home to a lighthouse and large numbers of guillemots and razorbills. Southward there is an enjoyable walk on the cliffs passing the remains of Ballone Castle to Rockfield, a small hamlet and well off the beaten track.

A good track heads south to the villages of Hilton of Cadboll and Balintore and on to Shandwick Bay. South of the village of Shandwick there is a Pictish stone, the Clach á Charridh, marking the burial spot of all the area's unbaptised children. Ahead is Nigg Hill from which the walker can look down into Nigg Bay, an oil rig construction site. South, across the water is Cromarty, many miles of walking away.

Many walkers will prefer to take a bus or train,

Looking south past the lighthouse on the point of Tarbat Ness

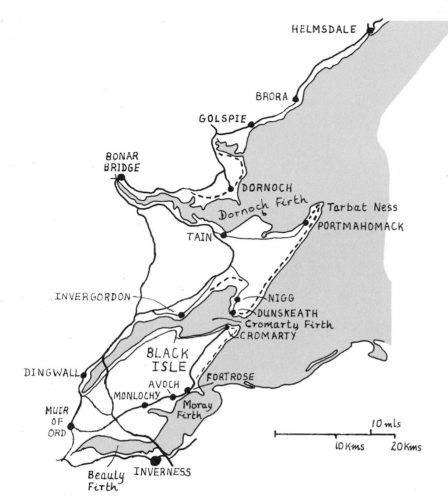

sandstone houses. The Groam House holds a good museum, while inland is the Fairy Glen, a superb wooded valley once studied by Hugh Miller.

The walker passes the golf course on the way to Chanonry Point where there is a memorial stone to Kenneth McKenzie, known as the Brahan Seer – Brahan from the castle near Dingwall – a man claimed to be able to foretell the future, who lived locally in the sixteenth or seventeenth centuries. His death reputedly came as a result of being flung into a barrel of burning tar by a local countess who was not enamoured of being told that her husband was having an affair. History does not record whether the seer was right, although his dying statement that the countess' line would end did come true.

Fortrose, on the other side of Chanonry's finger of land from Rosemarkie, has a ruined cathedral which dates back, in part, to the thirteenth century. Its current state is due to Oliver Cromwell who is said to have taken the stone to build Inverness Castle. From Fortrose the walker must follow the road to Avoch with its pretty harbour and then detour inland along country lanes to round Munlochy Bay.

Leaving Munlochy by road the walker heads for Kilmuir through the Kessock Forest, continuing to Craighton and the mouth of the Beauly Firth. From here Inverness is just over the Kessock Bridge, though the real enthusiast will go by way of the delightful lane that follows the northern shore of the Beauly Firth to Milton, taking the main road from there to Muir of Ord.

From that romantically named village it is road again to Beauly, a fine town with the remains of a thirteenth-century priory, where the River Beauly is crossed. The southern shore of the Firth must also be explored by road, though the railway – there is a station at Muir – hugs the shore closely all the way to Inverness.

experiencing the undoubted delights of the Cromarty Firth from a slight distance. The shore can be reached at several places for views of the fine bird life attracted to the sheltered Firth.

Invergordon is a busy maintenance base for North Sea oil rigs, while Dingwall, at the head of the Firth, is the 'capital' of Ross and Cromarty. There is a fine museum in the town, which is dominated by the tower on Mitchell Hill, built as a memorial to General Sir Hector McDonald, the Victorian soldier.

Beyond Dingwall, at Conon Bridge, where the walker crosses the River Conon, Inverness is only a dozen miles (19 km) away, and many will question the merits of rounding the Black Isle, the jut of land that lies between the Cromarty and Moray Firth. Its northern shore is hardly worth following, as it is road walking all the way to Cromarty, though the views across the Firth are excellent.

Cromarty, a Royal Burgh between 1264 and 1688, was the home of Hugh Miller, a stonemason and leader of the Free Church. Miller became interested in geology and discovered many fossils in the local Old Red Sandstone, giving his name to a species of fish. Some of the fossil beds that Miller worked can still be seen, the most accessible ones being on the shore at Eathie, to the south of the town. Miller's cottage, built in 1711 and the only thatched one left in Cromarty, is now a museum in the care of the National Trust for Scotland. Miller is also commemorated by a monument on the hill above the town. East of Cromarty are the Sutors of Cromarty, huge cliffs from which the views are excellent. A couple of miles away to the north, across the water, is Nigg Hill.

On the southern side of the Black Isle the walker can make good progress past the fossil beds at Eathie and on to Rosemarkie, a delightful village of red

Sutor Stacks below the headland to the east of Cromarty

Moray Firth to Firth of Tay

(OS sheets 26, 27, 28, 29, 30, 38, 45, 54)

Inverness to Lossiemouth (58 mls, 93 km)

DESPITE OCCUPATION BY Cromwell, and by Cumberland's troops after Culloden, the atmosphere of Inverness is indisputably Highland. The town is named for the River Ness, which takes Loch Ness' waters past pleasant promenades and under graceful bridges. The footpaths and suspension bridges of the Ness Islands are especially good, while the nineteenth-century castle on its green hill, and across the water St Andrews' Cathedral and the Eden Court Theatre, enhance the scene. The sixteenth-century Abertarff House is used by An Comunn Gaidhealach, the Highland Society dedicated to preserving the Gaelic language and culture. From the town the coastline offers little to the walker until Ardersier is reached.

From the north end of that village a walkway follows the turf-capped head of the shingle beach to Fort George. This virtually impregnable garrison was built after Culloden to consolidate Hanoverian rule in the Highlands. The fort itself is open to visitors, but eastwards an army training area and an oil rig construction yard prevent access to the coast, and the walker is forced inland to Nairn, a holiday resort with two fine beaches.

Eastwards lie the Culbin Sands, perhaps the most remarkable dune complex in Britain. Over the centuries, blowing sand has gradually submerged the farmlands of the Barony of Culbin and raised sandhills almost 100 ft (30 m) high. Now stabilised by pine plantations, Culbin's unusual landforms and fragile ecosystems are protected by a conservation management plan administered by the Forestry Commission in consultation with the Nature Conservancy Council. The forest is home to the capercaille, crested tit and red squirrel.

The walker should be aware that here the inherent navigational problems posed by sand dunes are magnified by tree cover and, on the coast, by rapidly changing shorelines which quickly render maps out of date. Despite an extensive forest road system, foresters themselves have become lost in Culbin! Serious exploration warrants local enquiry, and the use of a compass together with the most recent OS map.

The walk eastwards from Nairn to the mouth of Findhorn Bay should only be attempted with local knowledge. It is impracticable to follow the beach. This area, neither sea nor land, is at once a lovely and a lonely place, with a solitude that matches the remotest parts of Britain. For the last 3 miles (5 km) to Findhorn Bay the high tide drags at unscalable

Capercaillie can be found in the Culbin Forest

sand cliffs, bringing down trees and sand alike. At one point, tree stumps hunch spider-like below the high water mark where they stand scoured by sea and sand, the last remnants of the land where once they grew.

The impasse of Findhorn Bay, and the extra miles and tricky route-finding involved in returning from a coastal walk, suggest that the walker may prefer to start at the Forestry Commission picnic site at Wellhill. From here forest roads can be followed for 3 miles (5 km) until the salmon fishers' bothy is reached. There a gap in the sand cliff gives access to

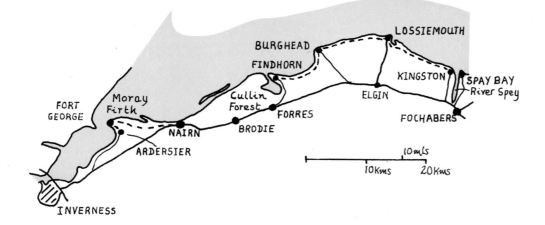

Looking along The Bar, a beautifully sculpted wedge of sand, towards Nairn

the beach. The walk westward along the shore from here cannot, however, be followed at high tide.

From Wellhill minor roads can be used to reach the charming clachan of Broom of Moy, where a substantial bridge – closed to vehicles – crosses the River Findhorn. A path now leads to Waterford and minor roads cross the head of Findhorn Bay.

Findhorn, reached from Kinloss which has a ruined abbey and an RAF base, was formerly an important seaport, and is now a sailing centre. The village we see is the third, the elements having conspired to bury the first village in sand and to cause the second, in 1701, to vanish under the tide. Even the present Findhorn is threatened by erosion and a substantial dune protection scheme is underway.

Burghead is reached via the beach, a splendid 7-mile (11 km) walk, starting from the shingle platform among the Findhorn dunes. As at Culbin, high tide should be avoided as its waters wash the foot of the unstable sand cliff along the mid-section of the walk. The promontory of Burghead ends in the white outline of the former coastguard station, not far from which is a fire-blackened sandstone pedestal. To this point, every 11 January, a burning tar barrel is borne through the village in celebration of the old calendar's New Year in a ceremony known as the Burning of the Clavie.

The massive building at the south-east corner of the village supplies malted barley to local whisky distilleries, of which there are more in Moray than in any other part of Scotland. From the maltings, the former railway line can be followed to Hopeman, a small fishing village.

The coastal path from here to Lossiemouth is delightfully varied: one small cove is appropriately known as Primrose Bay, while the impressive range of sandstone stacks and caves includes one cave used to stable the Laird of Gordonstoun's horses during the 1745 Jacobite uprising. Beyond the Covesea (pronounced Cowsea) Skerries Lighthouse the fishing port of Lossiemouth is reached.

Lossiemouth has a busy fishing harbour and is noted for two great men of their time: James Ramsay MacDonald, Labour Prime Minister, born here in 1866; and James Brander-Dunbar, Laird of Pitgaveny, who once ploughed up the town square during a difference of opinion with the town council, an action which, as landowner, he was perfectly entitled to take.

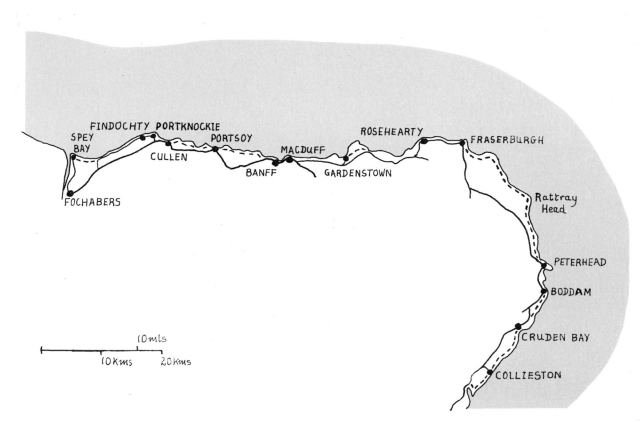

River Lossie to Banff (37 mls, 59 km)

The shore between the Rivers Lossie and Spey offers another fine beach walk, but beware of the army rifle range near the Bin Hill. When the red flags are flying a detour inland is necessary.

The mouth of the Spey is in a constant state of flux, and it is hard to believe that two centuries ago two men from Kingston upon Hull established a ship-building yard here, giving the name to the present village of Kingston. Their raw material came from the caledonian pine forests of the Cairngorms, the trunks, some as much as 4 feet (1.2 m) in diameter, being floated down the Spey. Today both Kingston and its near neighbour Garmouth are quiet places. There is a field path linking them as an alternative to using the road.

The deep and fast-flowing Spey would present a formidable barrier, were it not for the Great North of Scotland Railway, whose viaduct, built in 1886, is now a walkway giving impressive views of the river's shingle banks and winding channels. From the east end of the viaduct the Speyside Way heads south on the first leg of its 30-mile (48 km) route up the valley of the Spey to Ballindalloch, where it takes to the hills for the 15 miles (24 km) to Tomintoul, one of the highest villages in the Highlands.

The coastal walker should turn left on the Way, following it to its seaward terminus at Tugnet, a not inappropriate name for the salmon fishers' icehouse which has been converted into an interpretive centre featuring the Speyside Way, the salmon fishing industry, and the Fishing Heritage Trail.

From Spey Bay hamlet a track follows the coast east to Portgordon and on to Buckie where there is a fishing museum. Eastwards, Portessie, Findochty, Portknockie and Cullen are linked by paths along the coastal braes once used by fishers and smugglers. A natural arch offshore at Portknockie is well named the Bow Fiddle, while along the path to Cullen a sea

Loch Loy, a secret stretch of water set in the Culbin Forest to the east of Nairn

stack of sandstone is now stranded on dry land, providing dramatic evidence of the fluctuations in sea level due to the last Ice Age.

The approaches to Cullen from the west are dominated by the towering arches of railway viaducts. East of the village a shore track becomes a clifftop path to a point overlooking the ruins of fifteenth century Findlater Castle constructed in a niche of a narrow promontory. An overgrown path continues to the Sandend (pronounced Sann-ine) where a footbridge at the caravan site gives access to a wide stretch of sands. A short walk reaches the disused Glenglassaugh distillery from where a minor road leads to Portsoy, with an eighteenth-century fishing harbour. Here, a craft workshop specialises in working the local serpentine rock known as Portsoy marble.

Boyne Bay, with its wooded glen and ruined sixteenth-century castle, is a noted beauty spot, from where there is no established footpath to Whitehills, although a way can be made along the shore. Unlike Portsoy, Whitehills still flourishes as an active fishing port. The village's merchants have been selling fish from vans throughout the north-east since the 1920s, and today they can be met as far away as the streets of Aberdeen on their regular rounds.

The shore walk from Whitehills to Banff is straightforward, passing Red Well, a restored wellhouse protecting a mineral water well. The well's waters formed part of the recommended itinerary a century ago when Banff was favoured as a health resort.

Crossing the Burn of Boyndie by the footbridge leads to a fine sandy beach which can be followed to join the promenade along the rocky shoreline leading to Banff. Everything about Banff has an air of history. A number of the houses date from the seventeenth century, and many historic buildings have been restored. The oldest part of the harbour is eighteenth century but from far earlier times Banff traded with the Baltic ports. The silting of the harbour by the River Deveron ended its commercial activities, but it is now used by yachts and a Scandinavian link has been restored in the form of the annual Banff–Stavanger Yacht Race. Duff House, just inland of our approach to Banff Bridge, was an extravagance commissioned from William Adam by the first Earl of Fife, yet never occupied by him due to a dispute over construction costs which so soured his feelings for the house that he is said to have drawn down his carriage blinds whenever he passed by.

Macduff to Peterhead (49 mls, 78 km)

Across the River Deveron, Macduff's prosperous fishing fleet supports a late eighteenth-century town of simpler architectural style than its neighbour, and built on the steep braes above a busy harbour.

The coastline from Macduff to Aberdour is among the most impressive in Britain, although access is practicable at selected points only. Plunging cliffs and escarpments reach 500 ft (150 m) at More Head, while the cottages of Gardenstown, Crovie and Pennan huddle, gable-ends to the waves, beneath steep grassy braes.

St John's church, west of Gardenstown, dates from the eleventh century and niches in the inner wall of the seaward gable once housed the skulls of Scandinavian invaders slain in a battle nearby. Not far away are the Bloody Pits, where, it is said, the bodies of the vanquished were cast. A walk can be made from the church to Gardenstown by a little used path slanting down the side of a narrow glen, or 'den', to the shore.

A pleasant 3-mile (5 km) walk can be taken from Gardenstown's harbour along the shore path to Crovie and back by the country road above. This shore route is still used by Crovie folk for there are no shops among the 50 or so cottages tightly packed along less than half a mile (0.8 km) of shoreline. Only the sea wall surfaced with an irregular footway gives access, and storm-shutters protect the gable windows from the waves. Many of the people of Crovie left the village to live in Gardenstown after the great storm of 1953.

Northfield Farm is the best point for access to Troup Head. The route to the cliffs taking in the fields is from here. The head is excellent for its birdlife, with colonies of kittiwakes, guillemots, razorbills and puffins.

Cullykhan Bay is reached by a gravel track leaving the coast road. Across the gully to the north can be seen a hole, like a mine entrance, in the hillside. This is Hell's Lum (*lum* is Scots for chimney), a sea cave penetrating right through the headland. For the sure-footed, the opening can be reached by a signed route across the gully, involving some scrambling. Another more accessible tunnel, when the tide is low, pierces the north side of Cullykhan Bay under the peninsula, once fortified and known as Fort Fiddes, where old masonry suggests an ancient castle site.

To reach Pennan, location for the film *Local Hero*, it is necessary to detour inland via a minor road.

Apart from fishing, the coastline hereabouts supported smugglers using the sandstone caves. Millstones were also quarried. These were usually exported by sea, but occasionally overland, the millstone being rolled on its edge, its progress controlled by a long pole placed axle-like through the centre.

From Pennan an old road, now a footpath, reaches Aberdour Bay, passing the solitary, windowless hut – a fish-smoking hut – from the door of which smoke on occasion curls alarmingly.

Also en route is the ruined kirk of St Brostan and nearby is the memorial to Jane Whyte who, in 1884, plunged through the surf to bring ashore a rope from the wreck of the *William Hope*. Her heroism saved the lives of the 15 crew.

The old route continues eastward towards Rosehearty as a minor road from Mill Farm, though the coast is approachable at certain points. From Rosehearty the road must be followed as it hugs the shore through Sandhaven to Fraserburgh.

Fraserburgh, known as The Broch, is the turning point of the coastline, the point where the outer Moray Firth becomes the North Sea. Here, at Kinnaird Head, is Scotland's first lighthouse in a converted sixteenth-century castle. The town has an important fishing and fish-processing industry, though activity is reduced from the great herring fishing days. Then young women travelled the length of Britain to work, gutting and packing the 'silver darlings'.

Fraserburgh's beach, winner of a Keep Scotland Beautiful Award in 1988, gives easy walking for 2 miles (3 km), but a detour inland is necessary to cross the Water of Philorth. More fishing communities follow, the twin villages of Cairnbulg and Inverallochy, followed by St Combs.

Beyond, progress along the shore is impeded by a deep tidal creek and it is better to go inland, rejoining the coast at Rattray. Nearby is the Loch of Strathbeg, a National Nature Reserve which is the winter home for many thousands of pink-footed geese.

South of Rattray Head there is sand again, though near the North Sea Gas terminal, walkers are permitted only on the beach itself, access onto or through the dunes being prohibited.

Southward now, Peterhead is visible on its head-

Macduff, a small fishing village at the eastern end of the Moray Firth

land. One of the sights of Peterhead is the midnight departure on Sundays of the fishing fleet. Today, fishing, along with the oil industry, is the town's mainstay, its daily landings exceeding those of Aberdeen. The town had a brief spell as a health spa, displacing this later in the nineteenth century by whale processing, the town being one of the Scottish whaling ports that sent a fleet to Greenland waters. The Arbuthnot Museum deals with the local history. Before leaving, visit Keith Inch, the most easterly point on the Scottish mainland.

Boddam to Stonehaven (53 mls, 85 km)
At Boddam, easily reached from Peterhead, the islet on which stands Buchan Ness Lighthouse is entirely encircled by a path, making a short, but unusual coastal walk, which includes a bridge over the North Sea.

South of Boddam, the red granite cliffs are rather inaccessible, though the nature reserve near Longhaven and the Bullers of Buchan, an impressive blowhole, can be reached. The Bullers, no place for the faint-hearted, were described by Boswell as a 'monstrous cauldron' after a visit with Dr Johnson. On the clifftops at Cruden Bay, Slains Castle, now a gaunt ruin, is thought to have inspired Bram Stoker in the writing of Dracula.

A fine beach in the Bay of Cruden provides a welcome break in this hard coastline, though southwards the cliffs return for 5 miles (8 km) or so to the next large village, Collieston, and a minor road is best followed. The road passes through Whinnyfold, a good example of a 'heugh-head' village where the cottages are grouped at the top of the cliff, or heugh, due to the lack of level ground at the shore.

Collieston is not a heugh-head, its cottages being scattered among the trees. Just west of the village is the visitor centre for the Sands of Forvie National Nature Reserve. This 3 square miles (7.8 sq.km) of sand dunes and coastal heath between Collieston and the Ythan estuary is of great importance for wintering populations of wildfowl, waders and shore-birds while in summer there are arctic tern and eider duck colonies.

From Newburgh, beyond the Ythan, unbroken sands curve south to the mouth of the Don at Aberdeen, though care is needed at Blackdog, where there is an army firing range. The area should be avoided when red flags are displayed.

Aberdeen, Scotland's third largest city, lies between the Don and the Dee. The seaport grew up on the north side of the Dee: the oldest surviving house is Provost Ross' House, on the Shiprow, housing the maritime museum. The city has a fine array of buildings and streets in clean-cut grey granite. Especially notable is the unique, ornate granite frontage of Marischal College, completed in 1906. The granite came from the Rubislow quarry 2 miles (3 km) to the west. The harbour developed into a worldwide trading port in the nineteenth century, with clipper ships importing wool and tea. In the 1880s the steam tug *Toiler* was converted to a vessel capable of dragging nets cross the sea bottom, the start of a trawling boom with Aberdeen growing to become Scotland's premier fishing port. Although this position is no longer held today, the fish market is still a busy place and a fish festival is held each August.

It is, of course, North Sea oil which accounts for Aberdeen's status as one of the most prosperous cities in Britain, yet much of the extensive development that accompanies this has been accommodated away from the city centre in peripheral industrial parks and suburban residential areas. One sign of activity, however, is the continual traffic of oilfield support vessels to and from the harbour, best seen from the Torry Battery, high on the grassy headland south of the river mouth. From here the point of Girdleness can be reached, with its lighthouse designed by Robert Stevenson, grandfather of the author of *Treasure Island*.

To the south is the Bay of Nigg from where an excellent path leaves the road to follow the clifftop. En route is Burnbanks Haven, where an aerial ropeway serves the shore far below. In the days when several open boats fished from this haven everything would have been carried up and down the steep, winding path.

The walker must leave the clifftop when the cliff face is occupied by a vocal colony of kittiwakes for a path along the edge of a field east of the railway, heading for the village of Cove Bay.

The high cliffs south of here are inaccessible, but the coast can be rejoined at Findon, where the succulent smoked haddock known as 'Finnan Haddie' originated. South again are Portlethen and Muchalls, with interconnecting clifftop paths and field tracks. Here and there steep, tortuous paths lead to empty shores where once the fishing yawls were drawn up beyond reach of the waves.

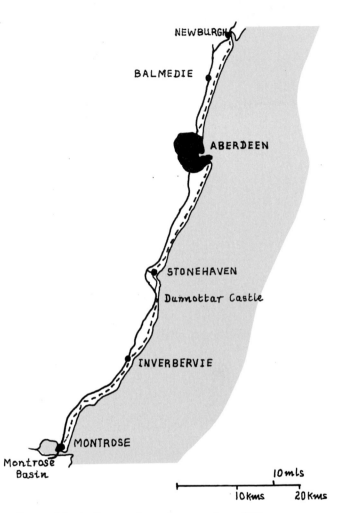

From Muchalls to Stonehaven the clifftops are overgrown and deep gullies interrupt the coast. At Mill of Muchalls a stream disappears underground to re-emerge intriguingly as a waterfall near the foot of the cliff.

Stonehaven is an attractive resort with some good local walks. North of the town a cliff path leads from Cowie to the ruined chapel of St Mary of the Storms. Northwards, the seaward edge of the golf course can be followed to arrive at wild Garron Point, northern extremity of the Highland Boundary fault and geologically speaking, the border of the Highlands and Lowlands. Stonehaven's harbour, in the 'oldest part of the town, was once a seaport of some

Beyond the sheltered harbour of Collieston are the Sands of Forvie and lowlands of old Aberdeenshire

North Sea Oil Rig off Aberdeen

importance, but is now largely used by pleasure craft. The harbour is overlooked by the historic Tolbooth, a former storage building and prison, built by the Earls Marischal, of Dunnottar Castle, for whom this was the nearest secure haven. The main street of the old town is the scene of the Fireball Ceremony at Hogmanay when local people parade at midnight with whirling baskets of fire, reputedly to rid the town of evil influences.

Dunnottar Castle to Dundee (62 mls, 99 km)

A steep path climbs the brae to the coast road above, taking the walker past the hilltop war memorial to Dunnottar Castle, whose ruins spread across a peninsula so well defended by crags that only at the last minute does the entrance appear. It was in a grim dungeon here that 167 Covenanters were imprisoned in 1685. Earlier in the same century, while under siege by Cromwell's forces, the Scottish Crown Jewels were successfully smuggled out of the castle and carried to a place of safety at the Kinneff Kirk.

The precipitous but practically inaccessible cliffs south of Dunnottar are home to vast colonies of seabirds. The RSPB have a reserve at Crawton, an abandoned fishing village, from where a minor road runs parallel to the coast, passing Catterline, Todhead lighthouse and Kinneff Kirk before rejoining the main road north of Inverbervie, birthplace of Hercules Linton, designer of the renowned clipper *Cutty Sark*. The town was granted its charter in 1342 by David II of Scotland, in gratitude for his friendly reception by the community on being driven ashore during a storm. The spot where he and his queen landed is still called the King's Step.

The shingle shore from Inverbervie south to Johnshaven and beyond is excellent for walking as a track known as the Low Road follows the shore for many miles. South of Johnshaven it deteriorates somewhat near the disused lime kilns. The now vanished village of Miltonhaven stood hereabouts, but continuing limestone quarrying so weakened its natural defences that eventually it fell into the sea.

South from the quaintly named Tangleha – 'seaweed haven' – the coastline becomes hard to follow, but should be rejoined, without fail, at St Cyrus for a view south along the broad curve of Montrose Bay. The cliffs here recede from the current shoreline,

Looking north to Stonehaven. On a headland to the south of the port stands Dunnottar Castle

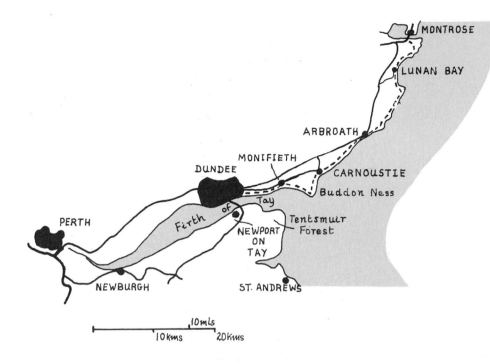

Figurehead of the Unicorn, *Dundee*

supporting rare plant communities on their inaccessible slopes. The saltmarsh, dunes and estuary of the North Esk combine to make the entire area of such environmental importance that it has been designated a National Nature Reserve.

A well-made path, once used by ponies carrying salmon up from the shore netting stations, winds down to the shore from where a track leads through the reserve. The North Esk is crossed by the eighteenth-century bridge still used by the main road and en route for Montrose the walker passes the Offshore Fire Training Centre. Montrose, like Aberdeen, lies between the mouths of two rivers, here the North and South Esk, and combines the activities of seaport, oil industry support base and seaside resort. A unique feature is the large area of tidal flats and saltmarsh known as Montrose Basin, now a nature reserve of considerable importance to wintering shorebirds, waders and swans.

The derelict fishing settlement of Fishtown of Usan is worth a visit, if only to see the 'dyke' of soft rock eroded by the sea into a perfect natural harbour. This tiny haven supplied fish to the Royal Court of Scotland when it was at Forfar, along a route known as the King's Cadgers Road.

The sands of Lunan Bay, backed by dunes and

topped by the ruins of Redcastle, are a scenic delight, and the area was used by Sir Walter Scott in several of his works. From the south end of the bay the coast becomes rocky again, the sandstone cliffs of the Red Head dominating views from as far north as Inverbervie. Southwards is Auchmithie, the fishing village which originated the famous Arbroath 'smokies'. A nature trail leads from Carlingheugh Bay near the town of Arbroath itself.

The town grew around the great red sandstone abbey where the Scottish Declaration of Independence was signed in 1320. Down by the harbour, smokies can be bought from the fish-houses. Nearby is the unusual Signal Tower museum, built as a signalling station for the Bell Rock lighthouse – made automatic in 1988 – on the infamous Inchcape Rock 11 miles (17.5 km) to the south-east.

The coastline from Arbroath to Carnoustie is low, largely bounded by a tidal rock platform, and can be followed from Elliot, south of Arbroath, to East Haven. At Carnoustie the sandy links have determined the town's international status as a golfing resort. Beyond is the dune and heath foreland of Buddon Ness, an army training area. Walkers are permitted to follow the coast from Carnoustie round Buddon Ness to Monifieth as long as they stay on the

beach, except when red flags are displayed. **Do not touch unidentified objects.**

Dundee's own seaside resort is the pleasant beach at Broughty Ferry, whose castle stands guard over the former ferry crossing to Fife, an important route until the late nineteenth century. During the early railway years there were even train ferries plying back and forth here from these massive slipways.

Dundee is an industrial city whose fortunes grew in the Victorian era with the jute industry. A little jute is still landed here but most of the surviving mills work with artificial fibres. Like Peterhead, Dundee enjoyed an era as a whaling port. Its maritime heritage includes the frigate *Unicorn*, a man-of-war built to be kept in reserve and thus roofed over to exclude the elements. Captain Scott's ship, *The Discovery*, was built here in 1901 for his 1910 Antarctic expedition. Now restored to her place of origin, her graceful combination of sail and steam propulsion is a proud addition to the waterfront. It makes a fitting backdrop as you cross the Firth of Tay on the Tay road bridge. Two miles (3.2 km) to the west, as the estuary narrows on its way to Perth, is the Tay railway bridge, scene of the famous disaster when, in December 1879, the central span collapsed during a storm, taking with it a train, its crew and 75 passengers.

Gourdon, a small, multi-jettied port between Montrose and Stonehaven

Firth of Tay to the Borders

(OS sheets 54, 59, 65, 66, 67, 75)

Tayport to Anstruther (40 mls, 64 km)

DROPPING DOWN TO the Fife shore the concrete pillars of the road bridge loom high above you as you follow the path past some old lighthouses into Tayport. Beyond, a track, bounded by forest and shore, leads to Tentsmuir point and the Abertay sands that stretch 5 miles (8 km) out to sea. Here the bird watcher can watch the waders frantically feeding on the rising tide as it pushes them closer to the shore. After the incoming sea covers the sands the birds are forced to roost on any mudbanks left above water until the tide recedes again.

A path follows a fine 3 mile (5 km) stretch of sand, skirting Tentsmuir Forest, and from it the lucky may see common and, maybe, a few larger grey, seals. Strewn all along this beach you will find the brittle 'shells' of sea urchins.

To avoid some awkward mud you must now take the path through the forest to Leuchars, an airbase town, the source of all the low flying jets that are a constant companion to the local walker. There, do not miss St Athernase's church with its ornate arcades and tower. Dating from the thirteenth century it is one of the best Norman churches in Scotland. We join the coast again just beyond Guardbridge where the fifteenth-century bridge, the oldest in Fife, crosses

the river Eden. The Eden estuary provides rich feeding grounds, attracting vast numbers of waders and wildfowl in winter. A disused railway line is followed along its southern shore, until it is possible to drop down onto the shoreline, to the edge of the world's most famous golf course. St Andrews, the home of golf, was where the rules of the modern game were first drawn up.

The town St. Andrews is named after the patron saint of Scotland, tradition being that his bones were buried here in AD 347. The twelfth-century castle was ransacked in the Anglo-Scottish wars and later in the seventeenth century much of it was demolished to provide stones for rebuilding the harbour walls. Much the same applies to the cathedral, started in 1160: all that now remains are the twin towers and Gothic arches of a gatehouse, along with the magnificent tower of St Rule's Church. In 1559 a mob of reformers, inflamed by the preaching of John Knox, set about the church destroying its ornaments. St Andrews University, founded in 1410, is the oldest in Scotland and dominates much of the city.

South of St Andrews the shore is quiet, but increasingly rocky, one fine outcrop being a sandstone archway called the Budd of Ness. Further along at Babbet Ness the low tide leaves a huge pillar high and dry on the beach. Fife Ness, the most easterly point of the Fife coast, is an excellent spot for watching passing sea birds.

Having turned the point the walker heads west along the southern coast of Fife. Six miles offshore (9.5 km) is the Isle of May on which are the remains of a thirteenth-century priory dedicated to St Adrian, who preached on this Forth island and was buried on May after being murdered by Danish raiders in 870. The mile (1.6 km) long island is now a nature reserve and sea-bird sanctuary.

The coast of East Neuk, as this part of Fife is called, 'neuk' being the old Scots word for corner, is largely unspoilt and dotted with traditional fishing villages. In medieval times there was considerable trade from

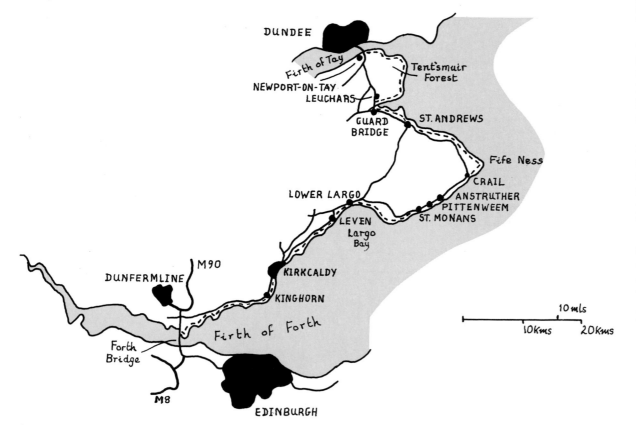

The twin fishing villages of Anstruther Easter and Wester

The 'Royal and Ancient' Clubhouse, St Andrews

these small ports with Europe, especially Scandinavia, where wool, coal and fish were traded for timber and other goods. The villages were very prosperous and there is an obvious Flemish influence in the architecture of the merchants' houses. Typically they are whitewashed, with red pantiled roofs and characteristic crow-stepped gables. When sea trade with Europe declined, fishing took over and in the nineteenth century large herring fleets were based at the ports. Today the villages struggle on with smaller fleets, their economies boosted by tourism.

The first village is Crail, with a history going back 4000 years. It is the epitome of a Scottish east coast fishing village, sturdy stone-faced houses crowding together around the harbour. The obvious Flemish influence contrasts with the harbour walls built of regular-sized blocks of standstone. The excellent museum next to the sixteenth-century Dutch town hall tells the natural and maritime history of the village. John Knox preached here in 1559, at the church of St Mary's.

Beyond Crail are the twin villages of Anstruther Easter and Wester. Locally called Anster this was the main herring port in Scotland but now the reduced fleet fishes mainly for shrimp, crab and lobster. Anstruther is the home of the Scottish fisheries museum, recording the heyday and decline of the trade. It includes a unique floating museum of many different boats, including the bright red North Carr lightship. Robert Louis Stevenson came from a family of engineers responsible for designing most of the lighthouses along the coast of Scotland and he was an apprentice engineer at Anstruther before ill-health made him leave the trade and take up writing.

Pittenweem to Edinburgh (71 mls, 114 km)

It is only a short way along the cliffs to Pittenweem, the next village which, with its cottages tightly packed around the harbour, has all the charm of Fife. The name means 'the place of the cave' after St Fillan, a seventh-century missionary who lived in a cave here, using it as his chapel. It can still be seen today, as can the stone slab on which he slept and the spring he used for water. Pittenweem has the last surviving fish market in East Neuk.

A mile (1.6 km) further along the coast is St Monans, where the main trade is boatbuilding rather than fishing. The, literally, outstanding feature of St Monans is the strange fishermen's church with its graveyard right up to the cliff edge. Named, like the village, after St Monan, it was built by David II in gratitude for being cured of an arrow wound at the saint's shrine here.

Leaving St Monans the geography changes as we follow the shoreline to Elie and Earlsferry, two villages sharing a mile of beautiful sand. Beyond are the rocks of Chapel Ness and at Kincraig Point there are caves said to have hidden MacDuff from Macbeth.

Westward the walker can follow the 6 mile (9.5 km) of beach which form Largo Bay. The village of Largo, backed by the volcanic hill of Largo Law, lies in the centre of the Bay amidst a group of rocks. It has been a popular holiday resort since the last century, a popularity that helped buffer the town against the decline of its fishing trade. In 1676, Alexander Selkirk was born here, the real-life Robinson Crusoe who was the inspiration behind Defoe's story. Following a disagreement with his captain Selkirk was marooned on an island 400 miles (640 km) off the coast of Chile and survived there alone for four years. A bronze statue of him, in his goats' skins, stands outside his home, and the local museum gives his full story.

The sheltered bay and rocky outcrops make Largo Bay a haven for bird life. Turnstones work the rocks and seaweed, but it is the sea ducks, particularly in winter, which bring the bird watchers. One of the most beautiful is the long-tailed duck.

Walking west along the bay towards the town of Leven the fishing ends and the industry begins, with Leven, Methil and Buckhaven all joined together into one sprawling ugly, industrial mass, servicing the North Sea oil industry. The coast from here never quite recovers its beauty until Edinburgh is left behind. The story is a familiar one, with fishing declining to give way to coal, which eventually gave way to oil. The coastal path, through Wemyss to Kirkcaldy, passes by the graveyards of the coal industry, the disused pits now having fallen into dereliction. This section is uninspiring and somewhat tedious, and a bus from Leven to Kirkcaldy is recommended.

Since Kirkcaldy was the birthplace of Adam Smith, the economist and Robert Adams, the architect, it might be expected that things would improve. But no, Kirkcaldy grew up as a textile town and made its

Looking west past Elie and Earlsferry to Largo Bay with Largo Law on the horizon

The Forth Bridges near Edinburgh (above)

John Knox's House, Edinburgh (right)

fortune from linoleum and is a child of this history. At its southern end the Seafield colliery, which mines coal from 2,000 ft (600 km) below the sea, maintains the industrial story. The train from here hugs the coast all the way to the Forth Bridge and is a good alternative to the walk.

If you do decide to walk from Kirkcaldy, the coast-hugging path passes disused mines but improves as it comes into Kinghorn. Beyond the grey stone streets of Kinghorn is Pettycur Bay, where, at low tide, the 'Black Rocks' are left high and dry, well over half a mile (0.8 km) out. Across the bay is Burntisland where the once busy shipyards now stand deserted. Next is Aberdour and the fine ruins of its fourteenth-century castle, from which there are excellent views of the islands of Inchcolm, Inchkieth and Inch Mickery, with the Edinburgh skyline looming. Just beyond 1½ miles (2.5 km) out in the Forth, Inchcolm can be reached by boat from Aberdour. The island's name derives from the Gaelic, 'Colum's Isle'. In the twelfth century a Columban hermit sheltered Alexander I here during a violent storm and in gratitude the king built an Augustinian abbey, regarded by many as one of the finest pieces of medieval architecture in Scotland. The island, which is about a mile (1.6 km) long, is now a sanctuary for seals, which can be watched close at hand, and seabirds.

Five miles (8 km) down the Firth from Aberdour are the Forth road and rail bridges. There is a

footpath across the 1964 road bridge, but everyone should take the train across the rail bridge at least once in honour of the imagination that conceived it. Opened in 1890 it is said to have taken 5,000 men to build, and is 1¾ miles (2.8 km) long and 360 ft (108 m) high. It does not take for ever to paint, as is proverbial, but three years.

From Dalmeny station, on the far side a beautiful walk takes the walker towards the uninhabited Cramond Island and along the river Almond to Cramond Bridge; hop on a bus here to reach the centre of Edinburgh.

Edinburgh is by far the finest city on the Scottish coast, steeped in history, tradition and the arts. Its buildings are as majestic as any to be found elsewhere and its skyline, seen from the castle which dominates it, is truly inspiring. This is no place to attempt to describe Edinburgh, but for anyone who has never visited the city, dump the rucksack, take a few days off and tread its beautiful streets, you will not regret it. A few days in the city will also revitalise your appetite for coastal walking.

Gosford Sands to Chapel Point (45 mls, 72 km)

To leave Edinburgh take a train to Longniddry, avoiding a long walk through the city's suburbs, past coastal industry and the power station. The shore is reached again at Gosford Sands from where a walk around Aberlady Point brings the walker to the Aberlady Bay nature reserve. The reserve is botanic-

ally important, showing a succession of plant life from mud-flat through to saltmarsh, and is also excellent for birds. The bay is bisected by a creek which can be easily crossed on an old wooden bridge just beyond Aberlady village. A path beyond takes the saltmarsh edge to Gullane Point and Hummell Rocks. From here North Berwick is a wild and beautiful stretch of coast that is important geologically. Offshore are numerous rocks and islands, the largest being Fidra, with a lighthouse and an impressive colony of birds, including eider ducks.

Inland is a golfer's paradise, the courses including

Looking east along the Firth of Forth towards North Berwick. To the right rises North Berwick Law while offshore to the left is the island of Fidra

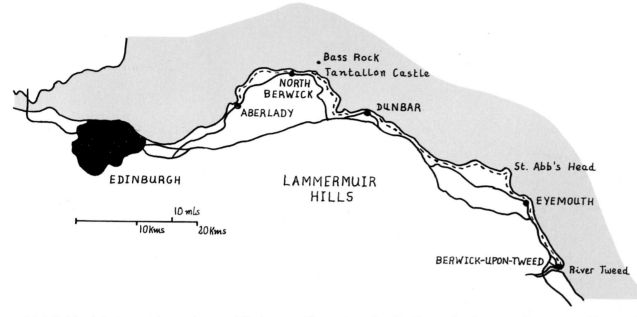

Leaving Dunbar, the way heads towards the lighthouse at Barns Ness. Between here and Catcraig a geological trail is laid out, enabling the walker to recognise the succession of limestone outcrops and abundant fossils. At Catcraig there is an early nineteenth-century lime kiln, standing 30 ft (9 m) high. Local limestone was burnt in the kiln to produce lime for use as fertiliser. Today the nearby cement works uses the limestone to produce three quarters of Scotland's cement. Around the next rocky outcrop, at Chapel Point, the impact of technology on the environment is re-emphasised by the massive grey cube of the Torness nuclear power station. A walkway is being constructed past it, so that the walker can avoid the A1.

Torness Point to Berwick (31 mls, 50 km)

Hurrying past Torness brings the walker quickly to Cove. Crammed into the rocks above its tiny harbour, with a steep track leading up to the hamlet by way of a 60 yard (18 m) tunnel through the rocks, it is surrounded by smugglers' caves and seems an ideal spot for them. Over the next headland lies Pease Bay, at the foot of a steep valley where Peaseburn cuts through the sandstone cliffs. Up the valley or 'dean', and well worth the detour of half a mile (0.8 km), is Pease Bridge. Built in 1786 to take a road over the valley it is 130 ft (40 m) high and said to have been the highest in the world at the time.

For the next 8 miles (13 km) there is a fine cliff walk, with contorted layers of strata running down the cliffs in all directions. The cliffs rise to 500 ft (150 m), then drop down again to the headland at Fast Castle. Standing just 70 ft (21 m) above sea level, and accessible only by a very narrow path this is a peaceful yet awesome place.

Beyond, the path continues in fine style to St Abb's Head, where the cliffs rise to 300 ft (90 m), producing some of the most spectacular geological formations to be found along our shores. St Abbs is named after St Ebba, a seventh-century princess of Northumbria, said to have been shipwrecked on the headland while escaping the King of Mercia. The headland is a National Nature Reserve and it is easy to see why, volcanic activity having twisted the rocks into turmoil, the sea assisting by scouring out caves and forming huge stacks. The result is a natural rock garden with huge stacks. The result is a natural rock garden with

Looking across the Firth of Forth past Tantallon Castle and Bass Rock to the Fife Coast

Muirfield, claiming to have the world's best golfing turf. As you pass the small island of Lamb coming into North Berwick, the volcanic North Berwich Law rises sharply to 613 ft (184 km) providing a focus and landmark all the way along this section of coast.

North Berwick nestling beneath the Law, offers, in summer, the opportunity of a visit to Bass Rock. Lying just 3 miles (5 km) north east, the Rock commands the eye from all parts of the local coast. Its steep sides rise sharply out of the sea, making the domed top seem much higher than its 350 ft (105 m). It is 1 mile (1.6 km) in circumference and home to around 9000 pairs of nesting gannets. The gannet take its scientific name, *sula bassana*, from the rock, such is their association with it. On the island is the ruined chapel of St Baldred. At one time soldiers were garrisoned in the island's fortress though the fortress was used as a prison in the seventeenth century before being dismantled in 1701. Of the town of North Berwick, the most intriguing part is the ruin of St Andrew's church by the harbour. Here, in 1591, over 200 local witches were said to have met to plot the death of James I of England (James VI of Scotland). The Devil himself was supposed to have appeared as a black goat.

To the east, the rising cliffs are dominated by the tall towers of the ruined Tantallon Castle, built by the

Douglas family in the fourteenth century. The castle was battered by Cromwell in 1651, but on this 100 ft (30 m) headland it is still an impressive and evocative ruin, even if its warm red sandstone now provides nesting places for fulmars. Clambering down the cliffs from the castle the huge, low slabs of Scoughall Rocks peter out into Peffer sands – which are followed to Baldred's Cradle. Ahead now is the wide sandy mouth of the River Tyne known as the John Muir Country Park. The park is named after a son of Dunbar, John Muir, born in the town in 1838 but famous as a pioneering naturalist, responsible for establishing America's Yosemite National Park. The Country Park has almost 2,000 acres of estuary, rich in wildlife.

Along the southern side of the estuary the coastal path goes through, mud-flats, sand, woodland, scrub, dune, and finally rocks as it climbs up onto the cliff tops to reach the harbour at Dunbar.

Lying on the main route between England and Edinburgh, Dunbar had the misfortune of being fought over many times. Cromwell severely damaged the town but then, a few years later, and for reasons best known to himself, he gave it money for a new harbour. Today there is a very busy harbour overlooked by the sandstone ruins of the castle on a site known to have been fortified for over 1000 years.

The Old Tweed Bridge, Berwick

pink thrift on red sandstone above forests of submerged kelp. Not surprisingly St Abbs is favoured by the diver and the botanist, but it belongs to the bird watcher: 10,000 guillemot are among the 50,000 birds that breed here, cramming the narrow ledges of the cliffs. There are fulmars and kittiwakes, puffins, shags, razorbills and gannets feeding on the abundance of marine life in the clean waters at the cliff base.

The harbour at St Abbs village, always an important refuge during storms, is still home to a small inshore fleet specialising in lobster and crabs. From the cliffs overlooking Coldingham Bay there are fine views of the short coastal stretch around Eyemouth, home of a much larger, ocean-going fleet. On the 14 October 1881, surprise gales claimed half of Eyemouth's fleet: 23 boats were lost and 129 men drowned. The town used to be a haven for smuggling, its alleyways being particularly useful for avoiding custom men, and the nearby caves lending themselves to storage. The local museum, an excellent place, recalls the town's history, its storms and smugglers.

Skirting the edges of the golf course to the south, the gently dipping and rising cliffs lead easily into Burnmouth. At the foot of a steep ravine the village houses are clustered around the harbour to form the last (or first) Scottish harbour on this coast. Burnmouth is a quiet place, but sturdily built to withstand the force of the winter gales.

Just outside Burnmouth you reach Ross Point. From here to the east, following the cliff tops to Berwick, is the mainline railway from Edinburgh to Newcastle and just over that the A1 trunk road runs by. In places the walker is obliged to follow the A1, so close does the railway hug the cliffs, but after a couple of miles, as Scotland becomes England near Marshall Meadows Bay, walkers have the cliffs to themselves again as they drop gently down to the mouth of the Tweed at Berwick.

St Abb's Head, north of Berwick-upon-Tweed

Northumbria

(OS sheets 75, 81, 88, 93, 94)

Lamberton Toll to Lindisfarne (21 mls, 34 km)

NO GREAT FUSS accompanies the entrance to England at Lamberton Toll on the A1. Even less is manifest on the cliff path which leads southwards to Berwick-upon-Tweed. What is Berwick, whose businesses and institutions are both Scottish and English? Is it a Scottish Burgh or an English Borough? Its turbulent history is marked with moments of pride and humiliation, prosperity and ruin. Under the Hammer of the Scots, Edward I, the streets ran with blood for two days in 1295, following the slaughter of 17,000 inhabitants. Berwick suffered greatly in all the Border disputes and had changed hands over a dozen times before 1482, when it was firmly annexed to England by Edward IV. Its legal incorporation into England took centuries. A well-worn tale relates how Berwick, independent of Scotland and England, entered into the Crimean War. Unfortunately, due to increasing English control over the town, Berwick was unable to conclude a peace treaty and is thus still at war with Russia!

A thorough exploration of Berwick ought to settle some of the questions prompted by the town's Anglo-Scottish affinities and allegiances. The town walls offer a fine 2 mile (3.2 km) walk, and several buildings of character are tucked away inside. The old castle, cruelly sliced by the railway, lies outside the walls. Most of Berwick's museums are military-oriented, hardly surprising in view of its history, though the Wine and Spirit Museum comes as an odd surprise. But despite it all, the impression is of Berwick as a buffer zone, and that it is across the Tweed where England really begins.

James I of England (VI of Scotland) set out in 1603 to embody in himself the idea of a United Kingdom. It seems disturbingly significant that he broke down in abject fear while crossing the rickety old wooden bridge across the Tweed at Berwick. The King ordered the 'Old Bridge' to be built, in stone with 15 arches, to replace the old one. Some years ago, as if to emphasis the comments above on where England actually starts, the ENGLAND signboard at Lamberton Toll, now replaced by a solid stone block, was removed and planted in the middle of the Old Bridge.

Industrial Tweedmouth is limited in extent and a promenade at Spittal shortly gives way to a clifftop track. The cliff line soon diminishes in height and is replaced by a line of sand dunes. The Northumberland coast, often proclaimed as a coast of beauty – indeed the section from Berwick to Amble is a designated Area of Outstanding Natural Beauty – is not tall and rugged, and sections of low cliffs and dunes will become familiar.

A wide sweep of sand seems to suggest an easy walk to Holy Island, but rapid tides, quicksands and unexploded missiles impose a route that goes via Goswick to reach the Holy Island causeway. The island spends more time connected to the mainland than cut off by the sea, but the flats flood quickly and it is essential to study the tide tables posted at the causeway before crossing. A hut on stilts half-way is the only sanctuary on a mis-timed journey. As an alternative to following the causeway a line of recently restored posts marks the old Pilgrim's Way across the sands.

Lindisfarne, as the island was called, became a Christian centre following the arrival of St Aidan in 635. Its priory grew in stature as a renowned place of learning and achievement, producing the lavishly illustrated Lindisfarne Gospels. One famous resident

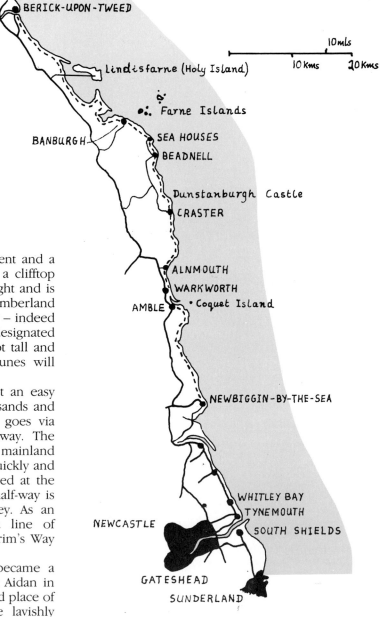

The ruins of the Priory, Lindisfarne

was St Cuthbert who undertook a great mission of conversion on the mainland. The Danes invaded, sacked and burnt the priory in 875, though it was re-founded in 1082. Dissolution came in 1537, when it was stripped of its treasures and roofing materials. A new museum sited at the priory details Holy Island's history. Some of the stonework from the priory was used in 1539 for the construction of Lindisfarne Castle which crowns a lump of rock once called The Beblowe and overlooks the harbour. The present structure is a thorough Lutyens restoration of 1902. Curious sheds built of upturned boats cut in half are a feature of the harbourside.

The Boat Storehouses near Lindisfarne Castle

Holy Island to Warkworth (43 mls, 69 km)

The Holy Island dune belt and all the tidal flats from Goswick Sands to Budle Bay form the Lindisfarne Nature Reserve, access to which, on foot, is freely allowed. Unfortunately though, there is no actual coastal footpath and the shoreline, which can be desperately muddy in places, with inlets that cannot be crossed at high tide, is only for the very persistent. If progress becomes impossible or distasteful, take one of a number of footpaths or minor roads inland for a road to the far side of Budle Bay, from where a path across a golf course leads to Bamburgh.

Bamburgh Castle, like Lindisfarne Castle, sits on a lofty lump of rock. The rock has been fortified since 547, though the first building was of wood and was easily swept away by the Vikings. A stone castle of the eleventh century had a lively history, suffering many onslaughts and becoming the first English castle to fall to gunfire. It was restored in 1704, but the current

Bamburgh Castle

form is a more thorough early twentieth-century restoration. Lord Armstrong, the restorer, was an engineering inventor and part of the castle houses a museum of his work and achievements. The castle dominates the little village of Bamburgh and offers sweeping coastal views.

Bamburgh village has a museum dedicated to the memory of Grace Darling and her daring rescue of 1838. Grace was the daughter of the lighthouse keeper on Longstone, the most distant of the Farne Islands. When she was 23 the *Forfarshire* came to grief on the rock of Big Harcar in a gale. As survivors appeared on the rock, father and daughter set out to rescue them, knowing full well that they would only be able to accomplish a one-way trip and would have to rely on the survivors to help them row back. There were nine survivors out of the ship's compliment of 52, and two journeys were needed to rescue them all. The Darling's boat was neither a lifeboat nor part of the lifeboat service, but the pair were awarded the RNLI silver medal and became national heroes. Grace stayed with her father at the light, despite offers of marriage, and died four years later. A monument to her can be seen at St Aidan's church.

A line of dunes links Bamburgh and Seahouses and walking the seaward side allows good views of the flat, but rugged, Farne Islands. Trips to the islands – there is a large grey seal colony and the bird life is

impressive – are run from Seahouses. Seahouses also has a fishing museum with a history of the local industry, particularly the herring trade.

A path around the rocky headland of Snook leads to Beadnell, a village in two parts. The tiny harbour, the lesser port, has a series of massive lime kilns in the care of the National Trust. After passing through a caravan site a path behind the dunes leads to Low Newton-by-the-Sea, a tiny village despite its long name. The coastline to either side of the village is National Trust property, as is the nearby bird sanctuary of Newton Pool. From the village a path, again behind the dunes, runs around Embleton Bay to Dunstanburgh Castle.

Dunstanburgh's active history was really quite brief. Building started in 1313 under the Earl of Lancaster, who was subsequently executed and is now said to haunt the place. Sir John Lilburn built a tower in 1325 and John o'Gaunt added a new gatehouse in 1380. By the 1460s, after several assaults and changes of ownership the castle was falling into a poor condition. Now, after 500 years of neglect it is a crumbling ruin, yet still it retains power and grandeur as is well-captured in the famous Turner water-colour. The visitor may find entry via the

Looking over Bamburgh Castle to the Farne Islands

massive keep unnerving, the enclosed land area ending in a sheer cliff which was left unwalled.

A delightful grassy path runs from Dunstanburgh to Craster, a little resort whose kippers are a speciality. Southward, the coastline becomes rather tame, though walking is easy as a series of paths and tracks run close to the sea. Rumbling Kern, a well-known feature, tends to disappoint, as the sea normally only slips and slops over the rocks rather than producing the famed organ-like compressions. The little village of Boulmer has a good harbour and had a lifeboat as early as 1825. In later years the boat was in the RNLI's service, but after 1968 the service pulled out, the boat continuing with voluntary support.

Easy walking leads to Alnmouth where a low tide ford across the River Aln is not recommended: it is better to walk round by road than to end up wet, muddy, both – or dead. Alnmouth, a steeply-sited village with tall buildings, was once a good port, but in 1806 a violent storm caused the River Aln to cut a new, more northerly, course to the sea, and the harbour was lost under sand dunes. A route is available behind these dunes or, alternatively, the wide, sandy beach can be followed. It is important, when following the beach, to cut inland to Warkworth long before Warkworth Harbour is reached, or a lengthy back-track will be necessary.

Warkworth Castle has an ideal defensive position, topping a hill with the tidal River Coquet forming a moat on three sides. A Norman foundation, the castle passed to the powerful Percy family, who increased and strengthened the fortifications. A bewildering number of Henrys inherited the castle and Shakespeare set three scenes from *Henry IV (Part I)* at Warkworth. Apparently inviolable, the castle was occupied by the Scots for a year in 1644-5. Despite being ravaged for stone in 1672 the ruins are still a commanding sight. The keep was partially restored as a home in the nineteenth century, though the current family seat of the Duke of Northumberland is Alnwick Castle. Warkworth is the last of the Northumberland coastal castles: southwards the coast becomes more industrial, losing its romantic image.

Amble to Marsden Bay (54 mls, 86 km)

Amble is reached by road and a walk through a harbourside picnic area. As its industry declines Amble is developing as a resort: its harbour already has a marina. Offshore is Coquet Island, where St Cuthbert spent time as a hermit. The saint's favourite

bird, the eider duck, is still known locally as 'Cuddy's Duck'. Southward minor roads and tracks are linked around Hauxley Haven to reach the Druridge Bay Country Park. The park has been reclaimed from an open-cast mining site, and though mining prevents the use of other tracks alongside the Bay, there is good walking along the wide bay sands. Come ashore at Cresswell and follow the road to Lynemouth.

Massive industry disfigures Lynemouth, but it has to be admitted that the combination is ingenious with coal from the mine being burnt in the power station to produce the power needed to operate the site's aluminium smelter. Nearby, sea coal, often reduced to grit sized pieces, is gathered into plastic bags for sale. Though relatively cheap, keeping a fire alight with the stuff is a real art.

A path through a wasteland leads to Newbiggin, a seaside resort more cheerful than Lynemouth. St Bartholomew's church, which stands on a headland, has served as a landmark for centuries. Be careful on the footpath leaving Newbiggin, as the mud-like cliffs are forever crumbling and collapsing. Beyond, a turn inland is necessary to cross the River Wansbeck by a bridge from which, there are two ways to reach Blyth. One is via the main road, and the other is via a minor road through industrial Cambois. The latter is to be preferred, if only for the interlude provided by a short ferry journey across the River Blyth. It would be unfair to be too hard on Blyth, for this one-time industrial eyesore is slowly changing its image. The Royal Northumberland Yacht Club has its headquarters here, and two museums, one an old wooden lightship, one concentrating on railways, offer a view of the town's past whilst much of the town centre is an architectural conservation area.

A good beach walk backed by dunes leads from Blyth to a place with the unprepossessing name of Seaton Sluice. Sluice gates were constructed across Seaton Burn in 1690, water being periodically released to scour the harbour of silt. The scheme was a brainchild of the Delaval family, who later commissioned Vanburgh to build the splendid Seaton Delaval Hall a short way inland. For over 200 years, until the 1870s, a flourishing port was backed by industries including mining, quarrying, brick and glass making. All these have now ceased, leaving a quiet resort with a massive sea wall protecting the town cliffs from erosion. To the south, a natural cliff line can be followed towards St Mary's lighthouse which stands on an island, the road to which is cut off

twice daily by the tides.

Whitley Bay is a popular seaside town reached by a variety of high and low level routes. Though the area towards the Tyne is built-up, the walk along the promenade is reasonable and has several points of interest – Cullercoats has a marine laboratory with an aquarium open to the public, while Smugglers Cave is a sea-cut arch.

Rounding Sharpness Point brings Tynemouth priory and castle into view. The priory – the earliest house dates from 650 – became wealthy and, as a result, became a target for sea-borne raiders. Records show that in 1296 practically all the house's wealth was spent on defence. The castle, part of those defences, is well sited, so well that Henry VIII took it over after the Dissolution of the priory.

The mouth of the River Tyne obstructs any immediate plans to press on southwards and a couple of choices present themselves. One is to walk to North Shields and take the ferry across to South Shields, the other is to visit Newcastle-upon-Tyne, several miles inland, but easily reached via the Metro system. From the city, the Metro offers a speedy trip to South Shields.

South Shields has a pleasant park alongside its promenade, though the effect is somewhat spoilt by the funfair blocking the seaward view. Be sure not to miss the 'Tyne' lifeboat which saved over a 1,000 lives before being retired. Alongside it is an anchor thought to be from a ship of the Armada. The town promenade gives way to a clifftop path which winds around the headlands of The Leas, where there is an irritating amount of fencing and warning notices. Is it all really necessary?

At Marsden Bay the National Trust and RSPB manage a nature reserve, though Marsden Rock is the more obvious focus for visitors. This huge but crumbling limestone stack is pierced by an arch, its broad top usually hosting a conference of cormorants. Kittiwakes also use the rock, while the shore usually has curlews, sandpipers, redshanks and oystercatchers. The neat and tidy surroundings of Marsden Bay end at Lizard Point lighthouse where a colliery tip is being reclaimed and a firing range can stop further progress. The cliff path can be used when the range is not active, access being restored to the walker immediately firing ceases.

Looking south along the Northumbrian coast from Dunstanburgh castle

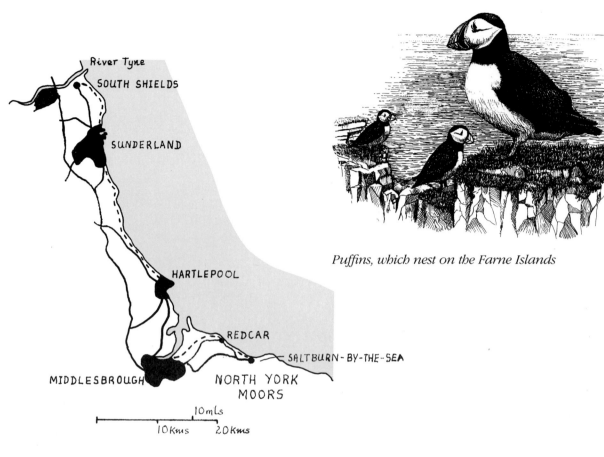

Puffins, which nest on the Farne Islands

Sunderland to Saltburn (53 mls, 85 km)

Entry to Sunderland is by beach or promenade. A huge memorial on the promenade commemorates the Venerable Bede, Sunderland-born, and now known as the 'Father of English History'. Bede wrote a contemporary account of the founding, in 674, of St Peter's, the ancient church in the landscaped area near the harbour. There are several other interesting churches in the town: St Andrew's, founded in 1902, was called the 'Cathedral of the Arts and Crafts Movement' because of its lavishly decorated contents, while St Timothy's is literally shipshape, even possessing an anchor. Today much of Sunderland appears modern, the town having been rebuilt after heavy wartime bombing, but there are several old gems tucked away for the persistent to find.

A cliff path leaves Sunderland for Seaham, though it is occasionally rather too close to a crumbling edge, making a move inland prudent. Seaham can seem a depressing place, with a 'Super Pit' blocking any coastal route out of town, necessitating a long detour through back streets and over wasteland, but things change for the better when a magnificent path, recently constructed alongside the railway, is reached. The path passes several deep, steep-sided, wooded valleys – locally called 'denes' – which are a saving grace of this section of the coast.

Horden Point, immediately southwards, has special significance, being the 500th mile of coastline to be purchased under the National Trust's 'Operation Neptune'. The emphasis will not be on preservation, but improvement, as the area is scarred by colliery wastes. Cleaning up the Durham beaches will undoubtedly be a long-term project. The path from Seaham will eventually be extended around Horden Point, but in the meantime it is as easy to walk along the beach. The first dene reached, at Hawthorn Hive, was a notoriously difficult place to walk but a concrete stairway and well-graded paths now offer a safe crossing. A path leads down to the shore which is a little sterile, though there is an interesting view through a hole in the headland to Seaham Colliery. Beyond the dene the path continues to Beacon Point, the most recent 'Operation Neptune' acquisition, though we are soon back with coal as a noisy conveyor over the path dumps a small mountain of waste from Easington Colliery into the sea. After that dreadful scene the path cuts inland alongside another dene.

Dene Mouth, which is by the shore, is ugly, but the scenery improves greatly on the way inland. The dene, Castle Eden Dene, is wide and wooded, sometimes narrowing to a rocky gorge. An assortment of paths and tracks are available and the area is an extensive nature reserve rich in flora and fauna. The Castle Eden Dene should not be confused with the celebrated Castle Eden Walkway, in another nature reserve much nearer to Billingham.

From Blackhall a reasonable cliff path can be followed, though it becomes clogged with caravans at Crimdon Park. Crimdon is another dene and beyond it a path over the golf course gives a route to Hartlepool. Old Hartlepool sits on a low headland, a town old enough to not only have been invaded by the Vikings, but to have had the event recorded in an Icelandic saga. A maritime museum charts the development of the port. The walk along Hartlepool Sands is excellent, but beyond the North Gare Breakwater progress is blocked by the mouth of the Tees.

To best circumnavigate industrial Teesmouth go to Middlesbrough using the transporter bridge to cross the river. The bridge – the only other one in Britain is at Newport – is a huge blue girderwork construction with a yellow, cable-supended cradle. From Middlesbrough a remarkable footpath follows the railway almost to Redcar, passing through every industrial complex imaginable, each strictly fenced off, but offering strange and intriguing smells. If the thought of this path fails to inspire the walker, the alternative is to take the train to Redcar.

The *Zetland* lifeboat museum is sited on the promenade at Redcar, the *Zetland* being the world's oldest lifeboat, built in 1800 and saving over 500 lives before being retired. Progress is easy to a clifftop walk at Marske which passes a cemetery where Captain Cook's father lies buried, close to the ruined tower of St Germain's church. The cliff line continues to Saltburn-by-the-Sea, a prelude to the Cleveland Way.

Industrial Teeside

Cleveland Way

(OS sheets 94, 101,)

THE CLEVELAND WAY, the second official Long Distance Path (LDP) to be opened, starts at Helmsley and skirts the North York Moors National Park to reach the North Sea Coast at Saltburn-by-the-Sea.

The original village of Saltburn was set where a moors-draining beck reached the sea, and there, at the mouth of the 'burn' the locals panned salt from the North Sea for shipment inland. Now all that remains of the original village is the Ship Inn, famed as a haunt of smugglers, shadowed by Cat Nab, a steep cone of glacial boulder clay, 200 ft (60m) high. The new town, Saltburn-by-the-Sea, is a mid-nineteenth-century piece of opportunism by one Henry Pease, who saw what railways and sea air had done for other men's wallets, and extended the branch line from Redcar to service his new resort. It was, he decided, to be a jewel, and the new town's roads were named appropriately – Diamond, Pearl and so on. It had a pier 1,250 ft (375 m) long, sadly cut in half by a boat in 1924, but it is still serviced by the world's oldest cliff railway. Saltburn today is a shadow of the town in its heyday, though the sands are still as long and flat, and the Rose Walk in the Valley Garden still as excellent when the colours are set.

The Cleveland Way runs beside the Ship Inn, taking the cliff edge past the remains of a Roman signal station on Huntcliff. The station was to warn of North Sea raiders and was excellently set for the purpose, Huntcliff being a superb cliff, nearly 400 ft (120 m) high. Excavation of the station revealed many bodies hurled into a well, the result, presumably, of a surprise attack.

Saltburn to Runswick Bay (13 mls, 21 km)
Ahead now, the view is dominated by the Skinningrove steelworks, the path avoiding the huge site by dropping down to the beach, crossing Skinningrove harbour and rising steeply up Hummersea Cliff. Soon Boulby Head is reached, often claimed to have the highest seacliffs in England, at 660 ft (198 m). This is not, as we have seen, true, but the cliffs are the highest on the eastern coast. Reputedly the cliff is the burial spot of Beowulf who chose it for its height. Certainly it is a superb vantage

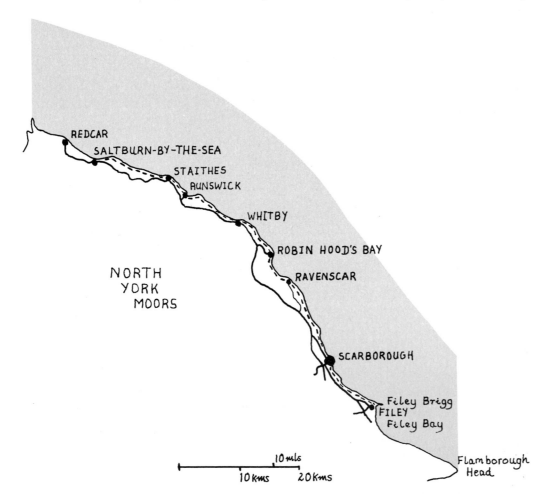

REDCAR
SALTBURN-BY-THE-SEA
STAITHES
RUNSWICK
WHITBY
ROBIN HOOD'S BAY
RAVENSCAR

NORTH
YORK
MOORS

SCARBOROUGH

Filey Brigg
FILEY
Filey Bay

Flamborough Head

10 mls
10 kms   20 kms

The Pier, Saltburn-by-the-Sea (above)

The Cleveland Way runs along the cliff line above Runswick Bay

Staithes

point, and the route forward to Staithes can be readily traced.

Staithes is one of the most photographed spots on the north-east coast and is often described as the Clovelly of the North. Such comparisons always seen back-handed compliments and they mask the village's considerable charms: Dog Laup is a narrow alley of great character; the boats – cobles – in the small harbour would be recognised by Captain Cook, who was an apprentice in a haberdashery here in a shop long since devoured by the sea; and the Cod and Lobster Inn which once had the bowsprit of a ship smash through its window so close is it to the harbour wall.

From Staithes the way keeps to the clifftops, passing the now disused Port Mulgrave, until it drops into Runswick, a far prettier village than Staithes, though not as neatly set. Today, the village is chiefly of holiday homes, a far cry from the community days in 1901 when the menfolk's fishing fleet was trapped in the bay by a ferocious storm, and the women and old men launched the lifeboat to bring them safely home. The walker can follow the beach around Runswick Bay passing, at about half distance, the Hob Holes, caves that were once the home of a goblin who could cure whooping cough in children. Near the eastern end of the bay the cliffs must be regained, offering an excellent view of much-mauled Kettleness. The headland of Kettleness was one of the largest local sources of alum – a natural mineral used in the tanning industry – and open-cast mining has reduced the cliff to half its original height. The

mining also made the cliff unstable, and on a stormy night in 1829 the rain-lubricated, mine-loosened boulder clay slid into the sea taking the village of Kettleness with it. Fortunately an alum boat was offshore and all the villagers were rescued, but the village was never re-built.

Kettleness to Filey (40 mls, 64 km)

Beyond Kettleness, the way reaches and follows a superb stretch of sand, from Sandsend to Whitby. Whitby is where Bram Stoker set the arrival of Count Dracula in England, and many features in the book can still be located. It was home, too, of the local jet industry, the hard black mineral having been known since Roman times, but only having achieved real popularity after Queen Victoria wore it as a funereal gem. The town's prosperity was not, however, based on jet, but on whaling, Whitby having been England's greatest whaling port in the mid-nineteenth century. The whaling was part of a great seafaring tradition: Captain Cook's first seafaring positions were on Whitby colliers, and his famous voyages were made in the same ships.

The Cleveland Way passes the uncompromisingly sited Whitby Abbey. The town's first abbey was founded in 655, and is famous for hosting the synod of 664 that decided in favour of the Roman, rather than the Celtic, church in Britain. That building was destroyed in the ninth century by Norse raiders, the present building being started in the mid-twelfth century and falling into disrepair after its dissolution. The east wall, the major remaining structure, is magnificent.

South from the abbey the coast is famous for its fossils, and equally good for its bird-life. Robin Hood's Bay is another pretty and beautifully located village. The name is a mystery: even the legends tying the Sherwood archer to the north-east coast are of poor quality. One suggestion is that the village was named for the forest sprite Robin Goodfellow. Certainly Boggle Hole, in the bay that shares the village's name, is named for a local sprite.

At Boggle Hole the Way leaves the beach to climb steeply to Ravenscar from where the view back to the bay is as good as any on the route. Ahead now is a ravishing piece of cliff walking, the view south extending as far as Flamborough Head, the local views being of 'wykes', small coves. Hayburn Wyke is a nature reserve through which a small beck runs, waterfalling its way onto the beach. Cloughton Wyke

is bigger, and is a noted sea-bird nesting site. Beyond, the cliff scenery is no less beautiful, especially at the hauntingly named Sailor's Grave. Thereafter the Way is followed easily to Scarborough.

Scarborough has a curious mixture of styles. The Way enters past the Yorkshire cricket ground and reaches the castle mound and old harbour. The castle has a long and interesting history, having played a major part in the Civil War. The harbour area has a fine array of old houses and the churchyard holds the remains of Anne Brontë. Beyond the harbour is the modern seaside resort, many a yard of amusements, etc., before the Spa town with its elegant architecture is reached. The Grand Hotel was claimed to be Europe's finest, while the Spa itself is a marvel of mid-nineteenth century building.

The Way leaves Scarborough along the splendid Esplanade, taking a cliff path around Carnelian Bay – named for the mineral that can be found there – and then crossing a less interesting stretch of coast to Filey Brigg. This extraordinary feature is said by local legend to be the start of a bridge the Devil was building from Yorkshire to Europe, but which he gave up after dropping his hammer. Another legend has it that a dragon died here, the Brigg being its fossilised bones. Either way it is a fascinating spot; the rocks oddly etched into hundreds of teeming rock pools. Be careful, though, the swift tides that cover the Brigg can surprise the unwary.

Filey lies at the end of the Cleveland Way, a failed spa town, now a quiet, restrained resort once home to the last man to be publicly executed in Scotland. That is, perhaps, not the lasting memory with which the town would have you depart, so visit the church, a magnificent, almost complete Norman structure, finely set above the sea.

Whitby Abbey standing above the twin-piered harbour entrance

Filey to Hunstanton

(OS sheets 101, 107, 113, 131, 132)

Filey to Patrington (89 mls, 142 km)

THIS SECTION OF coast divides into three distinct regions, the Holderness peninsula, the Lincolnshire coast and the Wash, though there is one constant factor binding the whole together – the wind. This dominant, unseen, force is a constant companion on any walk along a coastline that could, at one time, reasonably have been claimed as a colony of Scandinavia.

For 6 miles (10 km) from Filey firm sands sweep round Filey Bay taking the walker past numerous caravan and holiday parks to Speeton where the cliffs must, finally, be climbed. The path along the edge of the chalk cliffs rises to over 400 ft (120 m) at Bempton, and continues all the way around the nose of Flamborough Head into Bridlington. On it the walker follows a thin strip of vegetation between the cliff edge and cultivated fields. This narrow strip is covered with chalk-loving plants – field mouse ear, rough hawkbit, and many more, while the cliff has colonies of pyramidal orchid and red campion. The plants in turn attract the butterflies, and other insects. Look out for the vivid red and black six-spot Burnet moth on the deep yellow birdsfoot trefoil.

The locals used to descend these cliffs on ropes, a practice known as climming, to gather eggs for sale in local markets or for export to Leeds where the whites were used in leather manufacture. Thankfully, that is all in the past, and today the RSPB owns 5 miles (8 km) of the cliffs around Bempton. Here, among the gulls and auks, is Britain's only mainland colony of gannets.

Britain's only mainland colony of gannets at Bempton

At Thornwick Nab it is possible to descend to a small bay strewn with huge chalk boulders, though this means a climb up to Flamborough Head of 150 ft (45 m). The lighthouse here is 92 ft (28 m) high and was built without the aid of scaffolding. Nearby is a hexagonal tower built as a beacon in 1673. Two thousand years ago there was a fortress on this headland protected by the sea on three sides and on the landward side by Danes Dyke, running the whole 3 miles (5 km) from North Landing to South Landing. Its date puts it 800 years before the Danes, the name being from local tradition after a successful Danish landing near the Head. The chalk cliffs at the

Bridlington, a fishing port turned resort in the shelter of Flamborough Head

head are sculpted into stacks and arches which can be explored at low tide from Selwicks Bay reached by a steep path from close to the point of the headland.

Lying under the protection of Flamborough Head is Bridlington, a still busy fishing port which also doubles as a resort. A good museum to the town's history stands near the harbour whose piers were built from the stones of the town's fourteenth-century priory.

From Bridlington there is fine walking on low sandy cliffs and a narrow, firm beach all the way down the Holderness Peninsula to Spurn. The flat peninsula is prime agricultural land, its rich soil deposited by glaciers in the last Ice Age, but the sea is eating away at the shore by between 3 and 5 ft (0.9 – 1.5 m) a year. The cliffs crumble into the sea, leaving roads to end abruptly, and Second World War pill boxes, that once overlooked the North Sea, to lie under every high tide. At Hornsea – where a sixteenth-century farmhouse in the main street houses a museum on Holderness life – and elsewhere, huge concrete walls hold back the sea in an effort to halt the erosion.

Spurn Point has no rock base, and is built up of material eroded away from further up the coast, the sand and shingle spit now stretching one third of the way across the mouth of the Humber. It is an important nature reserve, famous for the birds that rest here during their migration. Spurn is constantly growing but about every 250 years the sea breaks through the neck and washes the tip away. Each time though, a new tip develops slightly to the west of the old one. On the very tip is a 120 ft (36 m) high lighthouse built in 1893 and England's only full-time lifeboat crew. West of the tip at low tide is a huge expanse of mud flats, a place for waders.

The walk along the Humber to Hull, by any of a number of routes that link road and paths to avoid the muddiest banks, can be depressing. The Humber drains one fifth of all of England's river water and its banks are strewn with oil refineries, chemical plants and tanker terminals that make it the third most polluted estuary in Britain. One highlight is the church of St Patrick at Patrington, with its beautiful 189 ft (57m) spire. The church was built on the lines of a cathedral in the thirteenth and fourteenth centuries, and is a near perfect example of English Gothic architecture.

Kingston upon Hull to Ingoldmells (73 mls, 117 km)

Kingston upon Hull, at the junction of the rivers Hull and Humber, was the hardest hit of northern towns in the Second World War and has been almost completely rebuilt, though parts of the 'Old Town' remain. The Kingston in the name – now usually shortened to Hull – is from 'King's Town', the King being Edward I who gave the port its first charter in 1299. Though known as a fishing port, Hull's modern docks, which take up 7 miles (11 km) of the Humber waterfront, are largely a container port and ferry terminal with only a small fleet of fishing vessels. The town was the birth place of William Wilberforce, the anti-slavery campaigner, and his house can still be seen in Old Town.

Take a bus from Hull to Hessle and the Humber bridge. Opened in 1981 it has the longest single span in the world at 4,626 ft (1,388 m) and took nine years to build. There is no toll for walkers and it is quite an experience, albeit windy, to cross. Daniel Defoe might have been pleased to try. In his day there was a ferry which took four hours, and he wrote that Barton – where the bridge ends – was 'noted for nothing . . . but an ill-favoured dangerous ferry'.

At Barton, the Romans commanded a 'ford'! Ermine Street, which linked London and York, crossed the Humber just west of here and it was possible to walk across at low tide – not something the walker should try. Today, Barton is a tidy market town surrounded by potato and turnip fields, with one of the best preserved Saxon churches – St Peter's – in the country. The footpath running right underneath the Humber Bridge is the beginning of the Viking Way which eventually wends its way inland across the Lincolnshire wolds. However, we go eastward on a shore path that leads all the way to Immingham Dock, from where a road must be taken to Grimsby.

If anything the southern shore of the Humber is more industrialised than the north: at New Holland is the rotting wooden pier of the old steam ferry terminal which the bridge pushed into retirement. From it the view of Hull and its docks at night is well worth seeing. Some of the Pilgrim Fathers set out from Immingham in 1608, though their departure point is now buried under a mound of concrete and steel, a legacy of the North Sea oil boom in the 1960s.

Named after a Danish fisherman called 'Grim', who landed here 1,000 years ago and started selling fish, Grimsby developed rapidly, in the nineteenth cen-

tury, into a major fishing port. Even after the limits imposed by the Cod Wars it is still impossible to think of Grimsby without thinking of fishing, though now it is more of a fish processing centre and distribution market. Around the old dock edge survives the largest fish market in Britain – fish are unloaded at night and auctioned in the early hours of the morning in a strange world of white coats, wellies, loud garbled sentences, furtive nods, glances and incredible smells.

Grimsby runs into Cleethorpes, where a plaque informs you that you are on the Greenwich Meridian, zero longitude, and that it is 9,895 (15,832 km) miles to the South Pole, but only 2,513 (4,020 km) to the North. Just south of Cleethorpes, at Tetney, about 5 miles (8 km) nearer the South Pole, amid a glorious saltmarsh full of sea lavender and samphire, lies the seaward end of the Louth Navigation Canal. Built in 1770 during the Industrial Revolution, it linked Louth, 12 miles (19 km) away, with the sea and was capable of carrying sea-going vessels. Like most canals, the coming of the railways sounded its death knoll. On the shore at Tetney Haven is an RSPB Reserve of ungrazed saltmarsh, deep creeks and low sand banks, which hold a colony of little terns, one of our rarest breeding sea-birds. High spring tides wash away many of their early nests and the wardens have to move nests higher up the tide line.

The lie of the land from here down to Mablethorpe has changed little since the Viking times, and many place names derive from the Danish, with the suffixes 'by' meaning settlement and 'thorpe' meaning farmstead. 'Much Pillaged' would have been a good name for a village hereabouts.

The shoreline can be closely followed, the walker dipping inland occasionally to avoid mud-flats or a danger area. The coast seems quiet and the beaches devoid of wildlife, but there are many burrowing creatures – cockles, tellins, razorshells and sea potatoes – living in the fertile sands which stretch out for miles at low tide, and support huge numbers of waders.

At Donna Nook, named after a ship wrecked here, the ancient dune systems are alive with rabbits, despite which the area is a haven for unusual plant communities. Protected by the MoD firing range – watch for the red flags – it is also a National Nature

Spurn Head, the narrow, moving sand spit at the mouth of the Humber

Natterjack Toad. These rare amphibians are found in the dunes at Saltfleet-by-Theddlethorpe

Reserve, as is the Saltfleet-by-Theddlethorpe dune system, home to the natterjack toad.

The shoreline south of here is followed by linking the promenades of small holiday resorts – Mablethorpe, Sutton on Sea, Sandilands, Ingoldmells – to reach Skegness.

Mablethorpe was chosen for its peace by Tennyson, who stayed on the day his first book of verse was published. He would find it less quiet today, unless he retreated to the dunes. Sutton is a quieter resort while Ingoldmells is different again, famous as the site of the first Butlin's holiday camp in 1936.

Skegness to Boston (27 mls, 43 km)

The best monument to this section of coastline is the town of Skegness. 'Skeggy', as it is affectionately known, was planned and built as a holiday resort in the 1870s and was much beloved by Tennyson. John Hassall's 'Jolly Fisherman' poster, commissioned in 1908 by the railway to advertise day trips, reads 'Skegness Is So Bracing', a gross understatement, but who cares about the wind when you are a kid? The resort boasts 6 miles (9.5 km) of excellent sand and a promenade garden with over 50,000 flowers, re-stocked annually.

Leaving the candy floss behind the walker meets yet more dunes where the Lincolnshire coast turns the corner into the Wash at Gibraltar Point. The Point Nature Reserve here covers the series of sand dune ridges that run parallel to the sea. The oldest dunes,

several hundred years old, are now covered in a thick, impenetrable forest of sea buckthorn whose bright orange berries are a feast for thousands of redwings, fieldfares and many other migrating birds in the autumn. In winter there are shore larks and snow buntings, with hen harriers and short-eared owls quartering low over the marshes, while out on the mud-flats, often miles out into the Wash, brent geese and waders feed. From the Point, on a clear day, the cliffs at Hunstanton, fourteen miles (22.5 km) away on the other side of the Wash can be seen.

South of the Point the walker is forced inland to Wainfleet. This small market town, which used to be a port but is now 5 miles (8 km) from the sea, stands on the River Steeping, which begins life as Tennyson's babbling brook deep in wolds at Somersby.

Southward from Wainfleet to the seawall the walker begins to get a real sense of the fens, and an admiration for the folk who live and work here. At Friskney, reclamation work has involved three sea-walls, the inner two now redundant. Here again the salt marsh is protected by an MoD firing range on Friskney flats, though it would be foolish to leave the guidance of the seawall: the salt marsh is a maze of creeks, subject to uncannily fast tides and the walker would almost inevitably get lost, bogged down or, more than likely, both. At Freiston Shore is a small village behind the meagre shelter of the sea wall. It has a much welcome pub, oft frequented by bird watchers, and is connected by a maze of small roads, criss-crossing the fens to other small hamlets.

Just beyond Freiston Shore the sea wall reaches the wide channel of The Haven which can only be crossed at Boston. Ships from Boston use the waterway – the last stretch of the River Witham to gain the Wash, taking the Boston Deeps from the shore to avoid treacherous sandbanks on their way out to the North Sea. On the seawall near Fishtoft is a memorial to the Pilgrim Fathers who tried to go that way in 1607 but were betrayed by their Dutch Captain, and gaoled in Boston.

At the end of the thirteenth century Boston was the most important port in England, a position it maintained until the fifteenth century, when the River Witham silted up. In the late nineteenth century The Haven was cut, and once again Boston is a busy port. The town itself is a fascinating mix of port and agricultural market town with some superb medieval and Georgian architecture. Its crowning glory is the

Boston Stump, the Tower of St Botolph's Church

'Stump', a 272 ft (81.5 km) high octagonal lantern tower at the church of St Botolph. St Botolph founded a monastary here in 654, but this was destoyed by the Danes 200 years later. The church was begun in 1310 though the stump was added later. There are 365 steps which lead to the top where a lantern was anciently used to guide shipping through the Wash. The view from the top across the Wash and fens is tremendous: on a clear day Lincoln Cathedral, 32 miles (51 km) to the north-west, can be seen. The cells where the Pilgrim Fathers were held can be seen in the old Guildhall, now a museum. The original Fathers fled to Holland before their famous journey in 1620 but a second group actually left Boston itself in 1630, founding the city of Boston, Massachusetts.

Between Boston and Kings Lynn in Norfolk, across the bottom of the Wash, lies the true fen country, though little true fenland now remains, most having been drained and tamed into agricultural land. The land is empty, dotted with the odd farm building, wind pump and spire, with dykes instead of hedges. In places, so little distinguishes the landscape that an old farm gate becomes a prominent feature. On the Wash side of the seawall is a wilderness of such beauty and isolation that its vastness becomes overpowering as salt marshes full of lapwings, reshanks and snipe give way to huge mud-flats and sand banks. Nearly half the area of the Wash has been reclaimed since Saxon times. Reclamation began in

Looking north along the sand dunes to Skegness

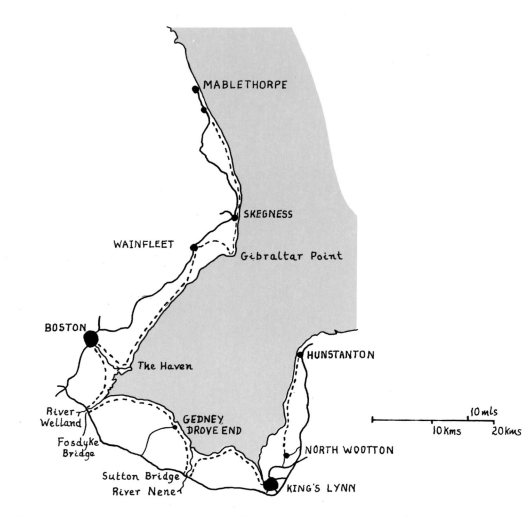

marsh. It was not the happiest time of the King's reign – he had just signed the Magna Carta.

The walker heads back to the twin lighthouses from the bridge, reaching Terrington Marsh and crossing into Norfolk. This area is the least inhabited part of the fens and also the least accessible. In summer it seems empty, though in winter it is alive with ducks and geese. The marsh wall curves gently round to reach the Great Ouse, the last of the five rivers which drain into the Wash, which is followed to King's Lynn.

Lynn, as it is known locally, was called Lun in the Domesday Book and was an important port in the fourteenth century. It was then known as Bishop's Lynn but the name was changed when Henry VIII granted it a charter. It is still an active port and a prosperous town, with an array of elegant houses spanning the ages from medieval to Georgian. The Guildhall of 1421 is faced in a chequer-board pattern of flint and stone and houses a fine museum, while the custom house by the river is an elegant seventeenth-century building.

North from Lynn the coast is difficult to reach, and it is best to go to North Wootton from where a road crosses familiar fen landscape as it heads for the seawall. Following the shore of the Wash north, however, changes soon become apparent: there is shingle and the sea is not too far away. The RSPB has a fine reserve at Snattishorn, with inter-tidal flats, shingle banks, and worked out shingle pits. Common terns nest on islands in the lagoons and the shingle holds its own unique flora of yellow horned poppies, sea rocket and sea beet. Following the shingle brings the walker to a large seaside village at Heacham where, in the fields surrounding the town, just a mile inland, is the centre of Norfolk's lavender growing industry. With the wind in the right direction July and August can smell very sweet.

earnest in the seventeenth century when Dutch engineers cut drains and built windmills, but now electric pumps lift the water into artificial channels, keeping the land dry. The weather does its occasional best to undo their efforts, the Lincolnshire dialect having words to cover the variety of rains. Here it does not rain – it kelshes, jugs, pelts and siles it down.

River Welland to Hunstanton (62 mls, 99 km)
From Boston the seawall goes south, cutting inland along the River Welland on its way to Spalding and the bulb fields. At Fosdyke Bridge, built in 1910, the Welland is crossed for a trek back out to the edge of

the Wash. A mile (1.6 km) inland you can see Holbeach St Matthew. The original town of Holbeach lies 8 miles (13 km) inland. It was once on the edge of the Wash, but as drainage pushed the sea further away it spawned satellite villages like St Matthew.

After miles of open marsh the walker passes the village of Gedney Drove End to reach Guy's Head, where the River Nene reaches the Wash. There are a pair of disused lighthouses on either side of the channel, one of which was once home to Sir Peter Scott. The Nene must be followed inland to Sutton Bridge where King John is said to have lost his treasures when a carriage carrying his belongings became bogged down and swallowed up in the

Sutton Bridge, where the walker must cross the River Nene to reach the southern shore of the Wash

The Norfolk Coastal Path and North-east Norfolk

(OS sheets 132, 133, 134,)

Hunstanton to Holkham (20 mls, 32 km)

HUNSTANTON HAS THE distinction of being the only 'west coast' resort on England's 'east coast' and has what is probably the shortest pier in the country – not even extending as far as the seaward edge of the promenade. The rest of the pier was swept away during the gales in 1978.

Near the town's war memorial is a second memorial to the 31 people – including 16 Americans – who died when the seawall to the south of Hunstanton was breached by the great tidal surge of 31 January 1953. Near to both is the first signpost for the Norfolk Coastal Path that runs from here to Cromer. The path starts along the top of Hunstanton's famous colour-banded cliffs, comprised of layers of brown carstone and red and white chalk, they are the northern extremity of the low range of chalk hills that form the East Anglian Heights. A little way along, just before the now disused Hunstanton lighthouse, ruined walls are all that remains of St Edmund's chapel – built near the spot that the soon to be King of the East Angles, and later Christian martyr, landed from Saxony in 855.

After a mile or so the cliffs drop away, to be replaced by drifting sand dunes and the official path follows the south side of the golf course (where on one gate-post a notice warns that there is 'no public right of way', beside the signpost for the LDP!). Beyond the Holme Dunes nature reserve and bird observatory – where almost 300 species of bird and over 350 species of moth have been seen – the dunes give way to a sea wall which heads back inland to the village of Thornham. Near here the Peddars Way – a Roman road that once ran from Colchester – meets a sudden and seemingly inexplicable ending. The most likely explanation is that a ferry once crossed the Wash from here as another road continues on the far shore to Lincoln. The ferry link between the two towns was probably preferred to the long and hazardous detour around the Fens.

The next stretch of marshes, around Titchwell, were drained in the late eighteenth century using techniques that avoided the construction of embankments and the walker is faced with either a couple of miles of road-walking (not advisable in the holiday season) or a slightly longer detour inland along the official line of the Norfolk Coastal Path. Either way the walker ends up at the village of Brancaster which, as its name suggests, was the site of a Roman settlement. A lane leads seaward here, but the walker must follow the landward edge of the saltings along a path that has now, thankfully, been laid with old railway sleepers. The line of the path itself is wet, even in midsummer.

A National Trust sign reveals the location of Branodunum – now little more than a grass-covered mound – the most northerly of the 'Forts of the Saxon Shore' built to defend Roman Britain against Anglo-Saxon raiders.

A little further on is Brancaster Staithe, the first of many yachting centres on the coast that now occupy what were once thriving ports. Though no longer a port, Brancaster Staithe is one of the few places where shell fishing, for mussels and whelks, continues. Much of this area was acquired by the National Trust in 1967 as part of their Operation Neptune. Offshore here is Scolt Head Island, a nature reserve. Access is restricted, and is by boat only. Do not attempt to walk across at low tide, the saltings are very dangerous.

Between Brancaster and Burnham the walker uses the windmill at Burnham Staithe as a beacon, following the seawall between saltings and drained marshland. The Domesday Book listed seven Burnhams and all but Sutton and Westgate remain today though most are missed by the walker, who keeps to the coast. Horatio Nelson was born at Burnham Thorpe where his father was the parson, which explains the number of local pubs with names like The Hero and The Victory. Burnham Deepdale church has, unusually, a round tower, the Normans finding that this shape was easier to fashion than a square when using the local flint.

The footpath along the seawall on the east side of Burnham Harbour carries the walker quickly along to Holkham Sands, perhaps the finest beach in England and another nature reserve, the largest coastal

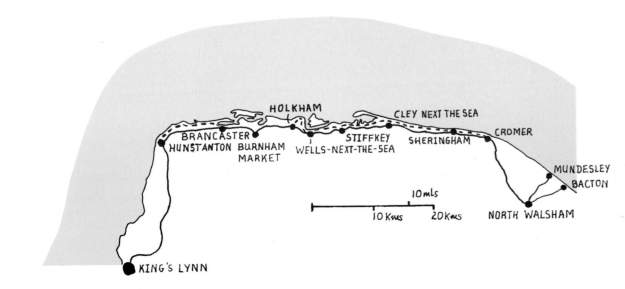

Looking west over Fresh Marshes. To the right is the sand bar of Blakeney Point while to the extreme far left are the Morston and Stiffkey Salt Marshes

The Saxon Round Tower, Burnham Deepdale Church

reserve in the country. This is one of the few stretches of the north Norfolk coast where it is actually possible to walk along the shore though, perversely, the Coastal Path takes an inland route along the southern edge of the dunes and on through the nineteenth-century plantations of Corsican pine. Holkham village is best known as the home of Thomas Coke whose experiments to improve cereal and animal stocks earned him the title 'first farmer in England'. The seventeenth-century Holkham Hall is the finest in East Anglia, with splendid gardens designed by Nesfield and later improved by 'Capability' Brown. Although trees screen the hall from the coast, the tall obelisk in the centre of the grounds can be seen – just – away to the south-west from the end of Wells harbour.

Wells-next-the-Sea to Cromer (24 mls, 38 km)

Nearing Wells the coast takes a dramatic turn inland at the lifeboat station, and a wide embankment carries the footpath and a road between the harbour and low-lying reclaimed marshland. Near the lifeboat station a marker shows the height reached by floodwater in 1953 and again in 1978.

Wells-next-the-Sea is the only working harbour left on the north Norfolk coast and as well as numerous fishing boats and yachts the occasional coaster is seen by the quay. Sadly, the atmosphere of the quay is spoilt by the trappings of a modern holiday resort.

After a short stretch of embankment the coastal path winds on along the inward edge of salt marsh for several miles to Blakeney. A distant gleam of white and the faint roar of surf are the only indications here of the sea, which at low tide may be over 2 miles (3 km) away. At high tide it creeps in, filling the tiny creeks almost to the edge of the farmland.

The vast expanse of salt marsh east of Wells is a continuation of the Holkham National Nature Reserve, and a few paths lead out to the sands at its edge. Further along is Stiffkey, once pronounced Stewkey and famous for its cockles, Stewkey Blues. Stiffkey Marshes are owned by the National Trust, who have an information centre at Morston harbour.

Blakeney church is a prominent landmark for some miles and is unusual in having a second, smaller, tower at the east end of the chancel from which a light was once hung to guide ships into the harbour. Blakeney is mostly a flint-built village with arguably the most picturesque waterfront in Norfolk. From it boats take tourists to Blakeney Point where the nature reserve is famous for its seals. Unfortunately a vast proportion of Britain's seal population died in the tragic epidemic of 1988 and this is, for the present, no longer the attraction it was.

A circuitous walk along the seawall around Blakeney marshes leads to Cley-next-the-Sea, where the windmill, now a private house, is one of the best preserved in Norfolk. Between Cley and Weybourne is a vast area of marsh and meadow used mainly for cattle grazing. Much of this is the Cley Nature Reserve, bordered on the south by the A149 and the north by the high shingle bank that continues westward to form Blakney Point. Substantial as the embankment seems, it has suffered serious erosion in recent years and has had frequently to be rebuilt. The local people fear it is only a matter of time before it is breached again, as it was in 1953 when all the land north of the road flooded.

The Norfolk Coastal Path follows the inward edge

The Old Windmill, Cley-next-the-Sea

of the shingle, since walking along the top only aids erosion, until the first low sand cliffs rise at Kelling Hard. Further on, Weybourne, with its fishing boats on the foreshore, is protected from the sea by just a low shingle bank between cliffs. In the past the village's position, a good anchorage and protecting cliffs, have made it a popular spot with invading forces. An old local saying is 'He who would old England win, must at Weybourne Hope begin.'

From Weybourne a clifftop path leads steadily upwards towards Sheringham with fine views inland to the wooded hills of the Cromer ridge, the remains of glacial moraine from the last Ice Age. Sheringham is a pleasant seaside town with a suprisingly short sea frontage as it too occupies a small gap in the cliffs. At the centre of the seafront is the old lifeboat house, now a museum and home to the *Henry Ramsey Upcher* believed to be the only remaining rowed lifeboat in existence.

Cley-next-the-Sea. In the village is one of Norfolk's best preserved windmills

The official line of the coastal path now takes another swing inland, but it is possible to continue along the clifftop and, better, along the shore past West and East Runton to Cromer.

Seen from the pier, Cromer seems to cower behind the 'Hotel de Paris', the hotel itself standing behind a high flint retaining wall. The town is best known for its crabs, and its lifeboat coxswain – Henry Blogg – who during 53 years service helped to save 873 lives. He won numerous awards including the George Cross, and the RNLI's Gold Medal no less than three times and was described after his death in 1954 as one of the bravest men that ever lived. The old lifeboat house is now a museum, in part a memorial to Blogg. Since 1967 the lifeboat has been launched from the end of Cromer pier.

Originally Cromer was an inland village, Shipden having been the fishing port. Today the strip of land on which Shipden stood has gone. It has been said that Yarmouth is built upon the remains of Shipden since much of the material taken from here is carried south.

Overstrand to Kessingland (53 mls, 85 km)

The Norfolk Coastal Path ends at Cromer, though it is possible to continue walking the coast to the Suffolk border and the start of that county's coastal path. Beyond Cromer the cliffs rise steeply to almost 300 ft (90 m) towards Overstrand. The church at nearby Sidestrand exists only because it was moved inland, stone by stone, in the last century: only the tower was left behind and that was claimed by the sea, just as a much earlier church had been.

At Trimingham a different hazard arose after the Second World War, when it was discovered that cliff falls had left dozens of mines – orignally planted as clifftop defences – strewn across the beach. A bomb disposal unit was permanently stationed here and the beach was only re-opened in 1966.

The shoreline can be comfortably followed now to Mundesley, a pleasant, quiet resort, despite the inevitable caravan parks. A couple of miles on, Bacton is the site of a Gas Treatment Plant, as the terminal is correctly known, opened in 1968 following the discovery of the 'Leman' gas field two years earlier. The plant is capable of supplying 60 per cent of the country's gas requirements.

The cliffs the walker follows are much lower here but still subject to severe erosion. At Happisburgh (pronounced Haze-borough) a wooden wall has

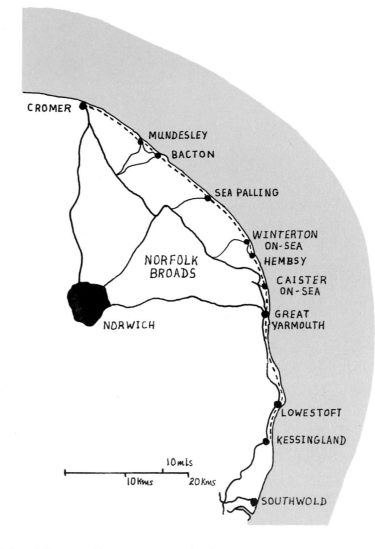

been built seawards of the cliffs, partially protecting them from the waves. Happisburgh Sands were a notorious graveyard for shipping and the church, with its 110 ft (33 m) tower, was used as a lighthouse until 1791. The modern lighthouse is safely inland, to the south of the village.

From the village the cliffs decline into marram dunes that continue southwards to Winterton-on-Sea. There is no footpath on this section and the walker has either to follow the road or to follow the beach if the tide allows. Eccles is another village that has all but vanished beneath the sea: it lost its church tower,

the last part remaining, in 1895. Sea Palling is like a desert town with sand blowing endlessly over its streets and in winter, when it is deserted, it looks even more forlorn.

A largely unfrequented beach, backed by high dunes, stretches south from here towards Winterton, a good place to escape the summer crowds, though this coast is also notorious for its sea-fret or 'haar' The wide expanse of established dunes to the north

Great Yarmouth, with its famous amusement park

of Winterton is now a nature reserve, home to adders and natterjack toads. These dunes formed at the foot of former cliffs, the line of which can still be seen in places, especially to the south of Winterton where tiny shacks that are used as holiday homes line the ancient beach, hidden from the sea by the dune ridge.

Staying on the shoreline we reach Hemsby, California and Caister, all now little more than holiday suburbs of Great Yarmouth, the old villages overrun by sprawling holiday camps that are hidden by the sandy cliffs. California is named after its pub, but Caister has a more distinguished pedigree, named after its *costa* or Roman fortress. In the second century it was capital of the Iceni, Boudicca's people. Its superb castle was the first in England to be brick built. It was built in the early fifteenth century by Sir John Fastolf, commander of archers at Agincourt and whose name, it has been suggested, gave Shakespeare his idea for Falstaff.

Yarmouth, which became 'Great' when Henry II granted it a charter in 1272, stands upon a long sandy spit extending out across the combined estuary of the Bure, Waveney and Yare rivers. This has formed since Roman times when the fort of Gariannon (Burgh Castle) on the south side of Breydon Water was built. Three miles (5 km) of glittering amusement arcades, theatre halls and funfairs back the wide sandy beach

Swallowtail Butterfly, found only in East Anglia

of one of the east coast's leading holiday resorts. But behind the holiday front Yarmouth hides a wealth of historic buildings: the twelfth-century church of St Nicholas is believed to be the largest parish church in the country while a few of the old 'rows' – narrow lanes, one only 30 inches (76 cm) wide – can still be seen, especially by the market place. A large stretch of the old town wall, built in 1285, also still stands towards the southern end of the town. Beyond this, housing gives way to a modern industrial estate with a caravan site backing the beach. Almost hidden amongst all this is Nelson's monument, erected in 1819 and topped by a statue of Britannia who faces not seawards as might be expected but to the north-west. The tower is open to the public during July and August. Nearby, at the old fish wharf – Yarmouth was once the centre of Britain's herring industry – a passenger ferry to Gorleston (not operating on Sundays) saves the walk back to the bridge over the Yare.

Gorleston is a quieter, more relaxed resort with a steep grassy slope dropping down to the promenade and its hotels and guest houses standing discreetly back from the edge. From it the cliffs take the walker in an almost unbroken run to Lowestoft, though the walk is occasionally squeezed by caravan sites and holiday camps. South of Hopton the walker crosses into Suffolk.

Lowestoft Ness is the most easterly point on the British mainland but has little in common with the country's other extremities. Once, fishermen's shacks and curing huts stood on the shingle foreshore, but now an industrial estate compares unfavourably with the lonely peninsulas of the Lizard, Ardnamurchan and Dunnet Head.

Lowestoft itself had, for centuries, been an important fishing port and great rival to Yarmouth, but by the middle of this century, the great herring shoals had gone. At first the town turned to shipbuilding, then to the servicing and supplying of North Sea platforms, but with the future of these industries too now in doubt only tourism remains. Unfortunately, for the tourist Lowestoft has little to offer that Yarmouth cannot better.

South of the harbour a promenade runs for 2 miles (3.2 km) along the foot of low cliffs until suddenly ending where the coast takes a step backwards at Pakefield. Between 1900 and 1947 the cliffs here receded over 500 ft (150 m) with the loss of dozens of homes, but since then the coast has stabilised and

now a wide shingle beach lies at the foot of the overgrown cliff.

Ahead the cliff offers easy walking to Kessingland, from where a wild and lonely coastline of low sandy cliffs, backed by empty heathland, is followed by the Suffolk Heritage Coast Path.

The Suffolk Heritage Coast

(OS sheets 156, 169)

Benacre Ness to Thorpeness (21 mls, 33 km)

THE PATH LEADS past Benacre Ness where a couple of disused gravel pits are now the preserve of wild ducks and gulls, and then, as the coast closes in again, along the top of low, crumbling sandstone cliffs.

At Benacre Broad the cliffs give way to a wide sand and shingle beach that holds back a small reed-bordered lake, an RSPB reserve with a hide on its south edge. The beach here, as with several other areas along the coast, is a nesting ground for terns and is fenced off during the breeding season.

Cliffs rise again for a couple of miles, then drop back again at Covehithe Broad, a shallow expanse of water that is rapidly decreasing in size as reeds spread and cause the broad to silt up. Once these reeds were cut annually for roofing, but as the trade has died they have been left to spread. The church at Covehithe has been constructed within the ruined walls of a much larger one. The original building was built by wealthy sheep farmers when Suffolk was, with its woollen trade, one of the richest parts of England and each village vied with its neighbours for the largest and most impressive church. When the wool trade decreased the villagers were unable to maintain the church and in the mid-seventeenth century it was demolished, a smaller replacement being built within the walls.

Easton is the third and last of the 'Suffolk Broads', formed like those at Covehithe and Benacre, where the shingle beach has barred a small stream. The cliffs beyond it are another scene of rapid erosion, although concrete defences have helped slow the action at the southern end. It has been suggested that at one time Easton Ness was the most easterly point in Britain, but the coast is now 2 miles (3.2 km) west of Lowestoft Ness.

Southwold, with its famous Adnams brewery from which beer is still delivered locally by horsedrawn dray, is built on an island formed by the River Blyth and the now silted Buss Creek, a haven for toads. It is a pleasant seaside town, largely unspoilt, except for the ill-placed short pier at its north end.

A jumble of old cottages crowd around the gleaming white lighthouse and a little further along cannons still guard Gun Hill, overlooking the scene of the battle of Sole Bay. It is recorded that townspeople lined the cliffs to watch the English and French warships narrowly defeat the Dutch fleet here in 1672, but this was only after the mayor had ordered the bridge over Buss Creek to be destroyed to ensure enough menfolk remained to defend the town had the outcome been different. The original cannons of Gun Hill preceded the battle, having been installed to defend the town against pirates from Dunkirk. The church contains 'Southwold Jack', a fifteenth-century soldier carved in oak whose axe strikes a bell when a cord is pulled, to record the start of services.

In summer a rowing boat acts as ferry across to Walberswick though it is only a short walk inland to

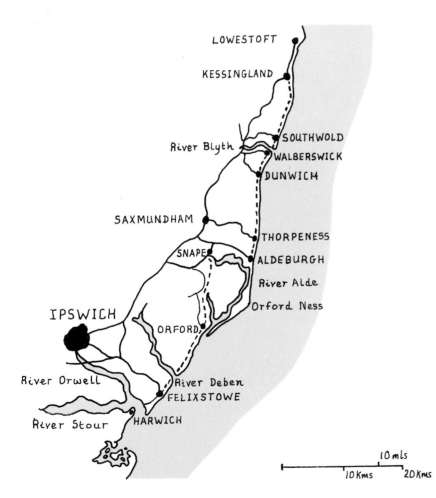

LOWESTOFT
KESSINGLAND
SOUTHWOLD
River Blyth
WALBERSWICK
DUNWICH
SAXMUNDHAM
THORPENESS
SNAPE
ALDEBURGH
River Alde
Orford Ness
IPSWICH
ORFORD
River Orwell
River Deben
FELIXSTOWE
River Stour
HARWICH

10 mls
10 Kms   20 Kms

the old Southwold Light Railway bridge that now provides a footbridge over the Blyth. Inland from the bridge is a desolate expanse of mud-flats and marsh, once drained but since reclaimed by the sea, the domain of black shuck, the phantom dog of Suffolk. Rising above the marsh is the high tower of Blythburgh church.

From Walberswick to Dunwich is a large expanse of freshwater marsh, threaded with footpaths along half-forgotten causeways and protected from the sea by a 20 ft (6 m) high shingle bank. Walking along the crest of this bank offers the finest views, but it can be slow and hard going. No place epitomises the sea's destructive power more than Dunwich. It is famous as the town that vanished and though that fate was common to many villages along England's east coast it was nowhere as dramatic as here. In the Middle Ages Dunwich was one of the most important seaports in England, yet all that today remains is a church, the pub and a handful of cottages, together with the ruins of a friary. A few fishing boats lie on the shingle and there is a large car-park and café while nearby notice-boards retell Dunwich's poignant history. At the time of the Norman Conquest Dunwich had a population of around 3,000 and was a port at the mouth of the River Blyth. It prospered greatly in the Middle Ages, being ideally suited for trade with Europe. Then, in 1326, a violent storm destroyed 400 homes, three churches and blocked the mouth of the river with a million tons of sand and shingle. The Blyth was forced to make a new outlet nearer its present position and from then on the town declined.

Although it is possible to continue along the shingle beach at the foot of Dunwich cliffs, a more pleasant path leads inland through woodland, carpeted, in springtime, with bluebells, to a quiet lane for Minsmere, one of the RSPB's foremost reserves. Access to the main part of the reserve is by permit only, but public hides line the seaward edge allowing the lucky a glimpse of the avocet – the RSPB's emblem – bittern and marsh harrier. More than 100 species of bird nest regularly at Minsmere.

Ahead the dominant feature on the skyline is Sizewell power station. The 'A' plant was completed in 1965 and work began on its companion in 1987, after the longest-ever public enquiry, held at Snape Maltings and costing £25,000,000.

More low cliffs rise beyond the village of Sizewell, a cluster of cottages, but these are protected by a wide foreshore. Thorpeness, with its popular boating lake and Tudor-style buildings is deceptive: it was built only at the beginning of this century as an exclusive holiday resort. The 'House-in-the-Clouds', a local landmark, is actually a watertower, while the windmill is now a Heritage Coast information centre.

Aldeburgh to Landguard Point (41 mls, 67 km)

Aldeburgh was once an important port but it no longer has a harbour, fishing boats and the lifeboat being launched directly from the beach, though

Avocets, the RSPB's emblem bird, nest at Minsmere

yachts congregate off Slaughden quay on the river Alde. The beach is also the scene of a spectacular firework display, preceded by a torch-lit procession, held each year as the culmination of Aldeburgh carnival. On the seafront stands the sixteenth-century Moot Hall, still used as a 'moot point', a place for public meetings: when it was built it was in the centre of the town. Today Aldeburgh is best known for its annual music festival, instigated in 1948 by Benjamin Britten and Peter Pears, and now held at Snape Maltings.

South of the town is the first in a long line of Martello towers built in Napoleonic times to defend south-east England. They take their name and design from a French fort at Cape Martello on Corsica which British troops had found particularly hard to storm.

The river Alde comes to within 50 ft (15 m) of the sea at Slaughden quay before suddenly swinging south, changing its name to the Ore and flowing a further 10 miles (16 km) to enter the sea at Shingle

The 'House-in-the-Clouds', a watertower near Thorpeness

Southwold

Street. The cause of this – Orford Ness – is the best example of a shingle spit, formed by the action of longshore drift, in Britain. Used during the Second World War for a radar listening post, access is still restricted, and the Heritage Coast Path is forced 6 miles (9.5 km) inland, following the old sailors' path through a pleasant mixture of sandy heath, water-logged meadow and woodland, to Snape Maltings. The beautiful buildings here date from the late nineteenth century and are of locally-made bricks. They ceased processing barley in 1965 and conversion to an arts centre began: two years later the Queen opened the concert hall. The complex now includes an art gallery and crafts centre.

The seawall to the east of Snape Maltings was breached in 1953 and the path now follows the inward edge of former fields to the picnic site at Ikencliff. From here the path leaves the estuary to cross Iken Heath, where clumps of Scots Pine stand in strange isolation amid ploughed fields, for Tunstall Forest. Southwards is Orford where, in 1165, Henry II built a castle to subdue the local barons. At that time the town stood opposite the end of Orford Ness, which gave its harbour welcome shelter from the sea. As the spit grew making access more difficult, Orford declined as a port. An interesting local tale is of a merman washed ashore here in 1197, who spent two months in the town before finally returning to the sea.

The path leaves Tunstall Forest at Chillesford and after passing the picturesque Butley mill regains the sea near the mouth of Butley river, tidal throughout its length. Burrow Hill, which the path crosses, is the site of an Iron Age hill-fort.

A seawall leads around Boyton Marshes and beside the river Ore to Shingle Street, an isolated row of former fishermen's houses standing on the high shingle bank. Shingle dominates the walk south past Martello towers and Second World War defences until sandy cliffs rise again at Bawdsey. Hidden away here is RAF Bawdsey, a radar station defended by menacing missiles. More picturesque are the fossils that are common amongst the debris at the foot of the cliffs.

Soon the red sands at the mouth of the river Deben (pronounced Dee-ben) are reached, from where, in summer, there is a passenger ferry across to Felixstowe Ferry. The alternative is a very long detour inland to Wilford Bridge, a couple of miles north of Woodbridge, where there are records of a tide mill in 1170 and where the present one was recently restored to working order. Also close to the Deben crossing is Sutton Hoo, site of the famous ship burial first excavated in 1939.

From the golf course at Felixstowe Ferry the land rises to low cliffs and the quiet suburbs of old Felixstowe. Here the sea has already swallowed the Roman fort of Walton Castle and work is in progress to prevent it from doing the same to the road. Felixstowe makes only a half-hearted attempt at being a holiday resort, its main attraction being the new swimming pool and leisure complex on the seafront by the pier.

Landguard Point, a narrow promontory stretching out across the mouth of the Orwell/Stour estuary, is dominated by the Second World War defensive posts that almost obscure a much older brick-built fort that is now a military museum. A nature reserve and sand and gravel workings co-exist here in uneasy alliance, while huge cargo ships pass by on their way to Felixstowe docks, the largest container port in the country. The port also serves cross-Channel ferries, and a passenger ferry to Harwich which will take the walker from the end of the Suffolk Coast Path to Essex.

Looking north past Shingle Street to Orford Ness. The River Alde runs for many miles between the Ness and the Suffolk Coast

Essex

(OS sheets 169, 168, 178, 177)

Harwich to Brightlingsea (41 mls, 66 km)

IN 1660 A NAVAL SHIPYARD was built at Harwich but the town's maritime tradition goes back to 885 when King Alfred defeated the Danes off Shotley Gate. The *Mayflower*, which took the Pilgrim Fathers to America was an east coast trader based at Harwich. In 1918 the German U-boat fleet surrendered here. Harwich town contains a wealth of old buildings, many of them old inns including the town hall,

originally built in 1864 as The Great Eastern Hotel. The building has a plaque to Samuel Pepys, diarist and MP for the town. On the east side, away from the bustle of modern port facilities, stands a wooden seventeenth-century tread wheel crane, believed to be the only one still in existence. Nearby stand the 'high' and 'low' lighthouses, the former a tall brick tower set well back amongst the houses, the latter on the seafront, a distinctive squat structure which is

now a maritime museum. Built in 1818 to guide ships in to the harbour around Landguard Point, they became obsolete in 1863 when shifting sands meant they no longer indicated a safe passage and new lights had to be constructed at Dovercourt.

To the south of the town, Hamford Water and its attendant creeks take a large bite out of the Essex coast. The 'bite' was probably formed when low sandy cliffs that once extended north of the Naze were breached, allowing the sea to flood the low-lying land behind. Though home for countless birds, and a playground, at high water, for yachtsmen, it is no place for the walker who is better off taking a bus to Walton on the Naze.

Walton stands astride a narrow strip of land leading to the Naze headland, but it is claimed that remains of the original settlement have been found 9 miles (14 km) out in the North Sea. The Naze has a long nature trail which offers good views to the Walton Backwaters, excellent for birds, especially during the autumn migrations, and butterflies, including the Essex skipper. The Naze, the word is from the same root as Nose and Ness, has the only cliffs of note in Essex, the soft Red Crag and London clays which form them being one of the most important sites in Britain for fossil birds. Back in the town the feature of greatest note is the pier, second in length of England's piers only to Southend.

Beach huts form an unbroken line along the promenade from Walton to Frinton-on-Sea, a more exclusive resort than its neighbour, that stands well back from the cliffs. A golf course and meadow divide Frinton from Holland-on-Sea which is now a suburb of Clacton, Essex's premier holiday resort and a popular destination for Londoners. Though holiday trade is perhaps no longer what it was, Clacton has maintained its prosperity by becoming a dormitory town for London, aided by the recent electrification of the east coast rail network. The town's seafront, with its array of Victorian and Edwardian buildings and the pier, is the archetypal seaside resort

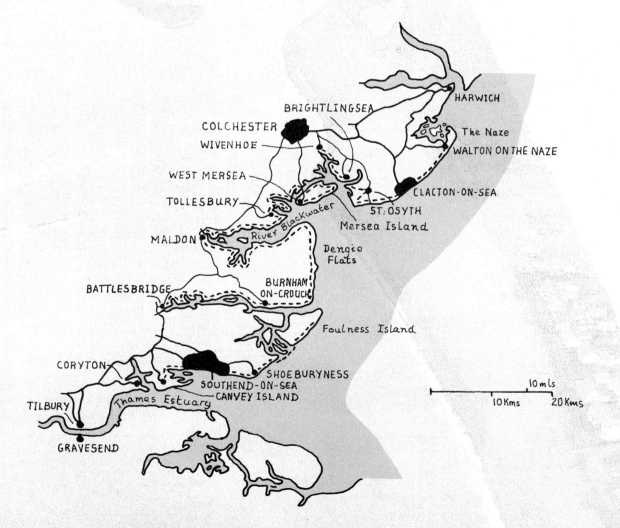

Looking across to Harwich Harbour and the River Orwell from the port of Felixstowe

promenade. Martello towers, which have been absent for some miles, reappear south of Clacton, the walker passing several en route to Jaywick where work has recently been completed on re-building the beach and constructing large breakwaters. Thirty-five people died here in the storm of 1953.

Beyond there is another Martello tower before the caravans of Seawick are reached. It is a relief to walk the simple earthen sea wall after the bustle of the resorts, and it can be followed around St Osyth Marsh to Lee-over-Sands, a ramshackle collection of cottages built up on stilts as protection against flooding. Here there is another important bird reserve.

The residents of Point Clear have extended their gardens onto the tidal marshes so a detour inland is necessary to reach St Osyth Stone Point, where caravans and beach huts surround a Martello tower which is now the East Essex Aviation Museum, dedicated to the memory of Raymond E. King of the USAAF and all 'who gave their lives for freedom 1939-45'.

In summer it may be possible to get a ferry over to Brightlingsea to save a frustrating 9 mile (14.5 km) detour around Brightlingsea Creek. The only saving grace of the detour is a chance to see St Osyth Priory, once described as the finest monastic building in Europe. St Osyth was Osgith, daughter of Frithewald, the first Christian king of the Angles and legend has it that while she was carrying a book to the Abbess at Pollesworth she fell into a swollen river and drowned, only to miraculously re-emerge from the water three days later. She was beheaded by Danish raiders in 653, but carried her head back to the church where she was later buried. The beautiful remains are largely Tudor and Georgian, but the thirteenth-century priory church survives.

Brightlingsea was once a Roman port though it takes its strange name from a later time – a local Saxon leader, Brihtling. In the Middle Ages the town was the only Cinque port outside of Kent and Sussex. Today, it is headquarters of the society dedicated to preserving the Essex fishing boat and races are held each September. It is also popular with water-skiers and windsurfers who enjoy its sheltered waters.

River Colne to Burnham-on-Crouch (82 mls, 131 km)

The dismantled railway line provides a pleasant walk along the shores of the Colne, with views across to the forbidden marshes of Langenhoe and Fingrinhoe,

The Boathouses at Tollesbury

to Alresford Creek. A 2 mile (3.2 km) diversion around this muddy inlet can be avoided at low tide by using an ancient ford which, though now buried under an inch or so of mud, still provides a firm crossing. In the days when the marshes meant that Brightlingsea was virtually set on an island, this ford was the main route to the town.

From Wivenhoe, with its derelict quayside, it is best to take the train into Colchester, a garrison town since Roman times, and then, as there is no path on the south side of the Colne, the bus to West Mersea.

Reached across the strood, a causeway frequently covered by high tides, Mersea island is popular with

both yachtsmen and holiday-makers. But despite this, it is possible to enjoy solitude at most times of the year on the low seawall that encircles the island. The Romans settled here and it has been suggested that Mersea was the headquarters for the Commander of the Saxon Shore Forts. The island is famous for its oysters, 'West Mersea Natures'.

Back on the mainland the seawall runs a winding course around the marshes and along the north side of the Blackwater to Maldon – although it does not

Harwich, with the River Stour to the left and the River Orwell to the right

become a public right of way until Salcot – passing the thriving village of Tollesbury, with its beautiful boathouses, to Heybridge, which still retains some commercial sea trade.

With most yachts staying round at Heybridge basin, Maldon is less cluttered than other local towns with, usually, half a dozen sailing barges with their distinctive rust-red sails moored alongside the quay. The stout tower of St Mary's church completes a picturesque scene little changed in 100 years.

A pleasant public park runs alongside the tidal mud-flats and a few kiosks and children's amusements are the town's only concession to seaside commercialism. Unfortunately, just round the corner is the public rubbish tip which must be passed en route to the site of the battle of Maldon. Here, in 991, Viking invaders were bravely held for many days by the townspeople of Maldon led by the Earl Brithnoth. Brithnoth was killed, and the English were defeated, but history shows that Maldon was never sacked. The battle was the subject of a tenth-century epic poem, *The Battle of Maeldune*. Today, Northey Island, in the Blackwater off Maldon, where the Norsemen first landed, is a nature reserve.

From Maldon the seawall continues uninterrupted around the Dengie peninsula. Lawling and Mayland Creeks cause long detours inland for the gain of half a mile (0.8 km). It is frustrating to stand at Mundon Stone Point looking over to the sprawling caravan park at Steeple Bay knowing it is nearly half a day's walk away, but only five minutes by boat!

The wide expanses of marsh on the shores of the Blackwater provide a winter feeding ground for huge flights of Brent geese, while at Steeple Creek herons, usually solitary birds, often congregate on the tidal islands. Beyond, there are more caravans at Ramsey Island and on the low hill-tops towards Bradwell. Bradwell Waterside exists mainly for yachtsmen and the nearby power station. From the older village of Bradwell-on-Sea, a mile (1.6 km) inland, a short stretch of Roman road leads to the isolated chapel of St Peter's-on-the-Wall. The chapel was built in the seventh century – and is, therefore, one of the oldest churches in England – by St Cedd, an apostle from Lindisfarne. Until the beginning of this century it was used as a barn but today it is a place of annual pilrimage. The wall to which its name refers is that of Othona another of the Roman forts of the Saxon Shore.

From Sales Point the seawall heads almost due

south with the magnificent desolation of Dengie Flats, shimmering brown at low tide, to the left – the sea is up to 2 miles (3.2 km) away here at low tide – until turning sharply at Holliwell Point into the Crouch estuary. Across the river and the low marshes of Wallasea Island the tower blocks of Southend can be seen, with the chimney of the Isle of Grain power station behind and the hills of Kent fading into the distance.

Burnham-on-Crouch has an annual boating regatta second in importance only to that of Cowes and even off-season the river seems crowded with yachts. In recent years the town has become increasingly popular with city workers, the regular rail link making it ideal for commuting, and large housing estates have appeared. Several buildings along the waterfront have also been acquired for re-development and the town is in danger of losing its charm.

Hullbridge to Tilbury (62 mls, 99 km)

The same railway does provides the walker with an easy alternative to the walk up the Crouch, past the half-submerged Bridgemarsh island, a warning as to what happens if sea defences are not maintained, to the new town of South Woodham Ferrers, where the footpath ends. Hullbridge, on the far side of the Crouch, with its squat church tower hiding behind a field of mobile homes, has been suggested as the site of a former bridge over the Crouch: certainly there was once a low-tide ford in use here. Alternatively, the village names of North and South Fambridge, on either side of the Crouch, might suggest the presence of a bridge, though the width of the river there would make a ferry more likely. Today Battlesbridge is the lowest bridging point.

Although it is possible to return back up the Crouch to Wallasea Island, even occasionally, to reach it by ferry from Burnham, and meander around the marshes of the Roach to Foulness, such a continuation serves little purpose as there is no sight of the sea beyond the seemingly endless salt marsh and mud. Much better is a 10-minute train ride into Southend-on-Sea.

From Southend it is possible to go east to Shoeburyness and the vast Maplin Sands. From these Foulness Island can be reached – be careful it is a restricted area – or seen. Here in winter as many as 40,000 Brent geese congregate. Southend itself is one of Britain's major seaside resorts with the longest

Marbled White Butterfly, frequently seen on the Essex Coast

pleasure pier in the world – it was badly damaged by fire in 1976 but saved for posterity, its famous railway still running – winkles and jellied eels and so on. Near Chalkwell station there is a granite obelisk offshore, erected in 1837 to mark the limit of the City of London's jurisdiction over the Thames, and replacing the earlier 'Crow Stone' which now stands outside the town's museum.

Further west is Leigh-on-Sea, which retains the impression of being a quiet fishing village – right down to the cobbled lane – despite now being a suburb of Southend. Fishing boats still shelter in the lee of Two Tree Island, while on the shore a line of

The Naze and Hamford Water, to the north of Walton-on-the-Naze

huts compete with each other to provide the freshest seafood delicacies.

The walking to the west, along a broad embankment around Hadleigh Marsh, is a pleasant, quiet change. To the right the stark ruins of Hadleigh castle, built in the fourteenth century for Edward III, offer a sharp contrast to the Coryton oil refineries just a few miles away across Canvey Island.

Canvey, divided here from the mainland by Benfleet creek, is the very epitome of man's resistance against the sea. Although first claimed by the Saxon chieftain Cana, it was not until the early seventeenth century that a permanent community was established. This followed work by the great Dutch engineer Cornelius Vermuyden who constructed the first of several seawalls around the island. Many of the Dutchmen employed in the project eventually settled there. In 1897 the island was half flooded during storms but the islanders persevered and rebuilt their seawalls. In the storm of 1953, 58 people died and much of the population was left homeless, but again the sea defences were rebuilt and now protect a population of 27,000. It is sad that the impressive achievement is housed behind an ugly concrete prison.

From Benfleet the coast eludes us: first behind the trackless wastes of Bower Marshes between East Haven and Vange creeks, then behind the oil refineries of Coryton and Shellhaven. The best option is to take either the train or bus from Benfleet to East Tilbury, where the Thames estuary can be regained for the final time at Coalhouse fort, another built in 1869 by Gordon of Khartoum.

Tilbury power station, unlike Sizewell and Bradwell, uses coal, delivered to its front door by ship. The path follows a concrete wall and crosses the roadway between the power station and its quay by an iron footbridge. Half a mile (0.8 km) further on is Tilbury fort, originally built in 1539 by Henry VIII. It was rebuilt in the late eighteenth century and altered again in the 1860s, but it has never fired a cannon in anger. The fort is a registered national monument, and has been restored and is open to the public. During the time of the Spanish Armada the British land forces were based here and in 1988 the riverfront served as the focal point for the 400th anniversary celebrations. From nearby we leave Essex, on a ferry to Gravesend.

Patterns in the mud at low tide, River Blackwater near West Mersea

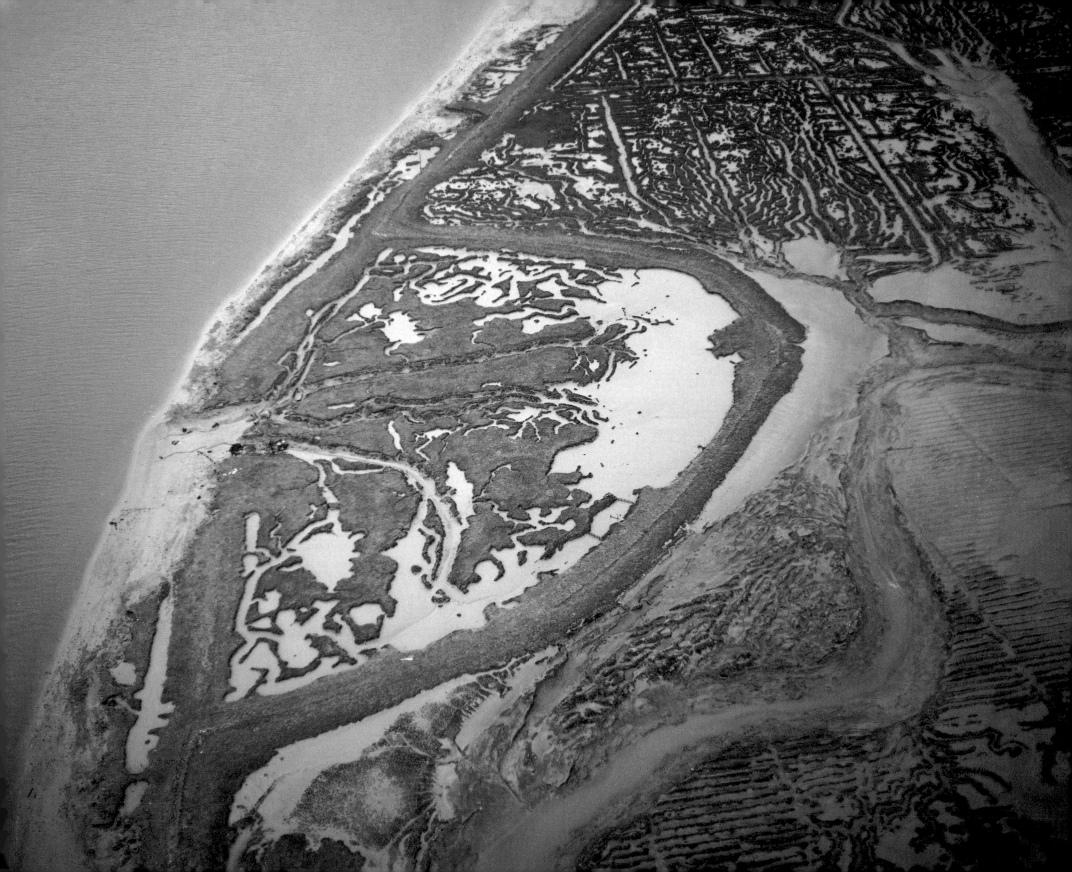

The Saxon Shore Way

(OS sheets 177, 178, 179, 189)

Gravesend to Motney Hill (27 mls, 43 km)

IN THE THIRD and fourth centuries the south-east coast of England was subjected to persistent attacks by the Saxon raiders, and Britain's Roman masters attempted to defend the area by building a series of forts stretching from East Anglia to Suffolk. The Romans called this stretch of the coast Litus Saxonicum, or the Saxon Shore. Troop movements and commerce forged a route between the forts – the Saxon Shore Way.

Today the Saxon Shore Way stretches from Gravesend, on the Thames estuary, to Rye in Sussex. It follows the ancient shoreline of Kent for 140 miles (224 km) and is waymarked either by the emblem of a red-winged Saxon helmet or red arrows on a yellow background.

The walker begins at Gravesend and follows the Thames river wall. There are still some active marine industries here, but most of the yards are now closed and derelict. Also in a state of disuse and dereliction is the Thames–Medway canal which used to stretch as far as Rochester. The entrance lock to the canal can still be seen and the old canal tunnel is still used by trains on the Strood to Gravesend line.

There are several old forts along this first stretch of the Shore Way: New Tavern Fort and Shornmead Fort were built to protect the river approaches to London, as companions to the defences at Tilbury on the other side of the river. Shornmead Fort, built in 1868, has been stripped of its heavy artillery but despite this and its overgrown state of disrepair, it is still an impressive sight and offers excellent views across the Thames. Further east, Cliffe Fort was built because it was believed that Napoleon might begin his invasion of England there.

Although the Shore Way does not actually pass through Lower Higham, it may be worth the detour to visit the village that many Dickens experts believe was the main inspiration for Pip's village in *Great Expectations*. Current thinking is that Dickens used Lower Higham but incorporated aspects of other villages in the area, in particular the lozenge graves in the churchyard at Cooling.

The Shore Way now heads away from the Thames, moving across the Hoo Peninsula towards the River Medway. Cliffe, the first village reached, was the seat of numerous councils of the Saxon Church in the seventh to ninth centuries, and from it the Way reaches Cooling, and the famous churchyard. Cooling Marshes to the north is where Pip met Magwitch, and there the convict was chased and captured before deportation. Cooling Castle was originally a manor house, fortified in the fourteenth century to protect against French and Spanish raiders. It was once owned by Sir John Oldcastle, a suggested model for Shakespeare's Falstaff, who was a follower of Wycliffe and was burned as a heretic in 1417. Today the castle is a ruin, not open to the public.

Just before High Halstow, the RSPB's Reserve at Northward Hill is reputed to have the largest heronry in Europe. The heronry is not accessible, but can be viewed from a signposted observatory.

The Medway is now visible, as are signs of the industry and commerce along it: the power station on the Isle of Grain can be seen towering in the distance and Hoo marina is soon reached. Two forts along this stretch of the river testify to Dutch aggression in the seventeenth century. Upnor Castle was an Elizabethan gun fort that failed to prevent a Dutch raid in 1667 when several English ships were destroyed, while Cockham Wood Fort, which is now gradually falling into the river, was built after that raid.

Strood, Rochester and Chatham make up the cathedral city of Rochester-upon-Medway, a city with so many places of interest that it warrants a visit in its own right. There are, of course, many Dickens' connections and each year the city celebrates their most famous son with a festival. Dickens lived and went to school in Chatham where his father worked as a clerk in the dockyard. Elsewhere, be sure to see the cathedral, a tiny place but with a memorable Norman crypt, and Watts Charity, the sixteenth century almshouses.

The route now continues through the Medway towns away from the river, which is virtually inaccessible for several miles. The former naval dockyard, dating from the time of Henry VIII, now

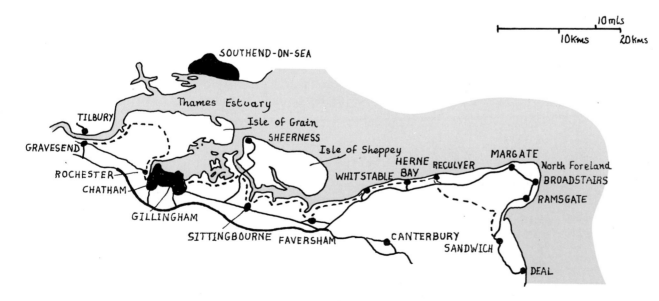

Nagden Marshes and Faversham south of the Isle of Sheppey

being developed by English Estates as a leisure facility, houses an excellent museum, staffed by some of the dockyard veterans. The naval architecture in the yard is outstanding, with several listed buildings. Gillingham and Chatham are separated by an area of open land known as the Great Lines, that was used in the eighteenth century as a military exercise ground. Here stands the famous war memorial, originally designed by Sir Robert Lorimer, to commemorate the Naval dead of the two World Wars. The Church of St. Mary the Virgin, the parish church of Gillingham, situated just above the river, is the last substantial building from the original village.

The Shore Way returns to the river from the Strand, a leisure park. Beyond are frequent signs of industrial decay – old barges lie rotting close to the bank and old jetties have collapsed from disuse. Further on, a section of the riverside, including Eastcourt Meadows, Horrid Hill, Sharps Green and Berengrave Nature Reserve, is being converted into a Riverside Country Park. The Berengrave site was formerly a chalk pit whose materials were transported to the pier at Motney, where the RSPB have an open reserve at Motney Hill. The joys of bird watching here are often offset by the 'aura' of nearby sewage works.

Upchurch to Reculver (73 mls, 117 km)

Things improve on the walk through Upchurch and Lower Halstow to the Kingsferry Bridge, which passes through farmland once famous for its cherries and still given over, in large part, to fruit growing. Although Lower Halstow has been spoiled to a certain extent by housing developments, it still retains some of its old charm and beyond the village, on the marshlands, the bird life is excellent. The village has a place in history: the Romans picked oysters from Halstow Creek and the monks from Canterbury bred the ancestors of the Romney Marsh sheep on their farm here.

At nearby Chetney Marsh, ships arriving from abroad were forced into quarantine following the outbreak of plague in 1665. The slight remains of an isolation hospital or lazaret can still be seen at Chetney Hill, while Deadman's Island is named for those who died during quarantine and were buried there. The later legacy of the prison hulks and their floating hospital ships that were moored here can be detected in the names of Slaughterhouse Point and Bedlams Bottom.

From the Marshes the Way reaches Kingsferry Bridge over the Swale Channel. Across the bridge is the Isle of Sheppey, not visited by the Saxon Shore Way, but whose northern end can be walked. Sheerness, the largest town on Sheppey, is the site of Charles II's dockyard, built under the supervision of Samuel Pepys, and from it Minster is reached. The church here contains a memorial to Sir Robert Sherland, a Lord Warden of the Cinque Ports whose imminent death as a result of his horse was foretold by a local prophetess. To avoid the death Sherland killed his horse, but soon after he stubbed his foot on its carcass – why was it not buried? – contracted gangrene and died Warden Point is named from the watch for ships kept there, and from it a walk around the eastern edge of Sheppey, past Shell Ness, can be made. This stops at the Isle of Harty, the Elmley Marshes, a large RSPB reserve for ducks, geese and waders, preventing travel westward.

From Kingsferry Bridge the Saxon Shore Way heads towards Sittingbourne past Ridham Dock and Kemsley Mill the former being the landing place for the wood pulp used in paper making at the latter. Paper making still continues at Kemsley, from where the Sittingbourne and Kemsley Light Railway used to carry paper between mill and town. After its closure in 1969 a preservation society took over and a stretch of the old line is now open for rides on steam trains. Sittingbourne is the home of the Dolphin Yard Sailing Barge Museum, a fine site.

From Sittingbourne the Way hugs the Swale shore to Faversham. This area was once famous for the manufacture of gunpowder, the last remnant of the explosives industry still being visible at Uplees. Faversham is a fine town, and its Heritage Centre should be the place to begin any tour. The town was once an important port and there are several reminders of those days: Standard Quay has an impressive row of old warehouses. Oyster fishing was also important, particularly in Faversham Creek and along the Swale, but pollution and over-fishing have destroyed the oyster beds. The church, to St Mary of Charity and dating in part from the fourteenth century, has an oddly carved tower, a well-known landmark from across the marshes. On those marshes in 1551, Arden of Faversham was saved by a fog that descended and hid him from his two assailants hired by Mosbie, the seducer of Arden's wife, though they later caught him up and killed him. Both Shakespeare and Marlowe have been attributed with authorship of the anonymous play on this local tale.

Most of the land between Nagden and Seasalter forms the South Swale nature reserve, a rich area for waders and wildfowl and, in winter, for Brent geese. Short-eared owls and hen harriers can occasionally be seen flying low over the grasses hunting for food. Beyond the reserve, the Shore Way reaches Whitstable. Whitstable's oysters have been famous for thousands of years: the Romans ate them and so did Shakespeare. Today, there is still a small fishing fleet, an annual oyster festival and the harbour has Europe's largest oyster hatchery.

The Shore Way is now firmly in holiday country, with caravan and chalet parks and holiday bungalows. Herne Bay's first pier was built entirely of wood in 1832 by Thomas Telford but this was soon destoyed, or, rather, eaten. The present pier is separated from its pavilion which stands majestically some 800 yards (732 m) out to sea. The connecting section was badly damaged in a storm in 1978 and had to be demolished. Once the second largest in England, the pier was a fine addition to a town claiming to have more hours of sunshine than any other coastal resort.

At Reculver, east of Herne Bay, the Shore Way turns sharp right and heads inland towards Richborough. Reculver was the site of one of the original Roman forts that were built to defend the Saxon Shore. Here the fort guarded the northern entrance of a channel known as the Wantsum. This channel, stretching from Reculver to Richborough, separated the Isle of Thanet from the mainland and was wide enough for a Roman fleet to sail through. Today, the Wantsum has been severely reduced by silting and is now no more than a small river, the Isle of Thanet being virtually a part of the mainland. The ruined church of St Mary stands on the site of the fort, its twin towers, known as the Two Sisters, a landmark for miles.

The Wantsum to Rye (67 mls, 107 km)

By heading inland the Saxon Shore Way misses the Isle of Thanet, a largely built-up area where easy progress is made following the promenades of Margate, Broadstairs and Ramsgate – the first raucous, the second quiet, the third hovering between the two. Ramsgate's ferry service to Dunkirk is an odd memory of its part in the 1940 Dunkirk evacuation, when over 80,000 men landed here.

The Way actually follows the old Wantsum to

Looking across North Foreland and Margate to the Thames Estuary

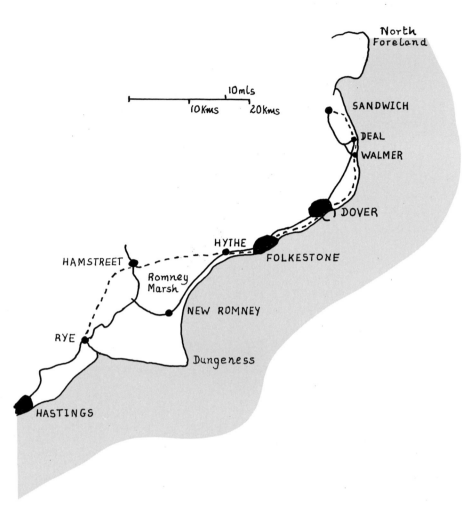

Cannon, Deal Castle

Richborough, also the site of a Roman fort, the remains of which, Richborough Castle, are still impressive. The fort occupied the central position of the Roman defences and was the headquarters of the Count of the Saxon Shore, the officer responsible for defending the coast from the Saxon marauders.

The Shore Way heads on to Sandwich, once a Cinque Port but now 2 miles (3.2 km) from the sea, or 5 miles (8 km) along the navigable River Stour. The town's long and exciting history has seen it ransacked by the French twice, in 1216 and 1457. In the latter fight the mayor was killed, and today's mayor still wears a black robe in mourning. Like most of the towns along the south coast it provided both men and ships to help defend the country against the Spanish Armada in 1588. Now, however, the town is a quiet seaside place best known for its golf links, the

famous and notoriously difficult Royal St George's.

Outside the town the Shore Way follows the coast road, across this and other golf courses. Out at sea the lightships signalling each end of the Goodwin Sands can be seen. Legend has it that the sands were once an island, the Island of Lomea, though there is little evidence for this. Named for Earl Godwinson, father of King Harold who died at Hastings, the sands are said to have claimed 50,000 lives.

Sandown Castle whose ruin the Shore Way passes, is the first of a trio built by Henry VIII, when there was a threat of Catholic invasion, that we pass in a very short distance. It had the reputation of being one of his most miserable prisons. The second castle at Deal, where the Roman invasion of Britain began in 55 BC, was built in the shape of a Tudor rose, and was the seat of the Captain of the Cinque Ports. It is

still an imposing fortress. Near it is the old Time Ball Tower, where a black ball fell at 1300 hours daily so that sailors could synchronise their clocks to Greenwich.

The third castle of the trio, at Walmer, is very well preserved and is the official residence of the Lord Warden of the Cinque Ports. It still retains much of its heavy artillery. Walmer Castle is open to the public, and is well worth the visit. South from Walmer the Shore Way stays on the cliff edge, passing the fine memorial to the men of the Dover Patrol and reaching St Margaret's at Cliffe with its huge bronze statue of Sir Winston Churchill.

Dover stands on the River Dour and has been a major port since before the Roman times. The ruin of the Roman lighthouse, the earliest in Britain, stands beside St Mary-in-Castro church. The beach at Dover has literary connections: here Matthew Arnold wrote his famous poem *On Dover Beach* and Dickens used it as the site of Betsy Trotwood's house in *David Copperfield*. The town has statues of Captain Webb, first man to swim the Channel, and C.S. Rolls, of Rolls-Royce fame, first man to fly the Channel in both directions. It also has a fine memorial, a granite plane, to Louis Bleriot who landed here after the first cross-Channel flight. Dover's medieval castle is an awesome sight still, it seems, standing guard over the town from its clifftop perch.

The route of the Shore Way now crosses the famous white cliffs of Dover from the tallest of which,

The White Cliffs of South Foreland to the east of Dover

Shakespeare Cliff, 300 ft (90 m) high, it is possible to see France, or so it is said. At Akers Steps the walker goes precariously down to sea level. Ahead now the Way passes, at times, through military firing ranges. **When the red flags are flying the marked alternative route must be followed**. In this area the Channel Tunnel, now under construction, may have an impact on the course of the Way.

Folkestone, at the end of the White Cliffs, is a pretty, genteel, old-fashioned English holiday resort. The Metropole Arts Centre is one of the finest in the country and plays host to the Kent Literature Festival each year. The town has no proper promenade, but instead a garden that extends to Sandgate, offering a delightful walk. Hythe, into which Folkestone runs, succeeded Lympne as a Roman defence point following a change in the coast line, and later the town became a Cinque Port. The church of St Leonard is famous for its huge, but macabre, collection of skulls and bones, not least because the bones do not correspond to a known community, the original owners being shorter and having differently shaped heads to those of the known ancestors of the locals.

Under the threat of invasion from Napoleon's France the Saxon Shore was fortified, and nowhere is this better seen than on the stretch from Folkestone to Rye. The Royal Military Canal, stretching from Hythe to Rye, was built as a means of transporting men and arms to strategic coastal areas. Now it is the site of an annual Venetian-type fête. There are also many Martello towers, built as watch towers and gun posts, though most have now been converted into houses, museums and cafés. Some experts believe that they are better suited to their present use than their original one!

The final stretch of the Shore Way, from Hythe through Ham Street to Rye, is all inland to avoid a danger area. Again shifting sand, mud and shingle have changed the shape and face to the coastline and claimed large areas of land from the sea. Oxney and a part of Romney Marsh were islands during Roman times. Dungeness, now the site of two power stations, two lighthouses and a scattering of holiday cottages,

was also, until relatively recently, surrounded by water.

The inland routes passes through woodland to reach Ham Street, never more than a small railway staging station but through which, at the turn of the century passed a host of famous literary figures. Henry James, Joseph Conrad, Ford Madox Ford and Stephen Crane lived or visited in the area and a literary circle to match the better known one of Bloomsbury grew up.

The Saxon Shore Way ends at Rye, an almost perfectly preserved medieval town, its buildings gabled and beamed and built with local stone. Do find the Mermaid Inn, a splended early fifteenth-century half-timbered building, its floor crooked with age. Here, in the eighteenth-century the Hawkhurst Gang drank,

their pistols on the table. The cobbled street they walked to the inn is still there today. In 1377 the French burned the town and stole the church bells. They were recovered a year later and were once hung in Watchbell Street to warn of future raids. Not for almost 150 years could they be re-hung safely in the church. This, and other stories from Rye's past, are told in the museum in Ypres Tower. Rye is now no longer a large port, as it once was, but it retains a nautical flavour even if the narrow harbour entrance can only be negotiated by small boats and sailing dinghies. Henry James, the writer, lived in the town for many years until his death in 1917 and his former residence, Lamb House, is now a museum of his life and work.

Folkestone

The Mermaid Inn, Rye

Sussex

(OS sheets 189, 199, 198, 197)

Rye to Cuckmere Haven (36 mls, 58 km)

THE COAST CAN BE walked from Rye Harbour – and for those who do an excellent series of charts helps the walker identify waders in the harbour's nature reserve – but those who visit Rye, and all should, may prefer to regain the coast by way of Winchelsea, taking the path from Rye that passes Camber Castle. The castle can only be reached by foot, but is not at present open to the public. It was built by Henry VIII as part of his defences against a Catholic invasion. This castle also has a Tudor rose plan, the circular walls being a defence against cannonballs.

Winchelsea is today a charming place, built to replace an old port with the same name that once stood in Rye bay but was engulfed in a great storm in 1287. The new town was built on a defensive grid-system, but was never completed: 12 of the original 39 grid 'quarters' and three town gates remain. The church of St Thomas bears evidence of the fury of French attacks, though these stopped when a shingle bar cut the town off from the sea. A museum in the Medieval Court Hall plots the history of port and town.

The seawall from Winchelsea Beach offers views of the Pett Level meadows, an excellent piece of wetland between the Royal Military Canal and the sea, and the old cliff line, as it takes the walker to Cliff End. Here there is a dramatic change of scene as a narrow, hedged path winds up between fields away from the beach with its erosion-preventing wooden stakes and the concrete debris of wartime.

The walker regains the shore at Fairlight beach, which can be walked if a wary eye is kept on the state of the tide. Beyond, the grass paths of the Fire Hills – named for the blaze of yellow gorse in spring, and usually alive with flowers – lead through the Hastings Country Park. The park covers over 500 acres of excellent sandstone cliff that is occasionally split by deep gorges called glens. The best of these, Fairlight Glen, is 2 miles (3.2 km) long and is explored by one of a number of waymarked nature trails.

Finally the path or, and much better, the cliff railway, descends to Hastings beach with its tall black net sheds. Hastings has long been an important port, one of the most powerful of the five Cinque Ports we have passed – Sandwich, Dover, Hythe and Romney being the other four. It was already important when William of Normandy came this way in 1066, bringing a fame that will last for all time. In reality William landed at Pevensey to the west and fought the battle that carries the Hastings name on a ridge above the Senlac stream 6 miles (9.6 km) inland, but reality rarely intrudes on myth. The story of the town from 1066 to the present is told on the 243 ft (73 m) Hastings Embroidery – a modern rival to the Bayeux Tapestry. Elsewhere the town has a fine Fisherman's museum, near the bottom station of the cliff railway, a Shipwreck Heritage Centre and the largest fleet of beach-launched fishing boats in Britain. The natural harbour, which once made Hastings the premier Cinque Port was blocked by the cliff erosion which also destroyed part of William the Conqueror's first castle near the top of the cliff railway.

Hastings is now urban-linked to Bexhill a nineteenth-century resort, famous for the De La Warr Pavilion, a 1930s entertainment extravaganza built as a rival to Hastings pier. Between the two towns, offshore at Golley Hill, are remnants of a forest that grew on the land bridge between the south coast and France, a bridge that may have vanished only 10,000 years ago.

For many walkers, despite Bexhill's charms, a fresh start may be preferred by taking a bus to Pevensey. The exact site of William's landing cannot be identified, the coast now is, in any case, very different from the way it was, though one nearby cove is known as Norman's Bay. As if to prove the point Pevensey Castle, part of the Roman defences of the Saxon Shore and re-fortified by the Normans, is at Old Pevensey, a mile (1.6 km) inland.

Beyond an extensive caravan site at Pevensey Bay, the land opens out towards the South Downs. Behind the shingle bank a firm track passes Martello towers built during threats of a Napoleonic invasion, one now housing a coastguard lookout, while another, in Eastbourne, houses the Sussex Combined Services Museum. Eastbourne also has a lifeboat museum housed in the old lifeboat house.

Eastbourne is another nineteenth-century built

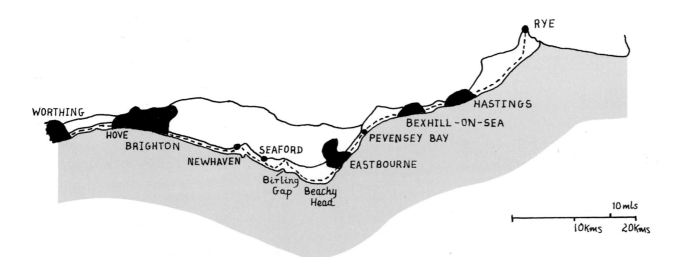

Looking west across Beachy Head to the Seven Sisters

here for Lloyd's since 1877.

A fine roller-coaster walk, equally enjoyable by full moon, begins from Birling Gap, above the remains of Belle Tout lighthouse that can be reached by steep smugglers' steps, along the Seven Sisters, chalk heights enclosing ancient truncated valleys. It is actually possible to count eight cliffs, but perhaps two are half-sisters! The view to Cuckmere Haven is excellent, but the River Cuckmere that reaches the sea here has been canalised, and can only be crossed by a diversion inland. A path that gradually descends the valley side and follows the river reaches Exceat Bridge, though a slightly longer track, skirting the river's old meanders, reaches the Seven Sisters Country Park where there is information on smuggling – the smugglers 'sowed' weighted tubs of gin or brandy for collection at low tide – and how the locals trapped birds during the 'wheatear harvest'.

Hope Gap to Emsworth (82 mls, 131 km)

From Exceat Bridge a beautiful path returns along the right bank of the Cuckmere to reach Seaford Head where the seats testify to the numbers of people who came to view the Seven Sisters. By common consent the best view is that from Hope Gap.

Westward a fairly level path passes fields and golf course before descending to Seaford, an uninspiring

town with the most westerly Martello tower. West again the River Ouse requires an inland detour to cross, the detour taking the walker through Newhaven where a jetty and pier enclose the harbour. This harbour was the 'New Haven', built in the sixteenth century when a storm changed the River Ouse's course, creating a port where there had not been one. The fort here was one of Palmerston's mid-nineteenth-century coastal defences against a perceived French invasion threat. Its construction was supervised by one Lt Ardagh a 22 year old officer, who used concrete for the first time in fortifications, produced by shingle being raised 120 ft (36 m) from the beach below. The gallery, candlelit despite the gunpowder cells, is just one of its many interesting features.

An easy path westward takes the walker into Peacehaven. This was designed and built after the First World War by Charles Neville. The original name of Anzac-on-Sea was changed, thankfully, to Peacehaven. The monument to George V on the cliff lies on the Greenwich Meridian and lists distances to cities of the Empire. London (Greenwich) is 48 miles (79 km) away, while Canberra is a little further, at 10,564 (16,902 km).

Brighton Pier

Clouded Yellow Butterfly, often seen on Beachy Head

resort town, though in this case a very elegant one. At night the floodlit Grand Hotel is the most impressive of the many smart hotels along the 3 mile (4.8 km) front where a network of coloured lights illuminates the bedding plant display.

From the town numerous paths penetrate the scrub on the South Downs to the west, some reaching the triangulation point that stands at 534 ft (160 m) above sea level on Beachy Head. The name is Norman French – *beau chef*, beautiful head – and is a good one, though the beauty can be more apparent from a distance than from the Head itself, where the view down to the lighthouse – only 142 ft (43 m) high – can be intimidating. The Head has a nature trail that points out the plant and bird life – rock pipits nest on the ledges and at the right time of year the cliffs are alive with migrating butterflies, the clouded yellows looking especially fine against the green of the grass and the white chalk – but many just take in the view, that extends eastward as far as Dungeness. One of several interesting commemorative tablets indicates that signalling has been conducted

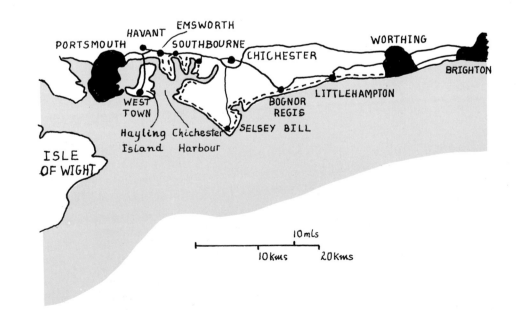

Brighton Pavilion

Windsurfing in the English Channel

From Peacehaven the promenade can be a dangerous place if a high tide is hurling waves and pebbles over the parapet, and some will feel that a bus to Brighton is preferred to the walk through Saltdean. The ride, however, would miss Rottingdean, a little inland, with its village pond, Elizabethan manor house and well-cultivated garden which once belonged to Kipling whose uncle, the Pre-Raphaelite artist Sir Edward Burne-Jones, designed the church's stained-glass windows.

Returning to the cliffs, Rottingdean's windmill and Roedean Girls' School command attention and later, Britain's oldest public electric railway – the Volks Electric Railway – links Europe's largest marina with Brighton pier. Brighton began as a small fishing village, but exploded into life 200 years ago when the Prince Regent, later George IV, favoured it as a retreat. From this start it 'invented' the seaside holiday and is today still one of Britain's major

resorts. If the resort as a whole is the Prince's general legacy, the Pavilion is his specific gift. Begun in 1812 by John Nash it has been applauded and reviled, but rarely ignored. Perhaps the best single phrase summing it up was by the critic who wrote that it was 'riotously extravagant'. It has recently been restored to its glorious former self.

For the rest, Brighton is a town of contrasts with a good old section of narrow alleys, some fine museums and enough entertainment to keep the most ardent pleasure-seeker happy for hours.

Westward from Brighton it is seaside all the way, the choice for progress being a walk along the beach or a trudge along the promenade. The walk takes in Hove, site of the British Engineerium, and Shoreham, where the Marlipins Museum is housed in an early twelfth-century building said to be one of the oldest secular buildings in Europe to have been in continuous, and still to be in current, use.

West again is Worthing, the biggest local resort, from where the Seven Sisters can be seen. Ahead now, at Ferring, a private road limits access.

There are rail and bus links to avoid walking but a stimulating alternative is to take a bus to Pyecombe to join the South Downs Way and to follow this via Devil's Dyke, Edburton and Truleigh Hill to the A283, and buses for Bognor, or to continue to Amberley before returning to Bognor, an eighteenth-century resort, beloved of Queen Victoria, and given the addition 'Regis' by her grandson, George V. From Bognor the walker must follow the promenade to Pagham Harbour.

Pagham Harbour was busy during the Middle Ages but then silted up. Later, in 1876, the harbour mouth barrier which allowed steam engines to link Chichester with Selsey, was breached by heavy seas. Today, the harbour is a nature reserve where Brent geese winter and little terns can be seen in summer. Paths circle the harbour, the walker visiting the pretty villages of Sidlesham and Church Norton, the latter with its chapel to the seventh-century St Wilfrid.

Ahead now are Selsey and Selsey Bill, the name

The Lifeboat Station, Selsey Bill

Little Tern, Chichester Harbour

deriving from 'seal island', a channel once separating the headland from the mainland. That channel, of which Pagham harbour is all that remains, was filled by silt, joining the 'island' to the mainland. From Selsey many will take a bus to West Wittering to avoid the explosion of caravans and shingle.

East Head is easily reached from West Wittering through a dune area now protected by fences from the tramp of feet. The walker can then follow the south-eastern arm of Chichester Harbour northward taking the ferry to reach a road for Bosham, a wonderfully picturesque village whose Saxon church is featured in the Bayeux Tapestry. It was from here that Harold sailed to Normandy where he swore the oath that led to the invasion of 1066. Here, too, Canute is said to have commanded the tide to retreat.

From Bosham no easy way leads to Thorney Island, though the island itself can be circled on the Sussex Border Path from Prinsted to Emsworth. It is the nesting ground of little terns, and offers excellent views of the tightly enclosed Chichester Harbour.

From Emsworth the Solent Way will take us towards Bournemouth, but first we shall visit the Isle of Wight, even though ferries for the island are only to be found further west at Southsea.

Little Tern's nest

Chichester Harbour

Isle of Wight

(OS sheet 96)

THOSE WANTING TO complete a full British mainland circuit may cross to the Isle of Wight by hovercraft from Southsea. This ferry arrives in Ryde, and from there, for a change, we shall go anti-clockwise.

Ryde itself is a Regency/Victorian seaside resort with an elegant pier, its end reached by an electric railway. During the Second World War, one end of the PLUTO fuel supply – PipeLine Under The Ocean – used to take oil to the Normandy beachhead, came ashore here. In the restored church of St Thomas's a computerised unit enables visiting Australians to trace both their convict ancestors and their ancestors' convictions.

Escaping from the town, paths cross the golf course and pass the grey grandeur of Cistercian Abbey ruins superseded by the present, early twentieth century Quarr Abbey constructed by Benedictine monks. A road is used to pass Fishbourne and its car

ferry, and to cross broad Wootton Creek. Beyond, quiet lanes lined with oak hedges and woods take the walker north-westwards. Just off the route, at Whippingham, there are attractive almshouses, once used by Queen Victoria's retired servants, and a church designed by Prince Albert himself. Many of the plaques in the richly decorated interior are associated with the Royal Family whose home, the Italianate Osborne House, is further on. The house, which is open to the public, was built for Queen Victoria to a design of Prince Albert, and has a Swiss chalet in the garden where the royal children played. The Queen loved both house and island, and it was here she died in 1901. Her son, Edward VII, was less enamoured of the site, and gave it to the nation in 1902.

There were shipyards at East Cowes from the twelfth century, much of the island's deafforestation dating from the eighteenth century, when the yards needed wood to build Royal Navy ships. Ironically,

the yards that built boats for the local smugglers also built the island's first revenue cutter.

A floating bridge takes the walker over the Medina to Cowes, world famous for yachting and especially for the events of Cowes Week. The Royal Yacht Squadron guards the harbour entrance, its 21 brass cannon at the ready. The squadron is housed in one of Henry VIII's defensive forts – thought to have been called a 'cow' and so giving the town its name.

Beyond Gurnard Bay, to the west of the town, a narrow cliff path, slippery after rain, descends across soft, shifting clay to reach firm shingle, before turning inland to Porchfield. Francheville, burned by the French in 1337 and rebuilt as Newtown, was once a busy harbour and the island's capital. Nowadays the silted waters form a nature reserve where 170 birds and 300 plant species have been recorded.

A tree-lined reach, an old mill, a twelfth-century church and charming stone cottages, are reached at Shalfleet, beyond which the Ningwood Lake footbridge and the path beyond Lower Hamstead jetty can disappear under water during spring tides. From Hamstead Point to Bouldnor the cliffs hold crocodile, turtle and shark fossils, though the coastal path stays on the tops, taking the walker through farmlands and mixed woodland.

Yarmouth has another of Henry VIII's castles, this one open to the public, and a pair of nineteenth-century defensive forts, called Victoria and Albert – how could the Queen have been amused? – are now separated by the Country Park woodland walk.

The path section from Totland to Freshwater is the finest on the walk, a steep cliff path bursting from trees onto the magnificent slopes of Headon Hill, its grassy ways bordered by willow-herb, gorse, hawthorn and honeysuckle. Seaward, the view takes in the mainland coast from Durlston Head to Hurst Castle, while ahead, beyond the green slopes of Tennyson Down, chalk rises in a series of terminal stacks.

Following the climb to the Old Battery, the National Trust have a gunnery museum in the old fort here, a spiral staircase and tunnel penetrate the cliff for a close view of those stacks – The Needles. There

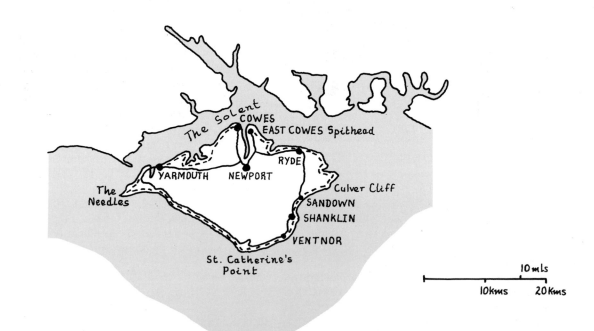

The Needles

Catherine's Point is threaded with paths reaching out to the neat white lighthouse complex. The very lucky visitor might see a Glanville Fritillary here, one of Britain's rarest butterflies and not found on the mainland.

Ahead now is St Boniface Down, at 747 ft (224 m) the highest point on the island, reached beyond the tiny twelfth-century church of St Lawrence, one of Britain's smallest. Nearby is a museum dedicated to smuggling, a glass-making works and a bird park. Eastward, pleasant surfaced paths lead to Ventnor, a Victorian resort in which many contemporary writers stayed and worked. Charles Dickens wrote several chapters of *David Copperfield* here.

Landslips in 1810 and 1928 beyond – one of which is grandly referred to as The Landslip – have left the coastal path to follow a tortuous, but interesting, course through trees, many less trees since the 'hurricane' of 1987. Luccombe Chine, after the landslip jumble, can be descended to the beach. It is a long, stepped descent, but the beach is a fine one, a just reward for the effort.

Shanklin is a popular Victorian/Edwardian holiday resort with a very fine chine that is followed by a nature trail. It was here that the pumping station for PLUTO was sited.

Northward there is a long climb up onto Culver Down with its monument to the first commodore of the Royal Yacht Squadron, Charles Pelham, the Earl of Yarborough. Culver Cliff at the end of the down is an airy spot and a fine nesting site for sea birds. Bembridge, a small town almost enclosed by the cliffs, has a maritime museum, a Ruskin gallery, the ruins of a tidal mill and the island's only surviving windmill. A causeway separating freshwater marshes from the harbour, and a dam wall, containing old mill ponds, open onto the pleasant and botanically very interesting St Helens Common. Over 250 species of flower have been noted here. The ruins are of St Helen's church, and are a reminder that sailors once used the pumice-like stone for 'holystoning' the decks of wooden fighting ships.

Easy made-up paths and tracks return to the shore at Seaview where two more Palmerston 'folly' forts are visible in the Solent and, beyond a track through woods reaches down to the promenade on the outskirts of Ryde.

are now three fin-like stacks, a fourth that once occupied the obvious gap having collapsed in 1764. It is sad to think that at any time one, or all, of the remaining stacks could disappear. The path now doubles back, passing, on Tennyson Down, a granite memorial to the poet who lived in Farringford House in nearby Freshwater. The chalkland grass here is covered with cowslips in spring, a preview of the next 13 miles (21 km) of walking.

In Freshwater Bay there is a fine natural arch through which the sea roars to shower excited children on the seawall. The next path section is mostly low cliffs, along part of the island that is still sparsely populated and was once infamous for its shipwrecks and smugglers. Blackgang Chine is named for a gang of smugglers. It is usually crowded and the walker who wants a peaceful beach would do better to go to Whale Chine, a little before Blackgang, where one can be reached down a flight of wooden steps. The word 'Chine' is well-illustrated here. It derives from the Saxon *cinan*, to crack.

Beyond Blackgang 'Chine, the headland of St

The Solent Way

(OS sheets 197, 196, 195)

Emsworth to Hythe (33 mls, 53 km)

FROM EMSWORTH, ONCE famous for its oysters, the Solent Way can be followed to Milford on Sea, a few miles to the east of Bournemouth. Taking the Way means missing Hayling Island, a fine angling and yachting centre, but compensates by offering a clearly defined route through a difficult walking area.

The causeway between harbour and millpond at the River Em's mouth is taken to paths through woods and fields to Warblington church, where two early nineteenth-century grave-watcher's huts suggest a local fear of body-snatching.

Langstone beyond is an ideal place to have a meal. Try the *Royal Oak*, where high tide comes up to the sea wall just outside, and, on rare occasions, into the pub itself. Neville Shute wrote part of *Pied Piper* in the restored windmill here.

Beyond Langstone the path loops around Farlington Marshes, a fine nature reserve, before following a track beside an extremely busy road. The route quietens soon, skirting Langstone Harbour for Eastney where the walker can visit the Royal Marines Museum or Eastney Pumping Station where, at weekends, the beam engines are in steam.

The Way now follows roads to Southsea where the castle, built by Henry VIII, and from which he watched as the *Mary Rose*, pride of his navy, capsized and sank with appalling loss of life, now houses the D-Day Museum. The collection includes the Overlord Tapestry, a 272 ft (82 m) tapestry that echoes that of Bayeux. While the walker is in Southsea consideration should be given to a boat trip to Spit Sand Fort, one of Palmerston's Follies. The fort, built as with the others in the 1860s, has walls 15 ft (4.5 m) thick and a

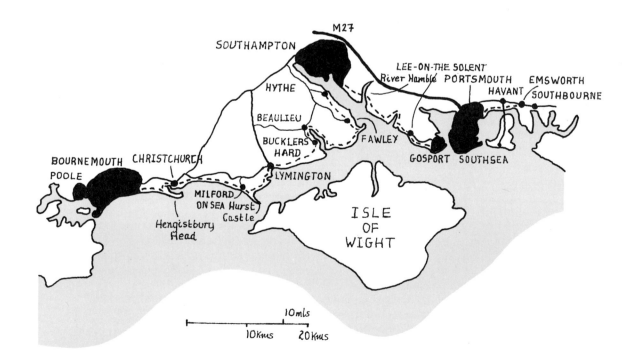

HMS Victory *in Portsmouth Harbour (above)*

The Dockyards, Portsmouth Harbour

well 400 ft (120 m) deep. The present owner bought it in 1982 after 30 years of neglect and vandalism and has dedicated himself to its restoration.

Portsmouth is reached from Southsea, one town running into the next, and it was to the Naval Dockyard here that the salvaged *Mary Rose* was taken for righting and exhibition. Both the ship remains and the museum objects are moving reminders of the tragic loss of life. The Dockyard also holds the Royal Navy Museum, and the *Victory*, one of the world's most famous ships. The ship, on which – as if anyone really needed telling – Nelson died at Trafalgar in 1805, is quite remarkably beautiful, and seems at the same time both sturdy and, when compared to the modern warships in the harbour, fragile.

The Solent Way avoids the rest of Portsmouth, taking a ferry to Gosport, but the town is a fine one and worthy of a visit. Take a boat in the harbour to see Portchester Castle, and on land go to the Round Tower, one of Portsmouth's first permanent defences built in the fifteenth century. The Square Tower is later, and now houses the 'First Fleet to Australia' exhibition, an intriguing show, using modern techniques to convey the chilling sights and sounds of the times.

Gosport is home to the fascinating submarine museum where visitors can try the cramped and claustrophobic conditions of submarines for themselves. Ahead now the Way passes Lee-on-the-Solent, home of the HMS *Daedalus* Fleet Air Arm base to reach Hill Head, an old smugglers' haunt. To the west the River Mean is reached near the Titchfield Haven Nature Reserve, renowned for its ducks. The Way follows the river to Titchfield where the Abbey, converted into a private house when it was dissolved, was where Charles I spent his last night as a free man. It is now a ruin. From the village the Way heads shoreward again, reaching the water beyond the Hook Park Nature Reserve.

The water is the River Hamble at Warsash, crossed by ferry for the village of Hamble, a popular yachting centre. Ruins dominate the path to the north. First, in the Royal Victoria Country Park, are those of the Royal Victoria Military Hospital, founded for wounded of the Crimean War, but now largely demolished. Then comes Netley Abbey, of which little survives. Netley Castle, originally Tudor but much restored, is now a convalescent home.

A road takes the walker to and over Woolston bridge and into Southampton. The city is not explored, however, the Way making for Royal Pier and the ferry for Hythe. There are those who will not regret the loss of time in Southampton, but though it is not a major scenic attraction it does have merit. From here, in 1620, the Pilgrim Fathers sailed, although it is true that they touched land again at Dartmouth and Plymouth before touching it in the New World, and before that the port had been used by the Romans and the Normans. Later it was the berth for the 'Queen' liners in the heady days of Atlantic Blue Riband sailing. There is, not surprisingly, a fine maritime museum in the town. Another good museum is dedicated to R.J. Mitchell, the designer of the Spitfire. The Art Gallery has a room dedicated to the work of Sir Edward Burne-Jones.

At Hythe an old train rattles 2,000 ft (600 m) down the pier to meet the ferry. The village's old cottages are sandwiched between a modern shopping precinct and an ultra-modern marina. Flying boats once operated from here, the town being the departure point for the Imperial Airways service to the East.

Fawley to Bournemouth (54 mls, 86 km)

Southward now the Way has to negotiate the oil refinery and power station at Fawley, no easy task to accomplish with elegance, to reach Calshot, where the Schneider Trophy races were held in 1929 and 1931. Later, the huge hangers here were used for flying boats, at a time when it was believed that commercial aeroplanes would never be able to operate from land because runways long enough would never be built.

Calshott Castle was rapidly, but beautifully, built by Henry VIII in 1539 with stone from the dissolved Beaulieu Abbey. A fine path by beach and cliff links the Calshot and Lepe Country Parks while beyond, the inland dip the Way makes is compensated for by Exbury Gardens where there are fine woodland walks, particularly in May when the rhododendrons and azaleas are in bloom, and during the autumnal display of brilliant foliage.

Beaulieu, the Norman French name is a translation of the Latin for beautiful place, is indeed well-set, and famous for the stately home of Beaulieu Abbey, though little of the thirteenth-century abbey now remains beside Palace House. The National Motor Museum is housed here.

To the south, the Way threads a way through the trees and meadows to Bucklers Hard, a village for which there is an entrance fee. The reason is that the entire village is a museum to the construction of wooden battleships, the men-of-war of Nelson's time, and earlier. For 150 years, until the early nineteenth century, this village was one of the most important construction sites in Britain, handily placed near both the oaks of the New Forest and the Solent. Nelson's favourite ship *Agamemnon* was built here by Master shipbuilder Henry Adams, whose house is now the hotel. One cottage houses the church, while others

Looking across Hengistbury Head to Christchurch Harbour

A Short Sunderland Flying Boat

are authentically furnished labourer's and shipwright's cottages. Later in its life, Francis Chichester sailed from the village on his voyage around the world.

As a link with the naval history of Bucklers Hard the Way twists and dips through oak woods to reach Sowley fishpond, ringed with trees. The pond was built for fish by Cistercian monks, but was used in the seventeenth and eighteenth centuries to power tilt hammers in an ironworks.

Five miles (8 km) of peaceful lanes follow, to reach the obelisk to Admiral Neale who, in 1832, gave iron columns to Lymington for the town lights. Beyond Lymington, a pleasant Georgian town, the Way uses 3 miles (5 km) of sea wall to circle the salt flats from which salt was once extracted until taxation and competition from mined salt ended production in 1865. Now the area is outstanding for its flora and birdlife.

A small ferry negotiates the mud-flats from Keyhaven's quiet harbour, taking the walker to Henry VIII's Hurst Castle strategically sited only 1 mile (1.6 km) from the Isle of Wight. The castle has never seen action, but has a long history of usage. Troops were even billeted there during the Second World War. From the castle the Way takes to the shingle for its last 2 miles (3.2 km) to Milford-on-Sea.

There is little coast left now before our starting point is reached. Beyond Milford, Hordle beach can be walked or avoided on the cliffs, the upper route negotiating the chine before Barton by golf course and heather.

Beach walking below the ruins of Highcliffe's neo-Gothic castle leads round to Mudeford's little peninsula from where a ferry crosses to the shingle spit which shelters Christchurch Harbour. The view to the Needles from here is excellent.

Hengistbury Head is soon reached, a disappointing headland only 118 ft (34.5 m) high, but with fine views eastwards to Hurst Castle, and west past the white cliffs of Ballard Down to Durlston Head. The head was occupied from Stone Age to Roman times, and was an important Iron Age port. Ironically iron, extracted from the ironstone of its southern sweep, almost lead to its destruction. The ironstone was quarried extensively in the mid-nineteenth century, the sea eroding the exposed soft rock quickly, reducing the spit's width, but also depositing the sand at the northern headland, almost closing the entrance to Christchurch harbour.

Inland, Christchurch, tucked in between the Stour and Avon, has a priory that took 400 years to build, beginning in the eleventh century, and is England's longest parish church. But Christchurch is not on our route. We follow the bracken and gorse lined path to Bournemouth, an elegant resort, famous for its gardens, its chines and its symphony orchestra. Bournemouth has a reputation for being a restful resort. It is a good place for the walker to stop.

Bracken Fern, New Forest

The start and finish of our Coastal Walk. In the foreground is South Haven Point, beyond is Sandbanks leading to Bournemouth. To the left is Poole Harbour

Index

Numbers in italics refer to illustrations

Abbotsbury 14
Aberaeron 64
Aberdaron 68
Aberdeen 140
Aberdour 150
Aberdyfi 64
Aberffraw 72
Abergele 76
Aberlady Bay 150
Aber Ogwen 74
Aberporth 63
Abersoch 68
Aberystwyth 64, *64*
Aldeburgh 184
Allerdale 86
Alloway 96
Amble 160
Am Buachaille *117*, 118, *118*
Amlwch 73
Amroth 54–5
Angle headland 58
Anglesey 6, 70, 72–4
Annan 86, 88
Anstruther *147*, 148
Applecross Peninsula 114
Appledore 42
Arbroath 144
Ardnamurchan, Point of 102, *103*
Ardrossan 96
Arisaig 104
Armadale 112
Armadale Bay *119*, 120
Arnside 82
Arran 96, 100
Arthur, King 32, 40, 56
Ayr 96, 98
Ayres, The 80

Badbea 128, *129*
Ballachulish 102
Ballantrae 94
Ballard Down 8, 10, 218
Balnakeil 120
Bamburgh 158, *158, 159*
Banff 138
Bangor 74
Bardsey Island 68
Barmouth 64, *66*
Barnstaple 42–4
Barrow-in-Furness 82
Barry 52
Barton 170
Basingwark Abbey 76
Bass Rock 152, *153*

Beachy Head *205*, 206
Beaulieu 216
Beauly 132
Beaumaris 73
Bede, Venerable 162
Bedruthan Steps 38
Beer 18, *19*
Bembridge 213
Bempton 168, *168*
Benacre Ness 183
Benbecula 108–9
Beowulf 164
Berry Head *21*, 22
Berwick 154, *154*, 156
Bettyhill 120
Bideford 41, 42, *43*
Black Isle 132
Blackmore, R.D. 46
Blackpool 81–2, *82, 83*
Blackwater, River 192, *195*
Blakeney Point *177*, 178
Blyth 160
Boddam 140
Bognor 208
Bonar Bridge 130
Borth 64
Boscastle 40
Bosham 210
Bossington 46
Boston 172, *172*, 174
Boswell, James 140
Boulby Head 164
Bournemouth 6, 8, 218
Bowness 86, 88
Brancaster 176
Brean 48, *49*
Bridlington *169*, 170
Brightlingsea 190
Brighton *207*, 208, *208*
Bristol 50
Bristol Channel 44, 48–50
Brixham *21*, 22, *22*
Broad Haven 60
Brodick 98
Broom, Loch 116
Brunel, Isembard 20, 50, *50*, 58
Bucklers Hard 216–18
Buck's Mill Mouth 42
Bude 40
Budleigh Salterton 20
Burghead 136
Burgh Island *25*, 26
Burnham (Norfolk) 176, *178*
Burnham-on-Crouch 192

Burnham-on-Sea 48, *48*
Burns, Robert 90–1, 94, 96, 99
Burrow Head 92

Cadgwith 32
Caerlaverock Castle 88, *90*
Caernarfon 70, *70*
Caister 182
Caithness *127*, 128
Caldey Island 56
Calshot 216
Camber Castle 204
Cambrian Coast Railway 64, 66
Canvey Island 194
Caolisport, Loch 100
Cardiff 50–2
Cardigan 63
Carlisle 86
Carregwastad Point 62
Carrick Coast 94
Carron, Loch 114, *115*
Castletown 79
Chapel Point 152
Charlestown 30
Charlie, Bonnie Prince 109, 113
Charmouth 14
Chatham 196–8
Chesil Beach 6, 14, *15, 17*
Chester 76, 78, 81
Chichester 210, *210*
Christchurch *217*, 218
Clacton 188–90
Cleethorpes 170
Cleveland Way 6, 164–6, *165*
Cley-next-the-Sea 178, *178*
Clo Mor 118
Clovelly 41, *42*
Cockington 22
Coleridge, Samuel Taylor 46
Coll 110
Colne, River 190
Colonsay 111
Colwyn Bay 76
Combe Martin 44
Constable, John 12
Conwy 74
Cook, Capt. James 26, 166
Cooling 196
Cornish Coastal Path 6, 28–40
Covehithe 183
Cowes 212
Crail 148
Creetown 91
Criccieth 66

Criffel 90
Cromarty 132, *132*
Cromer 180
Croyde 44
Culbin Sands 134, *137*
Culbone 46, *46*
Cullykhan Bay 138
Culzean Castle 94, *95, 97*

Darling, Grace 158
Dartmouth 22
Dawlish 20
Deal 200, *200*
Dee, River (England) 76, 77, 78, 81
    (Scotland) 140
Defoe, Daniel 46, 86, 148, 170
Dengie peninsula 192
Dickens, Charles 196, 200, 213
Dingwall 132
Dodman Point 30
Dornoch 130
Dorset Coastal Path 6, 8–16
Dounreay 120, *120*, 126
Dover 200, *201*
Drake, Sir Francis 26
Drigg 86
Dumfries 88–90
Dunbar 152
Dunbeath Castle *127*, 128
Duncansby Head 128
Dundee 144, *144*
Dungeness 202, 206
Dunnet Head *121*, 126
Dunnottar Castle 142, *143*
Dunoon 99
Dunrobin Castle 128–30, *130*
Dunstanburgh Castle 158–60, *161*
Dunwich 184
Durdle Door 12
Durlston Head 8, 218
Durness, Kyle of 118, 120

Eastbourne 204–6
East Neuk 146–8
Easton Ness 183
Eday, Isle of 123
Edinburgh 150, *150*
Edward I, King 30, 70, 72–4, 76, 170
Eigg 110
Eilean Donan *105*, 106, *106*
Emsworth 210, 214
Eriboll, Loch 120
Eriskay 109
Essex 188–94
Exmoor National Park 44
Exmouth 20

Falmouth 30
Farne Islands 158, *159, 162*
Faversham *197*, 198
Fawley 216

Felixstowe 186
Fife 146
Filey 166, 168
Findhorn Bay 134–6
Fishguard 62
Flamborough Head 168–70, *169*
Flat Holm *51*, 52
Fleet 14, *17*
Fleet Estuary 91
Fleetwood 82
Flint 76
Folkestone 202, *202*
Formby 81
Forth, Firth of 150, *153*
Fort William 102, *106*
Foulness Island 192
Fowey 30
Fraserburgh 138
Furness Abbey 82, *84*
Fyne, Loch 99, 100

Galloway, Mull of 92
Gardenstown 138
Giraldus Cambrensis 56, 76
Girvan 94
Glasson 82
Glenmaye 79
Gogarth Bay 73, *73*
Goodwin Sands 200
Goonhilly Down 32
Gorleston 182
Gosport 216
Gourdon *145*
Gourock 96
Gower Peninsula 52–4
Grange-over-Sands 82
Gravesend 196
Great Yarmouth *180*, 182
Green Bridge of Wales 56
Gretna 88
Grimsby 170
Gruinard Bay 116
Gurnard's Head *33*, 36
Gutterby Spa 84

Hadrian's Wall 86
Hamble 216
Hamilton, Lady Emma 58, 76
Harlech 66
Harris 108
Hartland 41
Hartlepool 162
Harwich 188, *189, 191*
Hastings 204
Hayle, River 36
Hebrides, Inner 110–11
    Outer 108–9
Heddon's Mouth 44
Helmsley 164
Helston 32
Henry VII, King 58, 60

Herne Bay 198
Hightveer Point 44
Hilbre Islands 78
Hinkley Point 48
Holderness Peninsula 168, 170
Holkham 176–8
Holyhead 73
Holy Island (Anglesey) 73
    (Northumbria) *see* Lindisfarne
Holy Loch 99
Hope, Inner & Outer 24–6
Hope Gap 206
Horden Point 162
Hourn, Loch 106
Hoy, Isle of 122
Hoylake 78
Hull *see* Kingston upon Hull
Hullbridge 192
Humber, River 170
Hunstanton 176
Hurst Castle 218
Hythe (Hants) 216
    (Kent) 202

Ilfracombe 44, *45*
Inchcolm, Island of 150
Ingoldmells 172
Inverary Castle 99–100
Inverbervie 142
Inverewe Gardens 114
Inverie 104
Inverness 132, 134
Inverpolly National Nature Reserve 118
Iona 111, *111*
Irvine 96
Islay 111

James, Henry 202
Jarlshof 124
John, King 174
John Muir Country Park 152
John o'Groats 128
Jura, Island of 111
    Sound of 100

Kent's Cavern 22
Kessingland 182
Kettleness 166
Kilve 48
Kimmeridge Bay 10, *10*
Kingsley, Charles 42
King's Lynn 174
Kingston upon Hull 136, 170
Kintyre, Mull of 100
Kipling, Rudyard 22, 42, 208
Kirkcaldy 148–50
Kirkcudbright 90–1
Kirkwall 122
Kishorn, Loch 114
Knott End 82
Knox, John 148, *150*

Knoydart 104–6
Kyle Coast 96

Lamberton Toll 156
Lancaster 82
Land's End 34
Langstone 214
Largo 148, *150*
Laugharne 54, *54*, 64
Lawrence, D.H. 36
Laxey 79, *80*
Lee 44
Leigh-on-Sea 192–4
Lewis, Isle of 108, *109*
Lindisfarne 156–8, *157*, *158*
Linnhe, Loch 102
Liverpool 78, 81, *81*
Lizard 32
Llanaber 66
Llanasa 76
Llanbedrog 66–8
Llanddwyn Island 72
Llandudno 74–6, *76*
Llanfairfechan 74
Llangranog 64, *65*
Llanystumdwy 66
Lleyn Peninsula 66–8, *69*
Lloyd George, David 66
Lochaline 102
Lochalsh, Kyle of 106, 114
Lochgilphead 100
Lochranza 98, 100
Logan Rock 34, *34*
Longships lighthouse 34, *34*
Looe 28, *29*
Lossiemouth 136
Louth Navigation Canal 170
Lower Higham 196
Lowestoft 182
Lulworth Cove 12, *13*
Lundy Island 44
Lune, River 82
Lyme Regis 14–16, 18, 48
Lymington 218
Lynemouth 160
Lynmouth 46
Lytham 81

Mablethorpe 172
Macdonald, Flora 102, 109, 113
Macduff 138, *139*
Mackenzie, Sir Compton 109
Madog 66
Maldon 190–2
Mallaig 104
Man, Isle of 6, 79–80, 86, 92
Manorbier 56
Man Sands 22
Manx Electric Railway 79
Margate *199*
Marsden Bay 160
Marsland Mouth 40, 41

Maryport 86
Mary Queen of Scots 90, 123
Mawddach Estuary 64
May, Isle of 146
Medway 196
Menai Strait 70, 72–3, *75*
Mersea Island 190
Mersey, River 78
Mevagissey 30
Mey, Castle of 128
Middlesbrough 50, 162
Milford Haven 6, 58–60
Minehead 6, 46
Minsmere 184
Moelfre 73
Montrose 142–4
Moray Firth 134–8
Morecombe 82
Moricambe Bay 86
Morwenstow 40
Mount Edgecumbe Park 28
Mousa, Isle of 124
Mousehole 32
Moyl Peninsula 90
Muck 110
Mull, Island of *101*, 102, 110
Mumbles Head 52
Mupe Bay *11*, 12

Nagden Marshes *197*, 198
Nairn 134, *135*
nan Uamh, Loch 102
Naze headland 188, *193*
Needles 8, 212–13, *213*, 218
Nelson, Horatio 58, 176, 216
Ness 76–8
Neston 76, 78
Nevis, Ben 102, *106*
Newborough Warren 6, 72
New Brighton 78
Newcastle-upon-Tyne 160
Newhaven 206
Newlyn 32
Newport (Dyfed) 62
   (Gwent) 50, 162
Newquay 38
New Quay 64
Newton Arlosh 86
Newtown 212
Norfolk Costal Path 176–80
North Berwick 150, *151*, 152
North Devon and Somerset Coastal Path 6, 41–6
North Ronaldsay, Isle of 123
Northumbria 156–62
North Wirral Coastal Path 78
North York Moors National Park 6, 164
Noss, Isle of 125

Oban 102, *102*
Offa's Dyke 76
Old Harry rocks 8

Orford Ness 186, *187*
Orkney 122–3
Osborne House 212
Osmington 12, 14
Owain Glyndwr 54, 64, 66

Padstow 38
Pagham Harbour 208, 210
Peacehaven 206, 208
Peak Hill 20
Peanmeanach 102
Peel 79
Pembroke 58, *58*, *59*
Pembrokeshire Coastal Path 55–62
Penarth *51*, 52
Pendine 54
Penmaenmawr Mountain 74
Pentire Point 38
Pentland Firth 128
Penzance 32
Pepys, Samuel 188, 198
Perranporth 38
Peterhead 138–40
Pevensey 204
Peveril Point 8, *9*
Pilgrim Fathers 22, 26, 170, 172
Pittenweem 148
Plymouth 26, *26*, *27*
Polperro 28
Poole Harbour 8
Poolewe 114
Porlock Weir 46
Portencross 96
Porthcawl 52
Porth Dinllaen 70
Porthmadog 66, *67*
Porthwarra 34
Porthland, Isle of 12, 14, *15*
Port Logan 92
Portmeirion 66
Portpatrick 92, *92*, 94
Port Penrhyn 74
Portreath 36–8
Portskewett 50
Portsmouth *214*, *215*, 216
Port Talbot *53*
Prawle Point *23*, 24, 26
Prestatyn 76
Preston 81
Prestwick 96
Pwllheli 66

Raad ny Foillan 79
Raleigh, Sir Walter 20
Ramsey Island 60–2
Ravenglass 84–6, *86*
Reculver 198
Redcar 162
Rhossili 54, *54*
Rhum 110
Rhyl 76

Ribble, River 81
Richborough 200
Ringmore 26
Rings Hill 12
Robert the Bruce 82, 94, 96, 98
Robin Hood's Bay 166
Rochester 196
Rockcliffe Marsh 86
Rottingdean 208
Rough Firth 90
Rousay, Isle of 123
Runswick Bay *164*, 166
Ruthwell 88
Ryan, Loch 92, 94
Ryde 212
Rye 202, *203*, 204

St Abb's Head 152–4, *155*
St Agnes Head 38, *38*
St Aldhelm's Head 10, *10*
St Andrews 146, *148*
St Anthony-in-Meneage 30
St Bees Head *85*, 86
St Brides Haven 60
St David's 6, 60, 74
St David's Head *61*, 62
St Dogmaels 62
St Govan's Head 56
St Ives *35*, 36
St Mawes 30
St Michael's Mount *31*, 32
St Osyth 190
Salcombe 24
Saltburn 162, 164, *164*
Saltfleet-by-Theddlethorpe 172
Sandown Castle 200
Sands of Forvie National Nature Reserve 140, *141*
Sandwich 200
Sandwood Bay *117*, 118
Sannox 98, *98*
Saundersfoot 55–6
Saunton Down *43*, 44
Saxon Shore Way 196–202
Scalloway 124–5
Scapa Flow 123
Scarborough 6, 166
Scott, Captain Robert 144
Scott, Sir Walter 91, 144
Seaham 162
Seaton 18
Seatown 14
Selsey Bill 208–10, *209*
Sennen Cove 34–6
Seven Sisters *205*, 206, 208
Severn Bridge 50
Shanklin 213
Sheerness 198
Shelley, Percy Bysshe 46
Sheppey, Isle of *197*, 198
Sheringham 178
Shetland 124–5

Shieldaig 114
Shingle Street 184–6, *187*
Sidmouth 18, 20, *20*
Silloth 86
Sittingbourne 198
Sizewell 184
Skara Brae 122, *123*
Skegness 172, *173*
Skipness 100
Skokholm Island 6, 60
Skomer Island 6, 60
Skye 106, 112–13, 114
Slapton 22–4
Smoo, Cave of 120
Snape Maltings 184, 186
Snattishorn 174
Solent Way 214–18
Solva 60
Solway Firth 86, *87*, 88
Sourlis 104
Southhampton 216
South Devon Coast Path 6, 18–26
South Downs 204, 206, 208
Southend 192
Southern Upland Way 94
Southport 81
Southsea 214–16
South Shields 160
Southwold 183, *185*
Speyside Way 136
Spurn Head 170, *171*
Stackpole Head 56
Staithes 166, *166*
Start Point 24
Stevenson, Robert Louis 102, 140, 148
Stiffkey Marshes *177*, 178
Stoer 118
Stoker, Bram 140, 166
Stonehaven 140–2, *143*
Stranraer 94
Strathy 120
Strome Castle *115*
Strontian 102
Studland Bay 8
Suffolk Heritage Coast Path 183–6
Sunderland 162
Sussex 204–10
Sutton Bridge 174, *175*
Swanage 8
Swansea 52, *53*

Tal-y-llyn railway 64
Tantallon Castle 152, *153*
Tarbat Ness 130, *131*
Taw, River 42, *42*, 44
Tay, Firth of 144, 146
Tayport 146
Tees, River 162, *163*
Teignmouth 20
Telford, Thomas 73, 130, 198
Tenby *55*, 56

Tennyson, Lord Alfred 40, 172, 213
Tetney 170
Thanet, Isle of 198
Thomas, Dylan 54, 64
Thorpeness 184, *184*
Thurlestone *24*, 26
Thurso 126
Tilbury 194
Tilly Whim Cave 10
Tintagel 6, *39*, 40, *40*
Tiree 110
Titchfield 216
Tollesbury *190*, 191
Tongue 120
Torness 152
Torquay 6, 22
Torridan 114
Trevose Head 37
Troon 96
Turnberry 94
Tynemouth 160
Tywyn 64

Uist, North & South 108
Ullapool 116
Ulverston 82
Upchurch 198

Ventnor 213
Victoria, Queen 20, 166, 212
Voryd Bay *69*, 70

Wallasea Island 192
Wallasey 78
Wallog 64
Walmer Castle 200
Walney Island 82
Walton on the Naze 188, *193*
Wantsum 198
Warkworth Castle 160
Wash 172, 174
Welland, River 174
Wells-next-the-Sea 178
West Highland railway 104
West Kirby 78
Weston-Super-Mare 50
Westray, Isle of 123
Westward Ho! 42
Weymouth 12, 14, *15*
Whippingham 212
Whitby 6, 166, *167*
Whitehaven 86
Whithorn 92, *93*
Whitley Bay 160
Whitstable 198
Wick 128
Wight, Isle of 8, 212–13, 218
Wigtown *87*, 91, *93*
Wilberforce, William 170
Williams, Emlyn 76
Williams-Ellis, Clough 66

Winchelsea 204
Winterton 180–2
Wirral Way 78
Woolacombe 44
Worbarrow Bay 12

Workington 86
Wrath, Cape 6, 118

Yarmouth (IOW) 212
  (Norfolk) *see* Great Yarmouth

Yell, Island of 125
Ynyslas 64

Zennor 36